A publication in
The Adult Education Association
Handbook Series in Adult Education

Serving Personal and Community Needs Through Adult Education

Edgar J. Boone
Ronald W. Shearon
Estelle E. White
and Associates

Serving Personal and Community Needs Through Adult Education

Jossey-Bass Publishers

San Francisco • Washington • London • 1980

Serving Personal and Community Needs Through Adult Education
by Edgar J. Boone, Ronald W. Shearon, Estelle E. White,
and Associates

Copyright © 1980 by: Adult Education Association
of the United States of America
810 Eighteenth Street, N.W.
Washington, D.C. 20006

Jossey-Bass Inc., Publishers
433 California Street
San Francisco, California 94104

Jossey-Bass Limited
28 Banner Street
London EC1Y 8QE

Library of Congress Cataloging in Publication Data
Main entry under title:

Serving personal and community needs through adult education.

(Adult Education Association handbook series in adult education)
Bibliography: p. 294
Includes index.
1. Adult education—United States—Addresses, essays,
lectures. 2. Labor and laboring classes—Education—
United States—Addresses, essays, lectures. I. Boone,
Edgar John, 1930–   II. Shearon, Ronald W., joint
author. III. White, Estelle E., joint author. IV. Series:
Adult Education Association. Adult Education
Association handbook series in adult education.
LC5251.B64   374'.973   79-9664
ISBN 0-87589-451-8

Manufactured in the United States of America

JACKET DESIGN BY WILLI BAUM

FIRST EDITION

Code 8012

The AEA Handbook Series
in Adult Education

WILLIAM S. GRIFFITH
University of British Columbia

HOWARD Y. MCCLUSKY
University of Michigan

General Editors

Edgar J. Boone
Ronald W. Shearon
Estelle E. White
and Associates
Serving Personal and
Community Needs Through
Adult Education

April 1980

John M. Peters
and Associates
Building an Effective
Adult Education
Enterprise

April 1980

Huey B. Long
Roger Hiemstra
and Associates
Changing Approaches
to Studying Adult
Education

April 1980

Foreword

Adult education as a field of study and of practice is not well understood by many literate and intelligent American adults whose exposure to the field has been limited to one or a few aspects of its apparently bewildering mosaic. Since 1926, when the American Association for Adult Education (AAAE) was founded, the leaders of that organization and its successor, the Adult Education Association of the U.S.A. (AEA), have striven to communicate both to the neophytes in the field and to the adult public an understanding of its diverse and complex enterprises. A major vehicle for accomplishing this communication has been a sequence of handbooks of adult education, issued periodically to convey a broad view of the mosaic. In 1934, 1936, and 1948 the AAAE published the first three handbooks. Although the Association had intended to issue a handbook every two years, that plan was not carried out for a number of reasons, including the outbreak of World War II and the termination of support by the Carnegie Corporation. Within three years of the publication of the 1948 handbook the Association itself dissolved in order to establish the AEA, which included the former members of both the AAAE and the Department of Adult Education of the National Education Association. It was nine years before the AEA was able to publish its first handbook, the fourth in the sequence, followed a decade later by the fifth version.

In the early 1970s both the Publications Committee of AEA and the Commission of the Professors of Adult Education (an affiliated organization of the AEA) explored the kinds of handbooks that could be designed to serve the changing nature and needs of the field. They found that different parts of the field were developing at different rates—in some areas information was becoming outdated rapidly, whereas in others a decennial handbook would be adequate to maintain currency. Moreover, the growing literature and the many developments in policies and programs led them to conclude that a single volume of traditional size would not be sufficient to treat the expanding knowledge base, the changing policies and practices, and the controversial topics in adult education. Accordingly, the Publications Committee decided that the next handbook would consist of several volumes, allowing the presentation of an increased amount of information on each of nine selected parts of the field and preparing the way for subsequent revisions of each volume independently on a schedule reflecting the pace of change in each area. The result is The AEA Handbook Series in Adult Education, which is being developed by the general editors with the guidance and assistance of the Publications Committee.

In this volume, *Serving Personal and Community Needs Through Adult Education,* the authors regard adult education as an effort by society to help adults acquire the knowledge and coping skills they need to meet and adjust to each change in role they must make during their adult life. The implicit value position is that adult education should be provided to assist adults to deal with the stresses produced by a changing environment. Adjusting to changes is therefore given more attention than is initiating or directing change, a philosophical stance that may disturb those who would employ adult education as a vehicle for facilitating radical alterations in governments and in social norms. Thus, the authors have chosen to focus on the ways individuals, families, communities, and sponsoring organizations can be aided in improving the quality of life within a given political framework rather than in stimulating and making possible a political reorganization.

In their effort to depict the comprehensiveness of the programming in adult education, the authors could not include every institution that provides programs. Instead, this book treats those aspects of programming that have changed the most since the publication of the previous handbook. The content emphasizes the diversity of the clients served, particularly those groups that appear to be receiving appreciably more (or different) kinds of educational services than did clients a decade earlier. Appropriately, the authors have also looked at how changes in delivery systems are affecting adult educators' ability to serve previously unreached groups.

In illustrating what can be achieved through adult education, this volume's authors have considered the ways in which learners' perceptions change when they know more and can cope better. And with respect to each of these changed views, the authors deal with four common elements: the providing institutions, the program objectives of the institutions, the delivery systems employed, and the distinguishing characteristics of the intended clientele. Utilizing a process analysis approach, the authors seek to demonstrate a common method of examining the diversity of programs and the delivery systems used to serve the ever-enlarging interests of adults.

Serving Personal and Community Needs Through Adult Education provides a sorely needed update, showing how selected parts of the field have responded to the technological and social changes of the 70s. Together with the companion volumes in the series, the book presents the adult education mosaic in a comprehensible and comprehensive manner for both workers in the field and others who seek to understand it.

Preparation of the series required the cooperation and dedicated efforts of scores of chapter authors, Publication Committee chairmen and members, and successive executive committees of the AEA. In bringing together the insights and perceptions of adult education scholars, the series is a major contribution of the Association to the advancement of an undertstanding of adult education as a field of study and of practice.

January 1980   WILLIAM S. GRIFFITH
                                          HOWARD Y. MCCLUSKY
                                          General Editors

Preface

During the past two decades the education of adults has become the fastest growing segment of the national and international education enterprise. Indeed, some analysts predict that adult education will be the only expanding segment in the years ahead. This prognosis seems logical when one notes that in the United States alone we now have the largest adult population and one of the lowest birth rates in the history of the nation. And the educational needs of those adults continue to expand in terms of both quantity and specificity. The most significant factor in this expansion has been adult educators' responsiveness to their clients' needs and interests. Since the early 1960s, the field has experienced considerable ferment as it has endeavored to expand and strengthen its research base and its professional education offerings. Today, adult education is widely regarded as one of the most responsive and relevant fields in the education enterprise. Speaking to the evolving nature of the field, this volume provides adult educators with information about the scope of current programs. The intent is to present a broad picture of adult education as a field of practice, with particular emphasis on its more significant program developments.

The following chapters are organized around five themes that offer an integrated view of programming and the types of learning needs it is intended to fulfill. These five themes—a sense of self, a sense of professional growth, a sense of opportunity, a sense of community, and a sense of experimentation—are not mutually exclusive but do provide a framework for understanding the growing differentiation of programs and clients. In developing these topics, we used the process analysis approach. Thus we treated the different kinds of programs as unique systems, emphasizing those concepts, structures, and functional relationships that have evolved and stressing their connections with the whole professional field. Using this technique allowed us to cut across client groups, delivery systems, and institutions.

The contributing authors constitute a balance of recognized scholars and practitioners from a wide variety of agencies and institutions, and they deserve special recognition by their colleagues. Some are administrators, some are teachers, and some are agency staff members. All have shown the ability to reflect on the developing nature of adult education and have viewed their particular subjects from the standpoint of practice. They and many others have collaborated in producing this volume. Of the other collaborators, we want especially to acknowledge five. Adele P. Covington served as technical editor, assisting in the organization, reorganization, and detailed revision of all the copy, and performed these demanding tasks in an exceedingly helpful way. And Lee M. Hoffman, Barry Adams, Robert Fox, and Rex Clay—doctoral students in North Carolina State University's Department of Adult and Community College Education—made helpful contributions to the preparation of the first draft.

Finally, we want to point out that during the two years this book has been in preparation, many developments have, of course, occurred. We regret that time pressures did not permit the incorporation of many of these changes in the sixteen chapters of this book.

Raleigh, North Carolina   EDGAR J. BOONE
February 1980   RONALD W. SHEARON
                                                     ESTELLE E. WHITE

Contents

Part Two: A Sense of Professional Growth

Part Three: A Sense of Opportunity

Part Four: A Sense of Community

Contents

Part Five: A Sense of Experimentation

The Authors

EDGAR J. BOONE, professor and head, Department of Adult and Community College Education, and assistant director, North Carolina Agricultural Extension Service, North Carolina State University, Raleigh

WILLIAM L. CARPENTER, professor of adult and community college education and head, Department of Agricultural Information, North Carolina State University, Raleigh

THOMAS W. CARR, director, Defense Education, Office of the Secretary of Defense, Washington, D.C.

J. LIN COMPTON, assistant professor of adult education, Cornell University

THELMA M. CORNISH, coordinator of adult continuing education, Maryland State Department of Education, Baltimore

JOHN K. COSTER, professor and director, Center for Occupational Education and Occupational Education Programs, North Carolina State University, Raleigh

ANN P. DRENNAN, executive director, Literacy Action of Washington, D.C., Inc.

HELEN M. FEENEY, associate professor of sociology, Queensboro Community College of the City University of New York

W. L. FLOWERS, JR., professor and associate dean of University

Extension, Virginia Polytechnic Institute and State University, Blacksburg

PHILLIP E. FRANDSON, dean, University Extension, University of California, Los Angeles

ROBERT J. HAVIGHURST, professor emeritus of education and human development, University of Chicago

HOWARD Y. McCLUSKY, professor of adult education, University of Michigan, Ann Arbor

SYLVIA G. McCOLLUM, education administrator, Bureau of Prisons, U.S. Department of Justice, Washington, D.C.

JOHN R. MacKENZIE, associate professor and director, Labor Studies Center, University of the District of Columbia

VIOLET M. MALONE, associate professor and state leader of extension education, University of Illinois, Urbana

EDWARD E. MARCUS, director, Elders Institute, Florida International University, North Miami

LEONARD NADLER, professor of adult education and human resource development, George Washington University, Washington, D.C.

RICHARD M. RIPLEY, colonel, U.S. Army (Retired), Raleigh, North Carolina

RONALD W. SHEARON, professor and associate head, Department of Adult and Community College Education, North Carolina State University

THOMAS R. SHWORLES, director, Center for Program Development and the Handicapped, Chicago City-Wide College, City Colleges of Chicago

MYRTLE L. SWICEGOOD, professor of home economics and district extension program leader, North Carolina Agricultural Extension Service, North Carolina State University, Raleigh

JOHN A. VALENTINE, professional associate for academic affairs, College Entrance Examination Board, New York

PAUL H. WANG, executive director, Taiwanese-American Service Center, Lincolnwood, Illinois

EUGENE R. WATSON, associate professor of higher and adult education, University of North Carolina at Chapel Hill

ESTELLE E. WHITE, associate professor of adult and community college education, North Carolina State University

Serving Personal and Community Needs Through Adult Education

Chapter One

Introduction: Serving Needs Through Adult Education

Edgar J. Boone

Perhaps never before in history has humanity felt the push of technological advancement so severely. In the contest between humans and machines, which are ever increasing in use and complexity, we have a tentative edge; yet this slight advantage is rapidly slipping away. In fact, the conditions under which humans can survive and grow may well be worsened by increasingly sophisticated technology. Almost imperceptibly the people of the world are having to adjust to dwindling energy reserves; the staggering costs of health care; critical food and water shortages; racial, ethnic, political, and religious upheavals; and a diminished role in participatory governance—to name but a few problems. Although these forced and often unwanted social changes have become the order of the day, few of us are willing to adapt our way of life to this new environment. An

1

added concern is that the world's population is expected to double before the turn of this century; masses of humanity could become congealed into a stagnant and listless collection of confused individuals, many of whom may be incapable of coping with institutionalized claustrophobia.

Today, the gap between innovation and application is closing rapidly, and the necessity for and probability of predicting the ethical, moral, social, political, and economic consequences of innovation are increasing. The impact of change is felt not only in the technological world but also in every part of life, including personal values, morality, religion, and the very nature of human beings themselves. This gap between the forced march of technology and the existential nature of the human organism is widening into an intellectual and emotional chasm. People cry out for accountability, relevance, involvement, and participation in life's daily affairs; yet their pleas often fall on deaf ears.

This book deals with the expanding role of adult education in its efforts to handle the closing gap between innovation and application and to bridge the widening gap between technology and humankind. Certainly as a society changes, the needs of its people also change. This concept of change has been a key element in the design and initiation of adult education programs since the inception of the movement. From its formative years to the present, the adult education movement has emphasized the planned acquisition of knowledge and coping skills by individual learners in their efforts to reduce the internalized anxiety brought on by the "age of innovation." As a mirror for society's current needs, adult education tries to help its learners identify, interpret, and resolve their specific requirements. Furthermore, the enormity and complexity of contemporary society's changing needs and interests demand continuous and comprehensive lifelong education. Adult education, therefore, may be perceived as one means by which society assists adults in gaining the knowledge and coping skills needed to adjust to the various role changes required in adult life.

Accepting this premise, I may begin rather cautiously the arduous task of defining the field of adult education itself. One might speculate that the field is a continual and generalized process and thus cannot be given definitive boundaries. It must be free enough to experiment with progressive concepts, to prevent technology from becoming dehumanized, and to broaden our world view, moving from the individual within the community to a philosophy of interdependence at a time when survival depends on cooperative adaptation to daily change and obsolescence. Houle (1972, p. 32) provided a useful framework by defining adult education as "the process by which men and women (alone, in groups, or in institutional settings) seek to improve themselves or society by increasing their skill, knowledge, or sensitiveness; or it is a process by which individuals, groups, or institutions try to help men and women improve in these ways." He suggested further that the fundamental system of practice in the field of adult education can be discerned only by probing beneath many surface realities to identify a basic unity of process. According to Houle (1972, pp. 32–40), the system rests on seven basic assumptions:

—Any episode of learning occurs in a specific situation and is profoundly affected by that fact.

—The analysis of the planning of educational activities must be based on the realities of human experience and on their constant change.

—Education is a practical art.

—Education is a cooperative art.

—The planning or analysis of an educational activity is usually undertaken in terms of some period which the mind abstracts for analytical purpose from complicated reality.

—The planning or analysis of an educational activity may be undertaken by an educator, a learner, an independent analyst, or some combination of the three.

—Any design of education can best be understood as a complex of interacting elements, not as a sequence of events.

On the basis of Houle's writings and those of other noted authorities, one is led to conclude that adult education is a "process system" that emphasizes both human development and the delivery of knowledge. From this conception arose the authors' decision to use the process analysis approach in organizing the book's content. Accordingly they treated those kinds of programming that were selected for discussion—usually new or growing kinds—as unique subsystems, showing how the concepts, structures, and fundamental relationships of those subsystems have evolved and how they relate to adult education as a professional field. This approach cuts across client groups, delivery systems, and institutions. What the editors envisioned is the expansion of a field or system of knowledge from its rudimentary definition to its currently complex state. From within the general field of adult education, program specialities have evolved, each distinctive yet sharing with the others certain basic knowledge. The rapid growth of these specialized types of programs continues as their clients' needs and life situations become more apparent, the expectations of society increase, and demands by "special" clients increase.

At this point in the field's development, we as adult educators stand on a new threshold. We must look at our conceptions of the field and at how further expansion will be affected by the learning needs of existing groups and of new, specialized clienteles. If such introspection reveals that we ourselves are unaware of the comprehensiveness of adult education as it exists today and what the future will hold, as professionals and leaders we must acquire a deeper understanding of the current and future differences in the learning needs of diverse client groups. Accordingly, it will be fruitful to examine programming in terms of the five thematic categories in which this book is arranged. These are not tidy, exhaustive, or mutually exclusive, but they do treat some of the current interests and needs of special adult learners, the efforts being made to serve them, and the problems inherent in those efforts.

A Sense of Self

Adult educators who are particularly concerned with learners' self-development typically want to expand the horizons of the individual student. Although educators can only guess about which bits of information will be needed in the world of the twenty-first century, by ensuring that adult learners fully use their own inherent resources, educators can increase the possibility of self-actualization. The adult who is well informed, creative, and responsible is likely to survive and deal effectively with the future as well as make a positive contribution to society. In pursuing these aims, adult educators must take into account that certain groups of clients have a greater need than others for self-development programs. Two of these groups at present are the aging and women, who together have a great deal to do with the social, economic, and moral direction of our society.

A Sense of Professional Growth

Professionals in any field realize that their social role is tied inextricably to their demonstrated competence in a specific art and that without proven competence they may soon lose institutional recognition and often, to an even greater degree, their self-respect or self-esteem. Yet professionals are finding it increasingly difficult to stay abreast of the rapid developments in their fields and maintain their competence. This difficulty arises not only because of the speed of knowledge expansion but also because of the way it expands. Instead of occurring in bursts, which would allow time for professionals to keep up to date, technological change in most societies is fast and continuous; as has often been noted, knowledge is expanding geometrically and exponentially. Thus, continuing professional growth and development become increasingly important.

Today a dynamic tension exists between people's dependence on experts and their desire to function independently. More than in the past, the layman is forced to rely on the knowledge and expertise of the professionals. At the same time, each individual desires to take more responsibility for and participate in all aspects of his life. This tension points to a need for the adult educator to perform the dual role of expert and consultant in helping the individual client make the most appropriate decisions. With this changing role must come a renewed interest among all members of the field in creating innovative programs to fit the professional's needs.

A Sense of Opportunity

The impact of technology on the lives of the world's population brings awesome problems for several segments of society—the physically handicapped, the educationally disadvantaged, and the socially deprived. Together, these people constitute a majority in most societies. In illustration of the immensity of this population in the United States alone, the 1970 census defined more than 45 million persons as technically handicapped and 23 million as economically disadvantaged, and 86 million had less than a high school education. Add to these surprising figures the millions of Americans who, owing to a lack of knowledge and coping skills, are unable to attain a sense of order in their lives. One need only visit the ghettos or the forgotten rural towns, villages, and open countrysides in the United States and in other nations to be reminded of the blighted conditions under which many of the world's people live.

Most of them are incapable of coping adequately in society. Although they might subscribe to the Protestant work ethic, employment of any type is often beyond their grasp. In effect they have no opportunities, and this has a debilitating psychological impact on them. Among these persons, efforts at self-improvement must be postponed until their basic needs are at least partially satisfied. As a consequence, the simple requirements of maintaining existence obscure any aspirations they might have for the future. Fortunately, however, there is hope for many. Motivated at the beginning by the desire to give upward momentum to those outside the economic and social mainstream, the adult education movement is accelerating its efforts to provide to all levels of society the satisfying harvest to be reaped from continuing self-development. Such efforts will bring into the mainstream those who are less fortunate. Disadvantaged subcultures are being helped to recognize the value of and the ways to adapt and use indigenous and research-based knowledge to cope with the many problems and obstacles with which they are confronted.

New programming—new assistance, both financial and psychological—is being engineered by adult educators to uplift the spirits of those who will avail themselves of these opportunities. The goals of these programs often are visionary, but visionary goals may be essential when the problems at hand are so immense. Among the current offerings are adult basic education and English as a second language, education for economic and social development, education for adults with special needs, adult education in corrections, perspectives on education for work, armed forces and veterans' education, and labor education in the United States.

A Sense of Community

The movement from the age of industrialization into the age of innovation and technology has obviously brought about changes in community and family life. Whereas communities formerly were well-defined, distinct geographical entitites, with norms that encouraged and supported a harmonious home and family life, they now have little sense of unity and identity, because megacities have banded them together into immense social groupings. As a result, communities are encountering increasing difficulties in attending to their members' needs. Community services, for example, originally were conceived of as autonomous units arranged to address church and family needs. But they have become impersonal bureaucratic agencies, unable to adequately meet the requirements of the masses of humanity caught in the backwaters of contemporary life.

In response to these changes, some people are returning to the simpler things in life. In the United States, the migration of youth and workers to the urban centers has slowed to a point where a repopulation of rural areas is now being recorded. And there seems to be a shift away from anonymous bureaucratic control to decentralized community help programs. Regardless of whether the setting is urban or rural, however, planned community development is imperative. Such activity begins with an educative process that involves local residents. Without their full participation in establishing the need for and initiating such programs, education for development will fail.

Although the family has not remained fixed throughout the evolution of society, it probably underwent its most profound alterations during the past three to four decades. Beginning with World War II, major transitions occurred in function and structure, as it endeavored to maintain itself as a system and yet respond to rapid technological and social changes. The resulting stresses have significantly affected its educational role as the chief architect and advocate for establishing, modifying, and maintaining social norms. Indeed, the family's role in transmitting knowledge, skills, and values to its members seems to have diminished. New family living styles have supplanted traditional ones. The nuclear family has largely replaced the extended family. Further, even the term *family* has changed, sometimes being used to describe arrangements such as communes, single parents with children, singles, unmarried couples living together, and two or more individuals of the same sex living together.

The future of the family and its educative role in society is the subject of much concern and discussion by educators and leaders at local, state, and national levels. The importance of the family in helping to maintain a stable and viable society is well established. So the major issue is not its existence but how to create educational programs that will genuinely help families cope with all facets of family living. Adult educators can play a central part in community development and the revitalization of home and family life. As role models and professionals, they are in the best possible position to recognize and to act on institutional inequalities and inefficiencies.

A Sense of Experimentation

The rapid changes that the world has undergone in the past half century assuredly will be followed by even more sweeping ones. The complexity of human existence mandates that new visions and delivery systems be considered for action now, so that we may at least try to prepare ourselves for the unknown. Two of the important directions for adult educators to consider are nontraditional education and the effect of mass and instructional media on education.

Summary

As leaders of the effort to facilitate the continuing self-development of adults, adult educators must design and implement various means of assisting these learners to achieve their highly personal goals; for as Lindeman (1926, pp. 8–9) pointed out so long ago, "The approach to adult education will be via the route of situations, not subjects. . . . In adult education the curriculum is built around the students' needs and interests. Every person finds himself in specific situations . . . situations which call for adjustments. Adult education begins at this point. . . . Texts and teachers . . . must give way to the primary importance of the learner." Indeed, the history of adult education's development as a distinctive field of study and practice shows that many specialized programs for learners have been created. But adult education today, like other established fields, also has a common knowledge base. And sometimes educators forget that exposure to this basic knowledge is not sufficient to serve the different needs and interests of their diverse clienteles.

Developments in adult education should spur its scholars and leaders to rethink and expand their conceptions of the field and its many ramifications and to evaluate their preparedness for the professional challenges ahead. If the world is to have the thoughtful, prepared, and involved adults it needs to assure positive social change and the survival of humanity, adult education must take the lead. Adult educators, whatever their specialty, can be expected to react to this coming age with their characteristic enthusiasm and curiosity and to be ready to make the adjustments and sacrifices necessary to upgrade their knowledge and skills. The authors of the ensuing chapters challenge them to begin their search for cognitive renewal in the hope that such renewal will benefit adult learners of today and those of tomorrow.

Chapter Two

Education for Personal Growth

Eugene R. Watson

Personal growth toward self-fulfillment has been described as a "struggle for identity and human values" (Moustakas, 1969, p. 1). This description implies an inward focus that challenges the external controls and demands placed on the individual. Yet it also suggests both instrumental and expressive social goals for the individual. As succeeding chapters indicate, other kinds of adult education programs have personal growth as a secondary component or objective; this chapter deals with programs undertaken primarily to achieve such goals as personal satisfaction, a strengthened sense of identity, the establishment or clarification of values, and increased effectiveness in adapting to an ever-changing society. Personal growth and the development of human potential are concepts that have precedents in antiquity, as in the striving for both mental and physical excellence in the Golden Age of Greece. They are manifested in our time in what has been characterized as the human potential movement. Developing an adequate picture of this movement would require a full volume or would result in a chapter resembling a roll call, with scores of tables. Since the first is impossible and the second undesirable, I decided to sketch its outlines and then discuss its relation to adult education.

Human Potential Movement

Many behavioral scientists have stated or demonstrated that a movement is under way to explore and use the vast untapped human potential. Gardner Murphy (1958) and Carl Rogers (1969), for instance, wrote convincingly of the need to develop this potential, and the work of Abraham Maslow also laid part of the theoretical foundation of the movement. In particular, Maslow's hierarchy of needs (1962) has proved a time-tested paradigm that helps to clarify adults' developmental goals, from instrumental to expressive. The most basic need in the hierarchy is the need to survive. Above this, in order, are the needs for safety; for love, affection, belongingness; for esteem; and for self-actualization. Self-actualization means developing one's potential to the limit of one's capacity. Maslow indicated that growth toward self-actualization is a condition of mental health. Indeed, in a volume published after his death (Maslow, 1971), his conviction was reaffirmed that neurosis is a failure to grow toward the fulfillment of one's potential.

The goals of the movement can readily be seeen as extensions of these basic ideas. According to one leader (Weir, 1975, pp. 293–294), most practitioners in the United States agree that the aims are "to help the participant become more self-accepting, more self-directed, more responsible, more effective in his relations with others, more efficient in the use of his biological energy, more in contact with his physical and psychic processes, and better able to discover and actualize his potentialities. The emphasis is more on the process of Becoming than on the content of Being."

It is difficult to estimate the size of the movement or the nature of its participants, because obviously millions of adults plan growth-enhancing activities without assistance from formal institutions, which keep records on such matters. As Tough (1971) pointed out in his pioneering studies of how adults learn, the most commonly used resources for learning are one's own experiences, family members, friends, neighbors, and self-discovered printed materials. Yet despite the independent nature of much of this learning, we can make some educated guesses about those who are working on their personal growth. Probably the majority are meeting their lower-level needs dependably, are at least high school graduates, and are female. Most are also between thirty and fifty, although many younger adults are planning personal growth activities in search of a way to respond to social conditions. And older adults, aged sixty or over, appear to be making such efforts in greater numbers too. The involvement of ethnic minorities probably is about proportional to their percentage in the overall population; much of their work toward personal growth is devoted to preserving and enhancing their cultural uniqueness and its meaning for their own potential.

Whatever their characteristics, these seekers usually require some basic reeducation in how to learn, how to explore their own potential, and how to continue to manage their own growth. The term *reeducation* has been used by many writers, with varying meanings. A direct approach to reeducating the adult was offered by Houle (1964), who outlined a strategy for learning how to learn that the individual can follow without taking part in classroom ritual. One of the most influential statements about reeducation came from Kurt Lewin in the form of a series of principles which have had a profound impact on the human potential movement throughout the world. As reviewed by Benne (1976), Lewin's principles basically are as follows: (1) the processes governing the acquisition of the normal and the abnormal responses are fundamentally alike; (2) the reeducation process has to fulfill a task which is essentially equivalent to a change in culture; (3) even extensive first-hand experience does not automatically create correct concepts (knowledge); (4) social action no less than physical action is steered by perception; (5) as a rule, the possession of correct knowledge does not suffice to rectify false perceptions; (6) incorrect stereotypes (prejudices) are functionally equivalent to wrong concepts; (7) changes in sentiments do not necessarily follow changes in cognitive structures; (8) a change in action-theology, a real acceptance of a changed set of facts and values, a change in the perceived social world—all three are but different expressions of the same process; (9) acceptance of a new set of values and beliefs can usually be brought about item by item; and (10) the individual accepts a new system of values and beliefs by accepting belongingness in a group.

Growth Groups. Lewin's tenth principle spawned a series of group approaches to personal development. Lewin's disciples insisted, and their early research (Watson, 1968) indicated despite counterclaims by professionals and laymen that groups actually induce conformity, the surrender of individual identity, and a consequent mediocrity of behavior, that cohesive groups can support the identification and valuing of individual differences and life experiences as well as offer support for self-direction and productive social behavior. Bradford (1974), an adult educator who was greatly influenced by John Dewey's experiential learning concepts, joined Lewin, Benne, and others in establishing the National Training Laboratories (now known as the NTL Institute for Applied Behavioral Science). The Institute became a means of implementing the principles for helping people learn how to learn in groups through the laboratory method of direct experience and immediate feedback. This process became known generally as sensitivity training, T-groups, or laboratory education. As Benne (1976) pointed out in his review of Lewin's principles and their influence after thirty years, they have received a substantial degree of support as a result of application and have stimulated many personal, organizational, and community development activities.

The basic form that emerged from the early NTL programs was a group consisting of eight to twelve individuals with heterogeneous backgrounds who followed a relatively unstructured format and were assisted by a "facilitator" from education or from one of the helping professions. This person helped the individuals become a group and studied the intrapersonal and group dynamics. Most facilitators seldom participated actively, acting instead as "nondirective" consultants and interpreters. But during the early stage of reeducation in how to learn, the facilitator often had to do some modeling. This phase, and eventually the overall process, depended on the creation of the following conditions: (1) concentration on "here-and-now" events as the basic data for learning; (2) the development of a system for providing immediate and potentially helpful feedback on behavior; (3) the "unfreezing" or freeing of participants from rigid, limited ways of perceiving, interpreting, and behaving; (4) the development and maintenance of a climate of psychological safety so that participants might be willing to risk new behavior and accept the consequent feedback with little defensiveness; (5) the maintenance of a participant observer stance by the members so that all might provide data, help others learn from the data, and learn themselves; and (6) the development of a "cognitive map" by participants for interpreting experiential sequences and learning "what leads to what," with help from brief lectures and selected readings (Schein and Bennis, 1965).

Another major center of influence, Esalen Institute, was founded in 1962 as an experimental center for "well" people to grow and explore their potential. The encounter group, an offshoot of the sensitivity group or T-group of NTL, became an early mainstay of Esalen's program. In their conditions and some of their general goals, encounter groups paralleled the NTL groups; but otherwise they placed less emphasis on maintaining a "here-and-now" climate and on learning about group dynamics, as such, and greater stress on introspection, awareness of intrapersonal dynamics, and the open sharing of feelings. These emphases stimulated experiments with implementing Eastern philosophies in groups at Esalen and in other organizations and programs emerging around the country. Other steps were the incorporation of the existential principles of Gestalt psychology, the use of sensory awareness techniques, and a renewed concentration on "holism," on how mind, emotions, and body function together to increase effectiveness and personal growth. The behavior of the facilitators or consultants in these cases ranged from virtual noninvolvement to active and directive participation.

Peterson (1971) describes more than forty personal growth methods or programs available to adults, most of which appear to have as goals a reeducation in how to learn and an awareness of one's potential. Among these approaches are the Gestalt techniques, pioneered by Frederick Perls; the TORI (trust, openness, realization, and interdependence) workshops, developed by Jack Gibb; Transcendental Meditation, as introduced into the United States by Maharishi Mahesh Yogi; Rolfing (structural integration of the individual), developed by Ida Rolf; and Life Planning workshops, designed by Herbert Shepard.

Social Influences. We must not suppose, of course, that the human potential movement sprang solely from a theoretical base in humanistic psychology and other social sciences. It has flourished partly in response to the unprecedented societal conditions of the past two decades. In this period, several converging forces—for the attainment of long-promised human rights, for political reform, and for recognition of the plundering of the environment—have confronted the restraining forces of the social order. These conflicts, in addition to the effects of the Vietnam war, produced some degree of alienation for many adults, whose counter-cultural activities included experiential learning groups or self-help groups very similar in purpose to those I have already discussed. Philosophically, they appear to combine Lewin's ideas with the humanistic psychology of Maslow and Rogers and with the new organic psychology, which treats the needs of the organism in a social context. One can also detect some roots in modern existentialism, in its emphasis on developing the individual's ability to shape his environment so as to give it personal meaning.

The negative tension produced by the conflicts and demands of society is another factor in the human potential movement. Many adults are seeking group-learning approaches that will help them relax as well as develop their potential for responding creatively to unpredictable environmental circumstances. Some group activities attempt to combine emphases on the development of alternative and strengthened coping mechanisms, peer support, self-awareness, the immediate application of learning, and a sense of freedom to learn.

Role of Adult Education

Adult education has responded to and been a part of the human potential movement in several ways. Since adult education reaches beyond formal educational institutions, permeating many organizations—business and industry, government agencies, health and welfare agencies, labor unions, libraries, the mass media, museums, art institutes, proprietary schools, religious institutions, and voluntary associations—we might say that a number of the personal growth activities already described constitute adult education. But beyond that, we find that adult education in the more formal sense has moved closer and closer to adopting the goals of the human potential movement, both theoretically and practically. For example, the term *andragogy*, which was coined to describe adult education's unique body of theory and practices, includes an emphasis on experiential techniques (Knowles, 1970, 1973) and on engaging the adult learner in active, self-directed inquiry (Knowles, 1975a). As a general principle of andragogy, those methods that encourage learners to analyze their own experience or to take the initiative in seeking out new knowledge, understanding, skills, attitudes, or values tend to bring about personal growth; and conversely, those methods that make learners dependent on authority figures run the risk of impeding personal growth. It follows, then, that certain conditions of learning should exist, at least ideally, in adult education programs: "(1) the learners feel a need to learn; (2) the learning environment is characterized by physical comfort, mutual trust and respect, mutual helpfulness, freedom of expression, and acceptance of differences; (3) the learners perceive the goals of a learning experience to be their goals; (4) the learners accept a share of the responsibility for planning and operating a learning experience, and therefore have a feeling of commitment toward it; (5) the learners participate actively in the learning process; (6) the learning process is related to and makes use of the experience of the learners; and (7) the learners have a sense of progress toward goals" (Knowles, 1970, pp. 52–53). We can easily see that these conditions are consonant with the aims of the human potential movement.

We find, too, that both the forms and the subject matter of adult education are moving toward such consonance. Continuing education courses, short courses, workshops, institutes, nontraditional study, external degree programs, and the like have been grafted onto the traditional foundation in order to meet the special needs of adults, and such activities increasingly have personal growth as a dominant goal. In addition, the standard academic subject-matter categories (English, history, and so on) are giving way in a number of cases to curricula geared to the tasks and roles of adult life. For example, Adkins (1970) of Teachers College, Columbia University, developed a Life Skills curriculum that included as its major tracks "Developing Oneself and Relating to Others," "Managing a Career," "Managing Home and Family Responsibilities," "Managing Leisure Time," "Exercising Community Rights," and "Opportunities and Responsibilities." Another example is a model developed for the UNESCO Institute for Education (described in Knowles, 1975b) in which learning activities are classified according to the abilities required to perform the life roles of learner, self, friend, citizen, family member, worker, and leisure-time user. The skills included in the category "being a self" are self-analyzing, sensing, goal-building, objectivizing, value-clarifying, and expressing. A third instance of the new ways of arranging subject matter comes from the Great Neck, New York, public schools, which in 1976 offered adult education programs on such topics as older Americans, human affairs, and communication skills. Some of these changes are due not just to the influence of the human potential movement but also to the insight that adults are problem centered or task centered in their orientation to learning (Havighurst, 1970; Knowles, 1970; Tough, 1971) and to the current recognition that adults, like younger people, experience developmental stages and therefore have differing needs at each stage in terms of their personal growth.

One notable institutional adaptation of published human potential materials and programs has been in the widespread use of McHolland's (1975) Human Potential Seminar format, especially by community colleges. The Community College of Baltimore, for example, is using the Seminar as an initial structured group experience for incoming adult students, some if not most of whom have experienced failure, frustration, and alienation in other educational ventures. The seminars stress self-affirmation, determination, and motivation; empathic regard for and sharing with others; value identification and clarification; the definition and achievement of realistic goals; and positive self-image. The college released research findings which indicate that these groups contributed to higher academic performance, a higher course-completion rate, and substantially fewer failing grades among the participating students as compared to a matched control group. In addition, students' reactions to the seminars were extremely positive. The findings support statements drawn from experience in other settings in which such programs have been used (Community College of Baltimore, 1976).

Another personal growth program useful as adult education is the Self-Differentiation Laboratory (Weir, 1975), which is presented in different locales throughout the year. These eight- to ten-day programs use a variety of experiential approaches to individual and group learning, to achieve essentially the following objectives: (1) an awareness of the unity of mind and body; (2) growth through the conscious use of experience; (3) the development of personal authority, autonomy, and responsibility; and (4) an awareness and acceptance of differences in others' perception.

Education or Therapy? An Uncertain Future

The foregoing examples have only touched on the overlapping of the human potential movement and adult education. Actually, adult educators have incorporated group approaches to personal growth in thousands of public and private institutions, organizations, and community groups throughout the United States. These activities currently are endangered, not for lack of either participant support or a large body of research that clearly indicates their potential for achieving positive results, but by continuing efforts, expressed in the media and in proposed legislation, to remove personal growth groups from the domain of adult education and place them solely in the domain of mental health.

History of the Issue. The reasons for these efforts are worth exploring. At about the time the NTL form of the adult experiential learning group began to receive the attention of adult educators, social scientists, and other professionals seeking more knowledge of applied group dynamics, the English psychiatrist W. R. Bion (1959) was developing a theory and practice of unstructured group psychotherapy in which the group was regarded as a therapeutic organism rather than as an audience for one-to-one therapy. Parallels between these developments were drawn quickly. Maslow (1962), on observing his first T-group in the early years of the NTL, commented about the power of such a milieu for either significant educational or psychotherapeutic outcomes.

As an educational innovation in the U.S., the intensive experiential learning group attracted many mental health professionals who were inclined to seek symptoms of psychopathology in group members rather than indications of growth potential. This preoccupation with the members' preexisting internal problems was anomalous in view of the original here-and-now, existential orientation of the NTL T-group. Compounding this tendency was a reliance by many clinically trained mental health professionals serving as group facilitators on theories of intrapersonal dynamics rather than interpersonal and group dynamics. By the late 1960s, it appeared to many observers that practitioners at Esalen Institute and even at NTL had shattered the always tenuous boundary between education and therapy.

In addition to this breakdown, other forces were combining in the late 1960s and early 1970s to jeopardize not only the educational role of such groups but their very existence. Ultraconservative factions claimed that the intensive experiential learning group was part of a conspiracy by U.S. enemies. Mental health professionals expressed a well-founded concern that some individuals suffering from a psychopathological condition would seek help in a personal growth group instead of appropriate professional attention. At the same time, some mental health professionals also recognized experiential groups as a major breakthrough for their increasingly maligned discipline and appeared to be interested in restricting the use of such approaches for the benefit of their discipline. Professionals from various disciplines were worried about the obvious lack of a pervading code of ethics for group work. From another sector came other complaints. Managers said there was little evidence that these group activities, as such, had benefited their organizations. Lastly, claims of excessive "casualties" were made by some researchers and participants; and although these were challenged by other researchers (Smith, 1975), they were widely published in the popular press.

The controversy was heightened by the burgeoning of thousands of personal growth programs and hundreds of "centers" (Peterson, 1971), which were frequently accused of being excessively antiintellectual and of being staffed by charlatans offering themselves as facilitators but possessing little preparation for such responsibility. In contrast, Leland Bradford recalled the early NTL commitment to well-prepared group facilitators or trainers and to action research and theory building (Reilly, 1976).

The economic recession of the mid 1970s, along with the publication of codes of ethics and standards for the selection of personal growth opportunities, and the emergence of certification programs (for example, that of the International Association of Applied Social Scientists), apparently resulted in a decrease in the number of "centers" and in reports of questionable practices. And in response to the concerns of management personnel, reputable group planners and staff members learned to be cautious about claiming that the programs can restructure personalities or cause overt changes in leadership behavior. They try to alert potential enrollees to the differences between programs designed to achieve educational goals and those designed for therapy.

Nevertheless, this differentiation remains problematic (Giges and Rosenfeld, 1977). In fact, the difficulties of defining the scope of personal growth groups, determining widely acceptable criteria for identifying competent practitioners, and distinguishing between changes within an individual brought about by learning and those brought about by psychotherapy led the International Association of Applied Social Scientists in 1977 to discontinue temporarily the accreditation of personal growth consultants. In doing so, the Association's board declared its intention to work diligently with other professions and with state legislatures to find ways to evaluate competence and establish criteria for adequate practice in group work. Clearly, the experiential group approach to adult learning—especially the personal growth forms—having spawned myriad offspring, is facing the responsibilities of maturity in an era of instantaneous malpractice lawsuits and endemic public questioning of practices in established helping professions.

The Future. Programs for the personal growth of adults initially were planned and conducted primarily by persons who viewed themselves as educators and who considered their clientele to be healthy persons seeking new dimensions in themselves, in others, and in their environments. Although no stigma may be associated with seeking help from mental health professionals, current trends are obviously causing an increasing number of adults to associate personal growth activities with therapy and a "not-well" condition needing treatment. Ironically, adults generally may come to view announced efforts to achieve the pinnacle of Maslow's hierarchy as attempts to recover from traumas and dysfunctions in their lives. It is quite possible, too, that adult educators will be on the periphery of the movement as other disciplines claim the right to determine the movement's goals and methods. Unless adult educators insist on collective action with other professionals to delineate and defend the primacy of personal growth as an educational goal, this kind of learning may become both restricted and constricted. If adult educators are successful in such action, personal growth activities will become an accepted and widely sought component of all kinds of adult education. And the more extreme versions and practices will eventually disappear.

In summary, adult education for personal growth derives its goals from the purposes of the learner. In general, current participants in personal growth activities are more likely than earlier participants to view themselves and their peers as potential resources for learning. Many formal adult education institutions have adopted task-oriented, problem-centered, learner-involvement emphases, usually requiring reeducation for learning through active involvement and direct use of experience. The promise of human potential and the impact of accelerating societal change on individuals have led to the development of a wide range of personal growth approaches, primarily with experiential group formats. Despite the demonstrated appeal and effectiveness of many such programs, they have been charged with questionable practices by various critics. And although the volume of these charges is diminishing, various professional groups are acting to control questionable practices, and research is refuting some of the charges, a strong possibility exists that adult education for personal growth will become the legislated domain of professionals concerned with and trained for psychotherapy rather than education. The nature and magnitude of education for personal growth as an element in adult education programming is at stake.

Chapter Three

Education for the Aging

Edward E. Marcus
Robert J. Havighurst

The chapter on adult basic education in the 1970 *Handbook of Adult Education* commenced, "This is a time of educational revolution—a time when adults of all ages and from all walks of life are returning to the education they missed when they were of 'school age'" (Cortwright and Brice, 1970, p. 407). The addition of men and women of advanced years to the new clientele of education was signaled at the 1971 White House Conference on Aging, where the delegates declared, "Education is a basic right of all persons of all age groups. It is continuous and therefore one of the ways of enabling older people to have a full and meaningful life, and a means of helping them develop their potential as a resource for the betterment of society" (1971 White House Conference on Aging, 1973, p. 6).

In this chapter we have undertaken to present a comprehensive though necessarily condensed view of the resulting new program area of education for the aging. First we consider its definition, general objectives, theoretical base, and guiding philosophy. Then we discuss the learning needs of the aging, identify certain kinds of impediments to educational progress in this field, and examine the status of the field as appraised by several national studies in 1974. Finally, we provide information about resources and guidelines for the interested student and administrator and take a look at future challenges. The treatment concerns only the situation within the United States as we have examined it. The content and implications of comparative studies covering other lands would have broadened the scope of the chapter but materially reduced its depth; we have no reason to suspect that our observations are fatally culture-bound. True, the details of resources and institutional arrangements mentioned are specifically American, but it is our conviction that the developmental model of aging which we present is universal.

Definitions, Objectives, Theory, and Guiding Philosophy

Education for the aging is distinguished from adult education in general only in the relative longevity of its customers. The word *aging* is used to avoid other terms, such as senior citizen, elderly, and older-aged, which are equally nondescriptive yet are offensive to many. Everyone is aging. In the absence of widespread acceptability of any term, we employ *aging* to mean past the half-century mark of individual existence, although we are aware that some programs for the aging, especially preparation for retirement, may also appeal to persons in their late forties. No substantive definition of the field of education for the aging is possible, since it includes every type of program and subject matter offered to younger persons; preretirement planning is its only exclusive program. The only reasons for singling it out for attention are that (1) historically, the aging were regarded neither as interested in education nor as feasible clients for it and (2) some minor modifications of setting and technique are advised for teaching the aging, which will be mentioned later. Education for the aging is not the same idea as "education for aging." The latter phrase refers to

special modifications of the common school curriculum and somewhat rare additions to professional and religious continuing education for the purpose of helping children and younger adults to
understand what old age is and to prepare for its advent in their
own lives.

The objectives of education for the aging include practically
all that would be specified for younger learners, including vocational training and retraining, preparation for "new careers," and
upgrading occupational skills. The only objectives that might be
added after age fifty are (1) exercising body and mind to keep them
alert and vigorous, (2) adequate use of the vastly increased leisure
time available to many persons following their retirement, and (3)
preparation for volunteer service of various kinds. Even these three
objectives are not unique to education for the aging, differing from
the overall objectives of adult education only in emphasis, not in
type.

Nature and custom, acting together, have set the last portion
of human life apart from the rest of it. By "nature," we refer to the
physiological and psychological concomitants of aging; by "custom,"
to social and cultural arrangements to accomplish the succession of
generations, which determine the positions and influence of those
who reach old age. Living is a process of continuous human development. Seeming discontinuities in it, such as retirement from occupations and age-related discriminations of the propriety of behavior,
are introduced by society. Thus, older adults are treated as different
kinds of beings from young and middle-aged adults, even though
growing old is an individual experience and the aging do not constitute a category of people who are all alike. Neugarten (1975)
advocated distinguishing between the "young-old," who are between
fifty-five and seventy-five and generally continue to be vigorous and
healthy, and the "old-old," for whom physical condition and health
may become a serious problem. The young-old ought to be regarded as all other adults in matters of concern to educators. Yet
because the aging are all too often considered a group apart, they
appear to constitute a separate clientele for adult education.

Moody (1976) grouped the philosophical presuppositions of
education for the aging in four models. The first, *rejection,* involves
avoidance, repression, neglect, isolation, and expendability; it pro-

vides no rationale for educating older adults. The second model is *social services,* an expression of political liberalism and the institutions of the welfare state; as a viewpoint, it gives rise to providing education for the aging as a form of entertainment to keep them busy. A model opposed to the denial of life and the elevation of passivity, *participation,* is a view which proclaims continuing activity as the norm for healthful human life. Education for participation consists of "consciousness raising," leadership training for advocacy roles, and preparation for second careers and other opportunities for genuine participation. The fourth model, *self-actualization,* depends on a conception of human life as possessing unending potential for development—that is, something must be uniquely possible in old age that is not realizable at earlier periods. Accordingly, educators have the responsibility to nourish the psychological growth that is most appropriate in the last stage of the human journey.

Moody's categorization is the fruit of an evolution of ideas about aging. In American thought, aging originally was accepted as a state of decline leading to death—the antecedent of the rejection model in any social system that accords honor mainly for continuing economic productivity. *Disengagement theory,* usually associated with the names of Elaine Cumming and William Henry, was a forward step in allocating to the aging responsibility for separating themselves voluntarily as well as involuntarily from their social roles at the same time that society presses them to do so because of their advancing age, the reward being unlimited leisure to pursue hobbies and recreation to the end of their days. The antithesis to this, called *activity theory,* equates ongoing engagement in life with successful aging and is the gerontological counterpart of the participation model. Meanwhile, the separate but cumulative contributions to human thought of such developmentalists as Erik Erikson, Abraham Maslow, and Robert Havighurst refocused attention on the meaning of existence. Does development persist through all phases of life? Is human life useless at any age? How much waste of time does nature program for in its biological cycles? Are efforts to increase human longevity mocked by immutable boundaries of function and potential?

Erikson (1963) postulated two "ages of man" built upon,

but going beyond, childhood stages: those concerned with generativity versus stagnation and ego integrity versus despair. Generativity has to do with establishing and guiding the next generation, a gradual expansion of ego interests, and a libidinal investment in that which is generated—in short, unflagging interest in the world fashioned by one's own production and one's progeny. Ego integrity is acceptance of one's one and only life as necessary, unique, and worthy. For Maslow (1971), self-actualization is the distillation of the peak experiences in one's life and is probably possible only in later maturity. Havighurst's (1976a) concept of the *developmental task*, which must be achieved at or about a certain phase in life if adults are to be judged and to judge themselves competent, makes a connection between human development and programs of education for the aging. A developmental task is set by both biological and social forces acting within or upon individuals. Some developmental tasks are closely related to instrumental forms of education; for others, instrumental education has relatively little value. For instance, many adults postpone until middle age the task of becoming responsible and informed citizens. And adjusting to bodily changes becomes critical after age forty-five. Both of the foregoing are suitable for instrumental education. In contrast, some of the expressive forms of education are particularly functional in enabling adults to become more effectively sociable with friends and neighbors after they have attained some of their most personal goals, and to profit from and enjoy increased leisure in retirement.

Like Neugarten, Havighurst distinguished between early and later old age. Between fifty-five and seventy-five, education "can be a way of helping to plan a strategy for the later years. It can diminish disengagement, particularly physiologically; even people severely disabled by the afflictions of old age can learn to reestablish some of their physical abilities. It can help in reengagement, giving people the ability to take part in new interests and activities. And it can itself be one of those activities, helping to occupy the time which the old person often has in abundance" (Havighurst, 1976b, pp. 48–49). After seventy-five, when individuals are engaged in learning, "it is likely to be related to a sense of personal need in one or more of the following respects: to live their lives with dignity, self-control and comfort; to spend their time with satisfaction and enjoyment; to make some contribution to society; to remain as far as possible a part of normal community life including interacting with younger persons; and most important of all, to maintain vitality of body and mind" (Havighurst, 1976b, p. 49).

Other models of aging have been suggested that also hold ideas of worth for educational practice. The *social roles model,* for example, implies the need for efforts to help older adults identify or devise and assume new roles in a society where the traditional roles of dispenser of wisdom and conservator of culture are either outmoded or rejected and the "plight of the elderly" is assumed to be their unwonted rolelessness. The *transactional model* attracts attention to the options for negotiation available to the aging; in this case, the educator's major contribution is to enable the aging to multiply and expand their choices.

The best justification for expenditure to educate the aging is a guiding philosophy of development that is superior to the considerations derived from the other models of aging. If productivity is the only publicly acceptable measure of the goodness of life, there can be no excuse for wasting money educating "old folks" who are not employed or will not be employed for long. The welfare model provides for grudging allocations as a form of charity to help "decayed relics" of better days endure their otherwise empty lives. Participation, as a philosophical model, yields a positive rationale based on the right of aging adults to continue to share in the common enterprise and to take courses that enable them to avoid dependency and to contribute to the social weal just as younger people do. But the belief that the development of the individual is a lifelong process, never fully completed until terminated by death, implies that denying the privilege of continuing education actually constitutes a form of deprivation for many, which closes off opportunities to continue growing and thus can prevent them from achieving the fullest actualization of their capabilities. What kind of society would systematically refuse its members—all of whom age—the chance to realize their highest level of development? Not the good society that is everyone's goal. This argument is strengthened further when combined with the observation that the aging have, in fact, already "paid their way" in the economy and deserve a decent return on their lifelong investment of work and taxes.

Learning Needs of The Aging

According to O'Toole (1974, pp. 12–13), "most Americans follow a path through life in which education is synonymous with youth, work with adulthood, and retirement with old age." Such segmentation of life produces the problem of segregated generations, in which education occurs at schools that are "youth ghettos," and the activity of the aged occurs increasingly in " 'leisure communities' cut off from the rest of the world, both spiritually and physically." The result is so little mixing of generations that only with difficulty does anybody escape from the track established by early experience, and the values of each generation are not freely transmitted within the society. An age-cohort effect prevails, which involves an entire generation of persons who participated in education to only a limited extent in youth, did not expand their participation during adulthood, and do not flood back into school after they retire from work—even when the opportunity is available to them. Finally, institutional inflexibilty hardly allows adaptation to cross-generational needs; and since educational institutions are accustomed to working with the young, they find it easier to identify and meet their needs than to meet those of the aging.

The outcome of these tendencies appears as a reduction with age in the amount of participation in education. Recent studies agreed that approximately 2 percent of persons past age sixty-five were enrolled in educational activities, as compared to over 33 percent between twenty-five and thirty-four, 21 percent between thirty-five and forty-four, 15 percent between forty-five and sixty-four, and 5 percent between fifty-five and sixty-four (Academy for Educational Development, 1974, Chart 2, p. 11). The survey findings of Harris and Associates (1975) regarding this matter were similar.

The effect of aging on the need for education is not well understood. If "need" is regarded as a psychological concept pertaining to the motivation to act, then action of some sort is the overt evidence of the existence of need. Yet if only two older adults per one hundred enroll voluntarily in educational programs, surely one cannot assume that so few of that age group need education. Their lack of involvement does not indicate that they might not benefit from participating in education. It does indicate that older adults are not conscious of the particular values that education may hold for them. So DeCrow's declaration (1974) that the learning needs of the aging are not significantly different from those of other adults should not be interpreted too literally, since the aging themselves may be unaware of the fact.

McClusky (n.d.) categorized the learning needs of the aging as the need to cope, to express oneself, to contribute, to have an influence, and to transcend. Our own feeling about this list is that three basic classes are sufficient: the needs for survival, self-esteem, and transcendence. The survival needs are life-and-death challenges that the older adult strives to overcome. The self-esteem needs relate to feelings of regret and nostalgia for the past, boredom and dissatisfaction in the present, and frustration with factors, such as fear of the ultimate loss of independence, that tend to limit life increasingly in the future. The need for transcendence refers to the continuing desire for fulfillment and personal growth (McClusky, n.d.), to the emergent generativity and ego integrity (Erikson, 1963), and to self-actualization (Maslow, 1971).

Adult educators believe they design and offer learning experiences useful to the aging in satisfying these categories of needs, but their success is debatable. Havighurst (1963) identified two basic aspects of education, instrumental and expressive, both of which are essential for lifelong learning. For the aging, education is instrumental when it helps learners master the particular skills they need to overcome external challenges, and expressive when it assists them to transcend their personal limitations. Londoner (1971) claimed that adult education for the aging is largely expressive, whereas the greater need of older adults is for education with instrumental value. Yet Marcus (1976) found that with age people's perception of which is more useful—participating in instrumental education or in expressive education—tends to shift, although the activities participated in may be classified by perceptive judges as instrumental. His finding suggests some of the complexity of the task of the educator, since today's older adults are apt to have learning needs that require instrumental programs in order to fulfill them, while they tend to perceive education as satisfying needs for expression. Accordingly, those older persons who participate in adult education are more likely than not to be affluent, because they can afford to indulge their expressive interests and because the more affluent are likely to have had greater experience with education and to be in the habit of participating in it. The predominantly middle-class cast of adult education persists in relation to age.

Participating in education appears to be a habit established for life. If it is not established early, it is not apt to be established. The data essential to understanding this matter indicate that (1) nonparticipation in adult education is generally associated with low levels of educational attainment and (2) the population of adults over age sixty-five has a lower average level of educational attainment than the remainder of the population. The combination of these two facts explains the seeming indifference of most of the aging to opportunities for continuing education. It does not speak to the absence of need, either ascribed or conscious.

However, for many decades census figures have reflected a steady climb in the educational level attained by the general populace. Those figures probably signify a progressive increase in lifelong participation in education. For the next half century, the aging population should display rising expectations of being served by educational institutions. Such growing demand for education by the aging will be bolstered by other kinds of anticipated demographic change, including continuing expansion of their numbers, both absolutely and in proportion to the other age categories. Approximately 22.5 million persons now in the United States are sixty-five or older; the figure is expected to reach more than 30 million by the year 2000. The proportion probably will grow from the current 10 percent of the population to about 15 percent by 2025, assuming constant levels of fertility and immigration and only a slight further increase in life expectancy. Moreover, prolonged health and vigor should be more characteristic of people attaining old age in the future than of those in the past, and these factors should add to their inclination to participate in education.

A variable closely related to educational attainment is economic status. The intellectual impoverishment that accompanies low educational attainment usually has its counterpart in physical poverty. The aging, caught in the spider's web of reciprocal reinforcements of physical poverty and intellectual impoverishment, display many tokens of social and cultural impairment, such as poor health and diet, inadequate housing, family dependency, and political powerlessness. Each of these deficiencies could be ameliorated through additional education. But the poor are not the only class of older adults with various kinds of educationally remediable needs.

The tradition of bygone times, when the elderly were honored more than they are today, is partially mythical. In past eras few persons survived to "ripe old age." Those who did usually worked up to the time they died. They retained control over their families and property; thus, they held on to power to assure that they received respect. Probably the respect which they were accorded also was tinged with some natural awe for the rare occurrence of long life. Today, longevity is not rare, young families are independent of control by their elders, and the institution of retirement separates the aging from positions in which they formerly exercised authority. Present-day society provides no alternative social roles that assure the aging a degree of respect equivalent to what they previously enjoyed. Furthermore, its goods, services, and physical layouts are not designed to be most useful to the aging. As a consequence, persons even in comfortable circumstances must learn to adjust to a variety of problems as they age.

To be added to the factors so far mentioned are trends toward more adequate and stable incomes and forecasts of tendencies that will influence future attitudes toward employment. Financial support for many older adults was poorly provided under the inadequate arrangements that prevailed in the past. But with the initiation, supplementation, improvement, and reform of both social security and private pension systems has come popular acceptance of the practice of retirement. The discriminatory feature of mandatory age-based retirement is expected to be eliminated in the years ahead through legislative and judicial action, leaving a variety of paths open to older-aged workers, including voluntary retirement, partial retirement, job retention, and new careers. The precedent for adopting sixty-five as the appropriate age for superannuation was established in Bismarck's Germany a century ago, when comparatively few individuals reached that age. The folly of applying the same rule today is increasingly evident, but merely elevating the retirement age across the board appeals to no one. For some, the opportunity to retire early voluntarily is a godsend—for example, leading to improved health in those whose work is physically strenuous or stressful. However, professional, managerial, and technical workers are less inclined to regard retirement as an unmitigated blessing, often preferring to reduce the intensity and pace of their occupational activities on their own initiative.

The continued impetus for the retention of forced retirement relies on the argument that jobs are scarce for younger workers. But proposed government policies favoring full employment, the decline in the birthrate that commenced about 1960, and the disappearance of cheap energy all foreshadow the possibility that pressures to remove the aging from the labor force will subside. Since 1970, the number of Americans between age five and age thirteen has declined. The dependency ratio of the young, or the total number of persons under age twenty per 100 persons aged twenty to sixty-four, dipped from 74.1 in 1960 to 67.5 in 1973 and is expected to go as low as 45.5 by the year 2010. Some interpret that projection as indicating the coming of a labor shortage after 1980 that will be severe enough to stimulate the return of many older workers to the work force; Peter Drucker foresaw a major training and retraining challenge as a result. Others do not expect the adult labor surplus to end very soon, but believe that the questions of need for the labor of older adults is going to depend instead on the cost of energy ("ASTD Has Good News . . . ," 1976).

The high standard of living that the U.S. has enjoyed was based on the ready availability of large quantities of fossil fuels, particularly of cheap petroleum. But petroleum is no longer cheap. If the current rate of consumption persists, petroleum will become almost unobtainable by the year 2010. The price of energy has more than doubled since 1972, and unless sources other than petroleum, natural gas, and coal are drawn on increasingly, the price can be expected to soar during the next quarter century. The result will be complex changes in our technology and way of life, such as those discussed creatively by Mesarovic and Pestel (1974) and Commoner (1976). The labor force of the future likely will be employed more in small-scale forms of production and service requiring fewer heavy machines and petrochemicals. This means that there will be more work of the kind that older adults can do easily and well, including many part-time jobs within walking distance of home. Corresponding to this development will arise the need for education and training to help older persons adjust to the new industries and work patterns. Indeed, the next decade probably will witness the emergence of a new, major emphasis in adult education on the preparation of people for an energy-sparing and labor-intensive technology.

Even should no increase occur in the demand for the services of the aging, another factor that will blunt the force of the recent drive toward eariler retirement will be the movement toward second careers and flexible careers. Just as the shortening of the work day led many workers to "moonlight," contradicting the notion that people would be content with an ever-growing amount of leisure, shortening the normal work life is beginning to lead many retirees to embark on another career after the termination of their first. Security in earned retirement income makes possible the gratification of a natural desire for a new start in life after families have been reared. In time, the idea of a mid-life career change generally may replace that of retirement. People will prepare for alternation between periods of continuing education and periods of renewed employment during the adult life span. The concepts of lifelong education and a learning society also are part of the comprehensive drift toward a path through life different from the one that heretofore prevailed.

The emergence of the aging as a massive population category brought into being a host of related social concerns, policies, institutions, occupations, and customs. Just as a whole system developed historically around the child, another whole system is developing around the aging, especially around the "old-old," who require a great deal of support and facilitation. This development also holds great potential for adult and continuing education. Perhaps it would be more meaningful to refer here to education about the aging than education for the aging. But since many older adults are going to be involved in the programs that are going to be developed, the distinction is arbitrary. Only the unfortunate view that most of the aging are incapable tends to limit the provision of the requisite training to young and middle-aged adults. With the growth of strong politically oriented advocacy organizations among the aging, any notion that only the youthful should be employed to serve the elderly will dissipate, and more older adults will ready themselves to provide the social, therapeutic, and supportive services that their agemates require. The following illustrate the kind of programs that we have referred to:

1. The provision of entry and in-service training to service providers in a multitude of fields—health, mental health, counseling, rehabilitation, welfare, manpower, education, homemaker assistance, nutrition, and community organization.

2. Extended family training to include not only parent and grandparent effectiveness but the roles of the second and third generation in nurturing their aging members and coping with the exigencies of three-, four-, and five-generation family constellations.

3. Preretirement planning, or preparation for retirement, which—if the prospect of retirement to inactivity continues to offer little allurement—will evolve into a generalized concept of life planning in which planning for mid-life career changes and active eventual retirement are elements.

4. Preparation of the aging for a host of specialized community service and leadership roles that will emerge as public acceptance and policies change regarding the positions especially suited to older adults. The outlines of some of these new roles already can be discerned, such as that of the volunteer (foster grandparent, court-watcher, nursing home ombudsman), the paid adviser (professional, technical, industrial, managerial), and the qualified member of a public commission, board of consumers, or other body charged with protecting the rights and welfare of the older population and representing it in social planning and setting goals.

The dividing line between education and service has become paper thin, and according to Houle (1975), education for the aging will become more involved in many settings outside the school such as extended-care facilities, retirement homes, senior citizen centers, local museums, travel clubs, and voluntary associations.

Goals and Impediments to Progress

The opportunity for a major expansion of adult education for the aging is apparent for the remainder of this century, but the actual increase in their participation is going to depend on the creativity and dedication of program sponsors and their capacity to adapt programs to the special characteristics of over-fifty learners. The difficulties and pitfalls the program sponsors face will include the following:

1. Generally, older adults do not perceive themselves in the image of students. Although many indicate that they are interested in learning various things, when asked why they do not engage in studying what they want to learn, they are inclined to respond that they are too old, no longer have enough energy, lack the time and money, have other responsibilities, or do not wish to conform to the requirements. Eventually, the improving health and vigor and rising educational level of the young-old should modify some of the low self-esteem and alienation which underlies these responses, but it will take more than the customary promotional techniques to convince many of today's aging that educational participation is worth the costs and risks. For one thing, it will take the active involvement of the young-old themselves as program stimulators, developers, designers, promoters, leaders, and teachers.

2. Tuition fees cannot be relied on as a major source of program support because of the stringent pecuniary circumstances of most older persons. Fortunately, the number of ways to pay for programs for the aging under both public and nonpublic auspices is increasing, although changes in the national economy probably will continue to pose serious problems for program administrators. Community-wide planning with thorough and well-founded development is going to be essential for the sustained growth of programming.

3. The old-old cannot travel by themselves to campuses out-

side their neighborhoods. Either suitable transportation will have to be provided for them, or adult education will have to be brought to them in their communities and institutions. This fact will contribute to the costs of programs and to the complexity of planning and administration.

4. Special preparation of teachers and special instructional techniques, materials, and facilities will be required. The aging are not a unique category; established educational principles and practices work with them. But an awareness of the qualities and infirmities that constitute aging is necessary for appropriate adjustments and empathic understanding to occur. Common knowledge usually is adequate for muddling through with regard to such matters as speaking loudly and distinctly, improving lighting, and using large-size print. But only basic gerontological grounding can help teachers cope with the different values and beliefs, attitudes toward authority, sets of age-cohort historical experiences, and perspectives on time and achievement that form the lines of demarcation among different generations.

Adult educators are responsible for meeting the changing learning needs of the whole aging population—for fulfilling the rising expectations of a growing clientele of better-educated, more physically healthy and mentally vigorous adults and helping them to prepare either for extended retirement or for new roles, jobs, and careers after the midpoint of life. Adult educators are also responsible for training relatives and service providers in the care of the aging, all in a variety of institutional settings. Already, more than half the national population above twenty-five years of age is more than fifty-five years old. That fact furnishes all the justification necessary for the burgeoning excitement about and interest in the prospects ahead.

Status and Issues

The 1971 White House Conference on Aging sparked a set of first-time surveys and studies, most of them reported in 1974, which provided a basic store of information about this kind of programming. Most comprehensive was the Adult Education Association's survey of about 3,500 programs presented by agencies presumed to possess the capacity to provide general learning opportunities for older adults living in American communities (De-Crow, n.d.). The American Association of Community and Junior Colleges' report covered programs of cultural enrichment for older adults offered by more than 340 two-year colleges (Korim, 1974a, 1974b). Educational opportunities for the aging in colleges and universities were described in the report of a study by the Academy for Educational Development (1974). A 1969 federal survey of participation in adult education resulted in initial and final reports published in 1972 and 1974, respectively, by the National Center for Education Statistics, which included data pertaining to programs for the aging (Okes, 1974). Another publication containing relevant information was the report of the Educational Testing Service's study of nontraditional programs (Cross, Valley, and Associates, 1974). The National Advisory Council on Adult Education's report the same year dealt with the aging as a target population. The following year, the Harris survey for the National Council on the Aging, titled *The Myth and Reality of Aging in America,* included questions and findings concerning participation in education. A much earlier ground-breaking study of participation by the National Opinion Research Center (Johnstone and Rivera, 1965) also supplied data still valuable to practitioners and students of education for the aging.

All these reports should be consulted for specialized statistical information about the state of the art in the early 1970's, as well as for descriptive and interpretative discussion, including illustrations of programs. Taken together, their findings indicated that (1) the field of education for the aging has only begun to be tapped but already is incredibly complex; (2) the capacity of the aging to respond to the initiatives of adult educators is not limited—the more education is provided for them, the more apt they are to desire and patronize it; (3) all educational sponsors have a role to play in expanding the field; and (4) undue emphasis on social and recreational programs in education for the aging is not justified. Indeed, the survey information concerning programs and components suggested that primary attention should be focused on moving education for the aging away from its past concentration on social and recreational activities, particularly in large urban areas, where the potential audience includes numerous persons of low socioeconomic status. Where the prevailing level of affluence is relatively high, older adults seem to prefer programs of general knowledge and cultural enrichment. Yet the practical skills, including vocational training, also are attractive to many adults of medium and high status.

A new development in Chicago may be worthwhile for urban adult educators to watch. Area institutions of higher education have formed a consortium called "The Metropolitan Chicago Older Adult Education Network" for the purpose of providing educational experiences and services for the aging. Specifically, the Network proposes to increase the participation of older persons as students, teachers, and staff members; expand interinstitutional communication and cooperation; involve business and industry; influence attitudes; and project education as the key to broadening the life options of the elderly. Information on the consortium may be obtained from the Chicago Community Trust, 208 South LaSalle Street, Chicago, Illinois 60606. Since no category of sponsoring institution or type of program emerges as best for the aging, it appears unlikely that any educational counterpart of the development of housing and communities just for older persons is in the offing. Few institutions founded to serve only the old have been successful for long, a conspicuous exception being the Institute of Lifetime Learning of the National Retired Teachers Association and the American Association of Retired Persons. The surveys indicated that the overall program area is still wide open for cultivation by any interested sponsor and planner.

The various reports described above dealt with what might be called the ground-zero situation, and trends cannot be deduced from them. We may presume that the trend most characteristic of the 1970s was the initiation of a great variety of programs organized along very diverse lines, and that it was inevitable that many, perhaps most, of them would prove unsuccessful in the long run and lead to abandonment of the kinds of approach represented in them. Yet undoubtedly it was a time of bustling experimentation that will lead to the identification and improvement of promising patterns of activity. Possibly some of the most prevalent and fruitful educational work with the aging during that decade was not adequately captured in the surveys cited but consisted of programs originated and conducted at senior centers and clubs, congregate eating sites, nursing homes, and other locations not under established educational auspices. If this surmise is true, the actual number of adults over sixty-five who are reached by organized educational endeavors may well exceed the 2 percent participation rate commonly reported.

Resources and Guidelines

Adult educators who are interested in increasing older adults' participation in adult education can get help from various resources and guidelines that are useful in designing and administering programs. Because so much innovative work is being done in this area, any published account is somewhat out of date by the time it is read. Nevertheless, the following information, which was current in mid 1976, should assist those who are not in the forefront of developments. The topics taken up include reference material, agencies and associations, financial support, personnel, facilities and materials, promotion and publicity, administration, noneducational services, and the aging as advocates of education. A note of caution is required here. Any major kind of programming that has developed since the mid 1960s is necessarily changing rapidly; hence the ideas we furnish here in the hope of assisting the reader reflect only our transitory, though reasoned, judgment as observers and practitioners at this time.

Reference Material. There has been as yet no systematic, comprehensive treatise on educational programming for the aging. However, the literatures of both education and gerontology offer much of value to readers seeking information. The compilation of papers published by the Adult Education Association, entitled *Learning for Aging* (Grabowski and Mason, n.d.), concerns various aspects of major interest. Basic references regarding the learning capacity of older persons include *Intellectual Functioning in Adults: Psychological and Biological Influences* (Jarvik, Eisdorfer, and Blum, 1973); *Cognitive Processes in Maturity and Old Age* (Botwinick, 1967); and the excellent chapter by David Arenberg in *The Psychology of Adult Development and Aging* (Eisdorfer and Lawton, 1973). Pertinent journals include *Educational Gerontology,*

Adult Education, Lifelong Learning—The Adult Years, The Gerontologist, and periodicals in other professional, scientific, and technical fields; all but the first-named have only occasional articles on the subject, and so it is necessary to consult their volume indexes for references. Specialized handbooks also exist, such as those published at Florida State University (Verner and Davison, 1971; Hendrickson, 1973). Detailed reading lists can be obtained from the ERIC Clearinghouses (for example, No. 37 from the Clearinghouse on Career Education), various university gerontological centers and institutes, and the National Multi-Media Center for Adult Education at Montclair (New Jersey) State College. Published proceedings of conferences, such as the Leadership Development Institutes at Florida State University, are other good sources of information.

Agencies and Associations. Federal, state, and local agencies, national and regional professional and membership associations, and college and university education and psychology departments provide publications and, in some cases, consultation and technical assistance. Federal agencies which offer various kinds of aid are the Administration on Aging and the Social Security Administration, both in the Department of Health, Education, and Welfare; the Manpower Administration of the Department of Labor; and the Cooperative Extension Service of the Department of Agriculture. The list of agencies that can counsel on and participate in educational programs for the aging includes health departments, law enforcement agencies, transportation authorities, employment services, divisions of insurance and banking, and divisions of public aid and welfare, in addition to state departments and area agencies on aging. Specific associations interested in the program area include the Gerontological Society, the National Council on the Aging (NCOA), the National Retired Teachers Association and the American Association of Retired Persons, and the National Council of Senior Citizens; educational societies such as the Adult Education Association of the USA, the National Association of Public Continuing and Adult Education, and the Association for Gerontology in Higher Education; and other organizations representing different kinds of services rendered to older persons, such as the American Public Welfare Association, the National Association of Homes for the Aging, and the American Library Association. The enterprising educator also can obtain a surprising amount of help from chambers of commerce, banks, newspapers, visiting nurses associations, travel associations, and ethnic societies. The major religious faiths and denominations also offer programs, services, and publications for the elderly, sometimes in cooperation with local educational institutions. Even so, this list is by no means exhaustive.

Financial Support. Federal revenue-sharing funds and grants under specific programs for older Americans, state and local matching and special-purpose funds, and "seed money" and services in kind from foundations, associations, and local groups and individuals can be expected to supplement regular tax support for education. It is a growing practice to eliminate or substantially reduce tuition fees for persons over a specified age, although in the long run serious ethical and legal questions may be raised about policies that discriminate on the basis of age. It may be more desirable to offer aid in the form of scholarships, transportation, domiciliary arrangements, and free books and supplies. Cooperation with community organizations also can reduce some of the special costs of operating programs for the aging.

Personnel. So far, only tentative answers can be given to questions about human relations which affect the aging, such as the best "age mix" in educational programs for older persons, whether or under what conditions classes should be age-integrated or age-segregated, whether teachers should also be older or younger than the students, and of what age the people who plan programs for older people should be. Program administrators must handle such matters on an ad hoc basis, but the following generalizations may be helpful. In courses offered as part of the regular curricula of the sponsoring institution, it is customary to integrate students of all ages in the classes and to use the services of regularly employed instructors, regardless of their age. Programs established especially for older adults usually are kept age-segregated, but their teachers may be any age. It is desirable now and will become increasingly important in the future that the training of teachers of adults also include exposure to gerontology to assure greater sensitivity to the physical and social attributes of aging, for example, the slowing of physiological response time and impaired self-esteem in some persons. An advisory committee of older adults working cooperatively with the administrator can do much to legitimate programs for the older members of the community. Such a committee should provide counsel concerning the content of the curriculum and the selection of instructors. And lastly, good social policy suggests the employment of qualified retired teachers, professionals, and technicians as part-time faculty and staff members.

Facilities and Materials. Until education is better accepted as a suitable activity for older adults, it will be difficult to attract them to participate. One way to do so is to hold classes in more desirable meeting places, such as churches, park fieldhouses, neighborhood social centers, senior clubs, and even private homes. However, many institutions have effectively lured older residents to their campuses for recreation and special events and gradually accustomed them to regard the institution as a community center. Where fear of crime prevails, classes should be scheduled during daylight hours.

In general, classes for the aging ought not to require them to climb flights of stairs. Adult educators should use ground-level rooms, or rooms at other levels at times when elevators, ramps, and staircases are reasonably uncongested. Activities involving reading, drawing, sewing, and other finely scaled behavior should be held in rooms that are well-lighted but without glare. Special sight-saving editions of some publications can be obtained. A lectern equipped with a public address system is very important. No other special furnishings are required, but the best setting is an informal arrangement of chairs and tables, preferably including some with firm arm rests to hold on to while sitting down and getting up. For the old-old, either programs will have to be held in the centers of homes where they congregate or reside, or many of them will need to be transported in vehicles specially equipped and adapted for their use to locations with particular features, such as ramps and toilet facilities with handle bars.

Promotion and Publicity. In general the promotional appeals of greatest potency for the younger-aged, such as those emphasizing preparation for an occupation or a career and the status conferred by earning a diploma or a degree, have more limited value in retirement. Older adults tend to eschew competition and taking examinations. Still, it is a mistake to offer "fun and games" as the reason to participate in any serious educational endeavor. A major handicap to promotion is that many of today's elderly are nonreaders and poor readers, which tends to present a formidable communication challenge to adult educators who wish to recruit them. Therefore, adult educators must develop a "transmission belt" with local organizations of older adults, using community agencies and spokesmen. Efforts should be concentrated on reaching out through family members, already enrolled elderly, and neighborhood churches, clubs, and employers.

Administration. A staff and faculty member should be designated the adviser or consultant on activities for the aging, to be the connection with the transmission belt for prospective students. The adviser also may be the actual director or coordinator of the program, but the most important function of the role must be to make contact. The adviser should be knowledgeable about the characteristics of older adults and able to interpret them to administrators and teachers. Separate functions, where staffing permits, can be performed by a program designer, a coordinator, and a counselor for older adults. Routines of enrollment and other procedures should be kept simple, especially if the older clients served are barely literate. Administrators should register the learners right in the classes or at convenient tables, keep the forms brief and clearly legible, and use monitors or large visual aids to direct learners through corridors to classrooms.

Noneducational Services. It is difficult to separate education for the aging from the provision of various social services to them because of the nature and range of their needs and the value of the point of contact in both time and place. Thus, arrangements for congregate feeding of older adults are easily adapted to the provision of interesting speakers, demonstrations, motion pictures, musical performances, the distribution of reading matter, and individual counseling concerning personal interests and problems. The institution can assist elderly persons to cope with bureaucratic requirements in connection with such matters as social security, Medicare, food stamps, and other rights and benefits. Interviews for employment and volunteer services can be held in educational settings and coupled with the provision of preparatory training, background information, and vocational guidance. An educational facility also can be the site of consumer assistance in connection with paying taxes, legal actions, health care matters, and protection in the purchase and maintenance of homes, automobiles, and appliances.

The Aging as Advocates of Education. The use of older persons as employees and volunteers in adult education benefits the educator, the older persons employed, the program clientele, and the community as a whole. Older adults can serve effectively as program coordinators, advisers, counselors, teachers, teacher aides, resource authorities, discussion leaders, registrars, monitors, illustrators, performers, demonstrators, role players, secretaries, supply clerks, and mailers. Every older individual incorporated in the program operations is a potential advocate of the worth of participating in it.

Current beliefs about the learning ability of the aging continue to depend on a biologically based age-decrement model. In combination with misconceptions about the so-called generation gap, these beliefs tend to perpetuate rejection of the aging as serious students and the classification of hobbies as "adult education" for the aging. But reviewers of research findings on adult and gerontological intelligence agree that the stereotype of decline is overdue for change. According to Baltes and Schaie (1974), the view that intelligence begins to slide downhill around the fourth decade of life was an outgrowth of the cross-sectional nature of early research and the age bias of I.Q. tests. These authors reported a longitudinal study by Schaie in which only visuomotor flexibility, which requires coordination between visual and motor abilities, decreased with age. Cognitive flexibility, or the ability to shift from one way of thinking to another, showed no strong age-related change, whereas crystallized intelligence, or the skills acquired through education and acculturation, increased right into old age. Other scientists have found age decrements in fluid intelligence—which consists of abilities thought to be relatively culture-free—but only on the basis of cross-sectional data that obscure the influence of generational differences. The distinction between competence and performance needs to be considered: in the case of the aging, the latter is susceptible to the effects of fatigue, dwindling reinforcements, intellectually and socially impoverished environments, and lack of compensatory education. The literature on the plasticity of adult intellectual behavior reveals the existence of large interindividual differences both within and between age cohorts and across ability domains, but the potential range of intelligence in the aging is still largely unexplored. However, most recent research shows no evidence of any age decrement in the ability to learn.

Experience in conducting programs for mixed-age groups has tended to undermine still another prevalent notion, that the age categories are mutually incompatible in the classroom. Studies of generational value structures suggest that the young and the old resemble each other in their attitudes more than either may resemble the generation between. There are numerous examples of youth welcoming the presence and participation of older-aged persons in their activities. A developing type of adult education activity is the intergenerational encounter workshop involving planned dialogue among members of three or more generations which provides a means for each to examine and redefine human and social attitudes. It offers promise as a useful tool for training and educating personnel in the helping professions.

The aging themselves are going to serve as the main resource for adult educators in developing effective programs for the older age groups. Information, even from authoritative sources, that is not supplemented by actual contact with many of the aging is insufficient to undergird attempts to provide for their education. Their collective characteristics influence mainly the consideration of facilities, materials, and means of promotion. Individually and in groups, they are indispensable allies in designing curricula, raising funds, manning staffs and faculties, and spreading the word in the community. The participation of the aging—as resource persons, as recipients of much-needed education-related services, and as fully capable learners—with persons of other ages tends to stimulate and enrich both the social climate and the intellectual discourse within sponsoring institutions. Age exclusivity in adult education has value only for certain specific ends, such as remedial education, and probably will decline in proportion to the amount of education that eventually will be provided on a mixed-age basis.

As a component of adult education, education for the aging affords probably the greatest opportunity left for novel institutional accomplishments. The client population is large and still growing;

its needs are great and substantially unmet. The prediction that older adults will participate in ever-increasing numbers during the remainder of this century seems well based. The greatest challenge to the field appears to be to find ways of moving beyond a concentration on social and recreational activities, especially in the large urban centers of the nation. A guiding philosophy of development provides positive justification for educational effort throughout the life span. Thus educational development is as important for the highest quality of life among the aging as it is for the preparation of the young to live their lives.

Chapter Four

Women's Education

Helen M. Feeney

The various dimensions of women's education in the United States today are not easy to define and describe within the confines of a single chapter. Nevertheless, we can gain a firmer conception of it by first of all taking a historical look at its continuous, though sometimes slow, development, then by examining the contemporary scene, and finally by considering what is needed in the future.

A Look Back

The reaction of a news reporter in 1870 on learning of the establishment of the Female Normal High School, now Hunter College, was that it was a mistake to educate girls above their station in life and that a higher education for women would decrease the

47

servant supply so much needed for the society of that day. Mary Putnam Jacobi, a physician and women's rights activist, wrote in 1891 that "women cannot maintain the same intellectual standards as are established and maintained by men. . . . Once past the common school, girls turned to music, manners, sewing, and French, while mathematics, science, and the social sciences were left to boys" (quoted in Smuts, 1971, pp. 112–113). In 1887 Rebecca N. Hazard wrote a paper entitled "Home Studies for Women," in which she recommended that women who desired enrichment and broader cultural horizons should form a home study club to read and discuss the great poets and writers of the world. Knitting and needlework were advised to occupy the members' hands while they sat in a cheerful, sunny room. These clubs were promoted by the progressive (of that day) members of the Association for the Advancement of Women as opportunities to study the treasures of knowledge so long withheld from women (Smuts, 1971).

Despite the attitudes manifested in the foregoing comments and proposals, women began to insist on admission to colleges, universities, and professional schools in the United States. In fact, by the end of the nineteenth century one third of American college students were women of college age (eighteen to twenty-two); and by 1937 women composed almost 40 percent of the national student body. Thus during the first few decades of this century, the women's education movement was doing pretty well, especially compared with the situation in Europe, where in Sweden, for instance, only 17 percent of the students were women in 1937. In British universities the percentage was a little higher, 22 percent, but in Germany (before Hitler) no more than one out of ten college and university enrollees was a woman. After World War II, however, the gap between U.S. and European enrollments by women greatly narrowed, partly because the women's education movement here had slowed— some even said regressed. Degler (1964, p. 202) claimed, for example, that there had been "no improvement in women's position in higher education; indeed it can be argued that women have failed to maintain the place reached much earlier. . . . A sign of regression . . . is that in the early 1950s women earned about 10 percent of the doctoral degrees in this country as compared with almost 15 percent in the 1920s."

These statistics must be carefully evaluated and balanced by others, however. We must remember that the percentages cited for the earlier period did not represent very many women in absolute numbers. In 1920 only 2 percent of all twenty-one-year-old women in this country graduated from college, whereas in 1965, 16 percent graduated. Moreover, the social class and age of women college students changed markedly after World War II. Like their male counterparts, women students before that were generally from the upper class and of traditional college age. Between 1950 and 1969, according to the U.S. Office of Education, the number of women college students more than quadrupled, and a noticeable part of this increase was due to the attendance of older, middle- and lower-class women. In this period, for example, the college enrollment of women thirty to thirty-four years of age increased from 21,000 to 215,000 (Women's Bureau, 1971). Although a good many of these older women are entering college for the first time, a considerable number are continuing interrupted educations.

Why have they done so? A complex set of social forces and personal motivations are at work. Fought (1966) found that the development of continuing education for women in this nation was the result of a number of factors, including (1) increased prosperity, (2) a reevaluation of women's education, (3) expanded leisure time due to technological advances, (4) the civil rights issue, which has reopened the need for psychological fulfillment for all, (5) women's need for education for teaching and technical jobs, (6) the higher status of women, (7) acceptance of modern psychological theories, (8) changes in the life patterns of women, and (9) increased emphasis on the need for continuing education for *all* owing to the expansion of knowledge. Another researcher and practitioner in the field of continuing education for women, Osborn (1963), found that among the top-ranking reasons for degree-seeking by mature, married women college students were enjoyment of learning and a desire for professional growth. Other motivations, not noted by Osborn, include a feeling of discontent and a sense of inadequacy. Some women resent their lack of education because it makes it difficult to find a job with the potential for upward mobility. Some are discontented because of an inability to use their training and intellectual potential. Some feel inadequate to match the professional advancement of husbands, either socially or educationally. Others are moved not by discontent but by seeing their own children become the first generation of college-goers in the family, and some are responding to the changing aspirations of all social classes.

The Contemporary Scene

Whatever the social or personal reasons, it is clear that women are entering or reentering college in record numbers, if not in record percentages. It is also true, however, that many of the barriers and difficulties which have plagued the women's education movement all along still exist in some form. For example, the life pattern of a typical woman still differs in predictable ways from that of a typical man. Most women, whatever their training, withdraw from the work world when they have children. Later, they have difficulty in returning to the labor market or to further academic achievement or, as the Minnesota Plan five-year report noted, "to critical, competent citizenship, because their intellectual skills and technical training have become rusty and out-of-date. Foreseeing this, many young women fail to begin or complete their higher education even when they have the necessary intellectual and financial security. The programs of many women in college lack direction because they cannot foresee a long-range vocational or professional objective" (University of Minnesota, 1967, p. 2).

Another limitation is the persistent belief that women have both special qualifications for and special handicaps in specific types of work. This view not only affects the type of educational programs offered to women, but also circumscribes their image of what they can do. Despite affirmative action directives, the human rights movement, and the Equal Employment Opportunity Commission, the fields of teaching, nursing, secretarial work, and social work—traditional female occupations—are chosen by the majority of females graduating from high school (Smuts, 1971). A survey of more recent data made by a large metropolitan university of its enrolled women students found them selecting similar career options in large numbers (City University of New York, 1972).

Similar limitations affect many women's attitudes toward

graduate work, particularly those of white women, according to Epstein (1971), who studied black women who had achieved success in the white male-dominated professions of law, medicine, university teaching, journalism, and public relations. Epstein found that while the white females surveyed generally supported the notion of college education for females, they were ambivalent about graduate or professional training. The black women in the study reported no family opposition to further education. The black women's education was considered to be an investment in the future, tied to "female role obligations such as becoming better equipped to help the family or a younger brother or sister get an education" and intended to yield economic rewards (p. 25).

How has higher education responded to these persisting barriers and to the varying needs of its female students—the middle-aged "freshmen," the returnees, the second-career aspirants, the women students of diverse social classes and ethnic and racial backgrounds? In many cases, not very well. Kreps (1971, p. 88) noted that the "guidance offered through continuing education programs for the past two decades was the only assistance from the education world to women returning to work." But thousands of women have been reached through these programs, and there is now an increasing public awareness that women's education must be improved in line with new knowledge about their need for learning throughout life.

During the 1960s, a number of academic institutions developed patterns of accommodation and sponsorship of an innovative nature that stressed individual attention to the returning women students. An example is the pioneering Center for Continuing Education for Women at Sarah Lawrence College (Bronxville, New York), established in 1962 by Esther Raushenbush. The Center carries out three types of programs: (1) an undergraduate liberal arts program for women who have not completed their undergraduate studies, who have been away from formal education for a number of years, and who want to return for a bachelor of arts degree; (2) a new design for graduate study for professions traditionally open to women; (3) two new professional programs, carried on by the Center independent of any university ("Preparation for College

Teaching" and "Medical Genetics"). The Sarah Lawrence student body, from generally affluent homes, could afford to participate in the experiment (Richter and Whipple, 1972).

The University of Minnesota's Continuing Education for Women program, the first special program for women at a university, provides extensive counseling services and testing as the heart of its Minnesota Plan. Special noncredit seminars are offered, and Minnesota Plan students also can work for either undergraduate or graduate degrees through the regular university curriculum. Under the Plan, all the resources of the institution became involved with the following objectives: (1) advanced planning for young women students for many aspects of their lives and (2) meeting the new educational needs of mature women, whether college graduates, persons with "interrupted" education, or ones seeking special training.

Another project, begun in 1960 and still in operation, is the Radcliffe Institute for Independent Study. The Institute is an integral part of Radcliffe College and thus of Harvard University. It is concerned with the advancement of learning and seeks to expand the choices open to women in scholarship, the creative arts, and the professions. The Institute is not a graduate school, however, but serves as a community of scholars, artists, and professional women. Full-time scholarships for projects and fellowships for research, the creative arts, and medicine are available. In 1967 a program of fellowships for part-time graduate study in colleges in Massachusetts, Rhode Island, and Connecticut was inaugurated. The Institute also maintains a guidance laboratory for women who seek advice on further educational, vocational, or volunteer opportunities. The Radcliffe Seminars, the adult education courses initiated in 1950, are now the responsibility of the Institute. The Seminars cover a variety of topics, such as research techniques, graphic arts, and abnormal psychology.

The University of Missouri, through its four statewide campuses (Columbia, Rolla, Kansas City, and St. Louis), conducts programs for the continuing education for women on the subjects of personal development, employment, public service, and home and family. The approaches vary and include consultation with individuals and groups, educational conferences and short courses, correspondence study (credit and noncredit), written materials for reference and study, mass media, and off-campus undergraduate and graduate credit courses.

Between 1966 and 1968, the New York State Guidance Center for Women was a state-supported pilot project established as a service for women of every educational and social background. When state funding ended, the board of supervisors of Rockland County appropriated money to continue the service as an agency of Rockland Community College. The Center has proved itself to be a valued community service. The two major categories of the Center's program are (1) educational and vocational counseling and testing for individuals and small groups and (2) educational and vocational information and advisory services offered through an educational and vocational library, workshops, public meetings on selected career fields, and two radio career information series. A report on the operation of the Center contains a recommendation of interest to educational administrators: "The experience of the Center seems to bear out the proposition of the original proposal that a community college is one kind of institution which is ideal for this purpose, in that the variety of services it offers and the variety of groups it serves tend to keep it free from being too closely identified with one or another sector of the population" (Westervelt, 1968, p. 1–14).

The College of General Studies of George Washington University began a program called "Developing New Horizons for Women" in 1960, under the direction of Ruth H. Osborn, now assistant dean for Continuing Education for Women. The Center's innovative programs and services have expanded to reach local, national, and international participants. Current courses treat career development and life planning, management, landscape architecture, publishing, and technical editing and writing. There are counseling and information sessions, special workshops and seminars, and fourteen off-campus centers for credit and noncredit courses that are held during the day, the evening, and on weekends. Since its establishment, the George Washington University Center has served approximately 7,000 women ranging from eighteen to seventy-eight years of age.

In 1975 the Center for the Continuing Education of Women

(CEW) at the University of Michigan developed five "trigger tapes" that focus on issues of concern to today's woman undergraduate. The videotaped vignettes, supplemented by a leader's study guide, deal with such issues as achievement versus affiliation needs, preplanning versus nonplanning of careers, sexuality, and making career and marriage work. The CEW Center, in addition to its courses, counseling services, and development of instructional materials, in 1975 sponsored a "Conference on New Research on Women II," with some fifty scholars participating (Center for Continuing Education of Women, 1976). Many other institutions are involved in specially designed educational programs for women, among them the Continuum Center for Women (Oakland University, Rochester, Michigan); Alverno College (Milwaukee, Wisconsin); the University of Pennsylvania; the Barnard Women's Center (Barnard College); the Miami-Dade consortium of colleges called the Council for the Continuing Education of Women; and a number of junior and community colleges located throughout the nation.

In the early 1970s, institutions of higher education rapidly developed community counseling programs and referral-information centers for women. In addition to counseling, the programs and services of these centers include educational and vocational components. For example, "Everywoman's Village," Van Nuys, California, serves as a transitional learning center for mature women. The Center sponsors a variety of courses that permit women to explore different directions for discovery of their special interests. The faculty comes from local colleges and universities, and special emphasis is given to the interests of individual learners. Another model, which started in New York City as the Women's Talent Corps, is the College for Human Services. Its main concentration is on training mature women from low-income groups for positions in community service agencies. Various other community-based programs include the Women's Resource Center (Columbia, Maryland); Everywoman's Center (East Lansing, Michigan); and the New Haven Women's Liberation Center (Yale University).

A number of nontraditional programs are also sponsored by voluntary organizations—the YWCA, the League of Women Voters, the National Council of Jewish Women, and the American Jewish Committee, to name a few. The Women's Center for Career Development, a program of the National Council of Negro Women initiated in 1976, offers education and career-planning services tailored to the needs of working women in New York City. Located in the financial district, it includes a career library and information service, career and education planning consultations, lunchtime mini-workshops, open forums, and an associate degree program sponsored jointly with Pace College. A unique, informal school is the F.E.M. Mini School, also located in New York City, which was designed to help today's woman enrich and enhance the quality of her life, to evaluate and strengthen her self-image, and to acquire and develop practical skills. Courses of short duration include "Time Management," "Assertiveness training," "Political Action for Women," and "Management Skills for the Woman Supervisor."

The New York State School of Industrial and Labor Relations (Cornell University) sponsors women's studies, with classes in the skills and knowledge women need to become effective members and leaders of their local unions. Sessions are held weekday evenings, and monthly "brown bag" seminars, without fee, provide opportunities for discussion and analysis of grievance issues, fringe benefits, collective bargaining, and changes in the economics of the labor market. In Washington, D.C., there is an active group of women dedicated to the working woman and the development of her potential. This is the volunteer project called the "Washington Opportunities for Women," or "WOW," as it is popularly known today. Begun as a counseling service by women graduates in the District of Columbia area several years ago, WOW helps the mature woman find fulfillment in satisfying commitment to renewed study, volunteer work, or a part-time job; endeavors to educate the community about its vast resources of untapped womanpower; and develops ways to serve both women and the community at large. This group pioneered in adapting programs to enable women to meet their requirements. For teaching and social work careers, projects, coordinated urban teacher training, and part-time teaching could fulfill certain requisites for a degree; for some women, part-time experience with the District Welfare Department could be translated into credit toward their master's degree in social work. The agency also worked with the Civil Service Commission to rate volunteer experience in the social welfare field in order to evaluate such experience when reviewing job applications ("WOW: A Model . . . ," 1970).

Women have been involved to some extent in the political process since they got the vote in the 1920s, but this participation has consisted mainly of canvassing, gathering signatures on petitions, and addressing envelopes. As the movement for equal rights progressed, another new objective inspired women to demand further education and training. The political arena beckoned—running for office or getting an appointment to an administrative post in government. To promote those goals and to encourage active citizenship by women through involvement in political activities at different levels, the Center for Policy Through Participation was inaugurated at Hunter College. In 1976 the project became the Women's Political Training Center with a program of seminars, workshops, and courses to train women in conducting meetings, organizing campaigns, and running for office. Though still a fledgling, the Center, along with the politically oriented Women's Institute at Rutgers University, is setting the stage for women who are determined to enter politics and to achieve positions of electoral power.

Any discussion of women's education would not be complete without a brief review of the growing field of women's studies. Developing out of the women's rights movement of the 1960s, women's studies is now one of the fastest growing fields in higher education. More than 100 colleges and universities offer majors or minors in the field; several offer master's and doctoral degree programs. Approximately 200 other schools sponsor courses or programs related to women's studies. Though not considered a discipline in the sense of economics or philosophy, women's studies is a field of investigation that endeavors to organize knowledge and make connections across traditional disciplines. This aspect and its newness to the academic arena have made women's studies controversial in many institutions.

The National Women's Study Association, an organization initiated in 1977, serves to unify and strengthen the various programs and to lend active support to women's studies on campuses and in elementary and secondary schools. Most of the members of the Association see women's studies as a long-range method of changing the whole curriculum, from preschool through graduate education. Regardless of the criticism about the legitimacy of the field and pressures on higher education budgets, women's studies is gaining identity and proving the quality of its scholarship and research (Maeroff, 1977).

The Road Ahead

What are the educational aspirations of women today—the young as well as the more mature? What values are being transmitted by women to the young in their own families, as well as in the culture at large? Are there significant differences regarding educational values and aspirations between differing socioeconomic groups in our society?

As factors affecting educational programming for women, concerns about role identity, labor demands and labor shortages, technological advances, diverse ways of life, and family patterns are as relevant in the 1980s and beyond as these social and cultural factors were earlier in this century. Women have become "a social problem," and their education and intellectual fulfillment are subjects of debate in contemporary society because they, as well as men, are the victims of the technological and social changes that occurred during the past century, and particularly since World War II. Women of all socioeconomic groups have been affected by these changes and by the demand for new freedoms. The recent burgeoning of interest in continuing education for women, the expansion of women's studies, and the growing awareness of a need for more definitive research in these areas indicate the type and amount of influence these social changes have generated.

It is currently assumed that women who return to school after age thirty usually are concerned with career options and goal-oriented programs. Yet in a study of older women in two social class positions (Class I—higher SES, and Class II—lower SES), the desire to learn and the enjoyment of learning were of paramount importance to both groups, despite the need for additional family income expressed by a number of women in Class II. Continuing their education offered a stimulus and an incentive they had never imagined previously and was possible only because of the availability of part-time schedules, evening and weekend classes, and academically flexible programs geared to their needs and interests (Feeney, 1972).

What is said here about women and women's education pertains to men as well, for there are thousands of older males who are returning to school, and many who are changing their life patterns for one reason or another. Smith (1964, p. 148) noted a need to reexamine the role of continuing education "in reshaping the careers that otherwise run down and in encouraging the development of alternate or even conflicting careers not on an emerging basis after the crisis but in preventative anticipation of the crisis." The life span of both sexes, but particularly of women, is longer than that of previous generations. Educational institutions ought then to become more flexible about admission and general academic policies for older adults, as well as provide innovative educational programs for the young. Neugarten (1972, p. 215) commented that "there must be more entrance points and exit points and a broader range of degree and nondegree programs for persons of both sexes, even though for the present it will be women more often than men who take advantage of more flexible educational arrangements." Another educator (Harbeson, 1970, p. 55) noted that "some leading educators have speculated about an extreme proposal that higher education for women should be tailored to take into account the domestic interlude in their lives, with early liberal education, but delay of specialization to the years following childrearing."

In an article entitled "Can Continuing Education Adapt?" Clarenbach (1970) listed the top priorities for programs of continuing education for women. Some of these priorities are to extend as broadly as possible the techniques and services developed over the past decade (1960s); to counsel the counselors and train the trainers to break down the traditional concepts of "women's fields" and "women's levels" of responsibility (the very young, the poor, and the high school dropouts have special needs here); to accelerate efforts to achieve institutional flexibility, significant financial aid, and expanded childcare facilities; to take affirmative action to ensure the employement of women in both faculty and administrative positions; and to educate faculty members and students by making positive efforts to inaugurate within the various disciplines courses dealing with women as subjects.

Though there is optimism today about the changes in attitude toward women's education and professional career development, women will continue to require special attention in higher education for some time to come. If women are to be prepared to enter new fields, more scholarships need to be made available, along with increased allowances for part-time study and time to "stop out" of graduate and professional study. Since 1888, the American Association of University Women has been providing scholarships and fellowships, national and international, to women for advanced study. But more assistance should be made available and on all levels of education. A number of women's professional societies, volunteer organizations, foundations, and trade unions have now taken up the challenge. The Business and Professional Women's Foundation, with its scholarships for women throughout the United States, is helping to further academic study and vocational study on a full-time or a part-time basis. The National Science Foundation provides grants supporting science career workshops for women at post-secondary levels. In 1976 the Foundation sponsored projects to facilitate science careers in ten states and the District of Columbia. These projects were designed to serve women who had received science degrees between 1961 and 1974 but who were not working in their degree fields. If such programs were offered in all disciplines, more women would be encouraged to pursue their earlier specializations.

Members of lower socioeconomic groups also are faced with limited support. Seifer (1972, pp. 70–71) commented thus on blue-collar families: "In the past, education for most working-class girls stopped with (or even before) high school graduation. In recent years, however, there has been a significant increase in the number of girls from working-class families who are beginning to attend college, especially the rapidly growing two-year or community colleges." Seifer made recommendations regarding the administration and curriculum of programs for this group, namely: more flexible schedules (weekend courses—not evening because of family responsibilities, lack of transportation, fatigue, and even fear for physical safety); increased awareness among counselors of the needs and expectations of working-class females; expanded humanities courses (creative writing, the arts, and the media—to allow for self-expression based on authentic working-class life experiences); courses on the contemporary role of women; and ethnic and working-class studies.

Most practitioners in the field of women's education would support these recommendations and such others as maintaining better records for women in various institutions, both educational and noneducational, so that data on their experience can be evaluated for academic credit. Experiential learning and credit for courses taught by nonacademic institutions are now being studied by the American Council on Education, the Educational Testing Service, and the New York State Board of Regents (Carnegie Corporation, 1975). More certification programs combining field experience and background preparation for the helping professions and community service are needed, as are increased opportunities for women who aspire to public service administration and to elective public offices.

There is no question, then, that women's education, like all future educational programs, must be increasingly responsive to the differences in background, preparation, and aspirations of individual women and men. Nontraditional education has pointed the way—it is now time for traditional academic establishments to take heed of what is happening outside the walls. Women's education, in terms of special programs and flexible curricula, will need to continue its separate identity until it has become more firmly established in academic institutions and until further education for women of all ethnic and socioeconomic groups has become more readily acceptable in our culture. In the long run, both sexes will benefit, as will the society. Margaret Mead has said that if the current expectations and educational patterns of girls and women were examined and revised, the performance of those tasks would be enlightening to educators themselves. She summarized her comment in this way: "The mother who can give her daughter confidence in her ability to understand mathematics will herself be more ready to use her own gifts in middle age. The father who is equally committed to his daughter's and to his son's education will find himself a less skeptical and more sympathetic employer and colleague of women" (1963, p. 6).

Chapter Five

Continuing Education for the Professions

Phillip E. Frandson

In one of the most haunting lyrics of the rock music era, the Beatles sang: "Once there was a way—to get back home. . . ." This expresses well the longing of many in the late twentieth century for a time when goals were clear, rewards were clear, "a way" was clear. Once there was a way to obtain a professional education, to be licensed, and to live happily ever after. But those days are gone forever. Degree obsolescence is today's way of life. The "half-life" of knowledge in any given profession may now be as little as two to three years. The degree, in short, is today the *beginning* of the education of a professional.

To carry this point forward, in this chapter we look first at the compelling revelations that have forced professionals to accept the fact that they must keep their knowledge and skills updated if

they are to retain a position of leadership. Next the arguments
pro and con about proper approach to continuing education for
professionals are examined. Then a discussion of the issues that have
contributed to the public's loss of trust in professionals is followed
by a look toward the future in which some searching questions are
addressed to adult educators.

The Progression

The change began slowly. First came the recognition of
many that after a number of years of practice, although experience
had advanced and enhanced the knowledge of the practitioner,
some of the book-learning might be a bit rusty and a refresher course
was in order. The concept of taking some time off and returning to
school to retake some of the courses became commonly accepted.
With the advent of World War II, and the sudden tremendous
government-financed acceleration of knowledge—particularly in the
sciences, including medical science, but to some extent in virtually
every professional field—refresher education became only a drop
in the bucket, and the era of continuing education began. The
seminar, the residential conference, the intensive short course came
into being, since very few professionals could any longer afford to
take time out for study. The updating and upgrading of knowledge,
the exposure to and absorption of new research and development in
the field became essential parts of professional life. The experience
of professionals in the aerospace industry, who found themselves
obsolete and out of jobs by the thousands because of technological
advances or changes with which they had not kept up, focused the
attention of others who were not already aware that they must swim
abreast of the current of learning—or drown.

It has now become clear that even continuing education is
not enough. The acceleration of knowledge has assumed something
of the nature of atomic fission—new knowledge whirling in at such
speeds that it does not merely occupy the seat next to the degree,
but actually blasts the nucleus out of much once-basic knowledge
and replaces it with the new. Thus, suddenly, reeducation has appeared. This is the need to restudy one's beginnings, to identify, then
discard, those portions of earlier knowledge that actually stand in

the way of the new, while reeducation's accompaniment, continuing education, feeds in a constant stream of the latest in discovery.

An additional complication is that there is no longer a clear straight line in any element of professional life. The expanding body of knowledge has forced the proliferation of specialization and subspecialization; one needs to remain enough of a generalist to understand the overall picture and yet also needs to know the chosen specialty well enough to make competent decisions in it. On top of all that, one has to study very intensely just to comprehend the depth and breadth even of a single subspecialty. The extrapolation of this problem has compelled virtually every profession, against much internal opposition, to depend on and delegate functions to the paraprofessions, a movement which has in itself brought on a whole new type of development in both basic and continuing education.

Finally, as knowledge acceleration forces the microcosm of specialization on the professions, on the other side of the picture, and in a sense providing its balance, is the macrocosm of multiprofessional involvement. The increasing overlap of professional fields generally has been highlighted by the need for this approach in all major national and international decision making. Hence, the final (at least as of this moment) component of the education of a professional: the need for interdisciplinary and multidisciplinary study. The simple overlap of "Engineering and Management" has been replaced by complex multidisciplinary programs having such titles as "Biomedical Engineering," "Systems Applications to Urban Productivity and Technology," "Ocean Resource Science and Engineering," and "Environmental Planning," which involves urban design, architecture, soil engineering, pollution control, and psychology. In short, any person who chooses to embark, or continue, on the road of late-twentieth-century professional life needs to grasp the whole matrix of implications.

Complete rethinking of what constitutes the preparation of a professional is now in order, and indeed is under way. It is no longer necessary, or even wise or feasible, to try to cram the "all" of professional education into undergraduate and graduate programs. Operating on the concept that obsolescence is the fate even of much basic cognitive study, undergraduate and graduate education become rather the gate of entry to a lifetime of challenge in broader, deeper realms of learning and accomplishment. Corbally (1976, p. 11) stated that "those who engage in the prolonged period of education and training through which professional knowledge and skills are attained and certified have an obligation to engage in programs designed to keep that knowledge and that skill updated and appropriately directed." Along the way there awaits the dual reward of self-fulfillment and of contribution to a society that cries for leadership from those who have the strength and dedication to devote themselves to the betterment of life through the professions.

Approaches

How shall continuing education for the professions be assured? Or, perhaps more appropriately stated, how shall continuing education for the professions be implemented and continuing maintenance of up-to-date knowledge and competence in the professional "public servant" be assured? As of the moment, three solutions have been suggested. Although they are not necessarily mutually exclusive, considerable disagreement currently exists among their proponents. The three are (1) mandated formal continuing education; (2) periodic redetermination of competence, demonstrated by examination, performance evaluation, or other agreed-on means of measurement; and (3) self-guided study, which relies on the professionals' sense of responsibility to their profession and clientele (as well as on their own survival instincts) to assure that knowledge and competence are maintained.

Arguments for and against the three approaches force out two general issues: first, the validity of the approach for accomplishing the desired ends and, second, the rights of all parties concerned. The second issue relates to all three of the means previously listed. Involved is of course the right of control by the profession, not only over its own mission, goals, and objectives but also—in somewhat less clearcut degree—over the lives of the individuals in its professional ranks. Involved, too, is the right of control by individuals, groups, and other bodies outside the profession. These comprise the governmental and private funding agencies that underwrite a vast proportion of professional research, development, facilities, and actual undertakings in practice; and the clientele or consumers of the professions, whether as individuals, or through voluntary consumer organizations, or through the governmental boards, commissions, and other agencies established to protect the consumer's interests. Finally, there are the rights of the individual professional over his own life, and the key issue of the extent to which such rights may be forfeited when professional service is undertaken as a life goal. In this later regard, Pennington and Moore (1976, p. 6) raised a series of significant questions, among them perhaps the single most important one for all professionals and the public they serve: "Is practice a right or a privilege?"

Returning now to the first issue—that is, the matter of the validity of the approach for achieving the desired ends—we find that this topic, though no more crucial, is even more complex. It therefore seems appropriate to deal with mandated formal continuing education, periodic redetermination of competence, and self-study as they relate to this issue.

Mandated Formal Continuing Education. Those who favor mandated formal continuing education—or accept it as more or less inevitable—contend that it is absolutely essential, in the interests of society as a whole, that formal control be exercised to assure that all professionals are cognizant of recent research and development in their fields. In notes on a workshop session, Greek (1976, p. 72) stated: "The consensus of the group was that mandatory continuing education was clearly the direction that the professions were going. The central question raised was: what can the professional associations do, and what role could and should they play in that process?" Greek then outlined the role he saw for them: "Because of the sense, 'if *we* don't do it, someone else will do it for us,' it is obvious that mandatory requirements should evolve within the professional association. It should establish minimum standards; identify competencies; develop self-directed study material; and set performance capabilities that general practitioners should have. The professional association should clearly make the decisions on what the guidelines of continuing education should be, . . . be responsible for what happens to the professional after career entry, and assure competence of the professionals in their field."

The implication seems to be that without such formal control, many individual professionals may neglect to maintain knowledge and competence. Implicit in this contention is the idea that many professionals not only will be deficient in a sense of responsibility to their profession and to the public they serve, but will be curiously blind to the consequences for their own future if they fail to maintain viability in their chosen profession. The advocates of mandated formal continuing education acknowledge these implications but, in support of their views, point to several kinds of questionable responsibility prevalent in the professions today. We discuss these later in more detail under ethical issues.

If one accepts the premise of mandated formal continuing education, a host of subsidiary problems and arguments within arguments arise. These stem essentially from the controversy surrounding the question. Who shall plan, develop, present, and evaluate these formal continuing education programs? Universities and colleges hold that because they are both the primary sources of new professional knowledge through their research activities and the primary storehouses of the knowledge of the ages through their professional and research libraries, they should be the central resource for the development of continuing education programs. But even within their own ranks there is disagreement about whether the direction of continuing education should be vested in the faculty of the professional schools, as those most directly associated with professional expertise, or in the academic specialists in continuing education or extension divisions, as those specifically trained in the development of instructional programs for the adult.

Professional associations contend that their members, having the broad cognizance of the whole field of service in which they are engaged, are best equipped to visualize the total professional educational need. Hence, they should be in control of program development. Less powerful but nonetheless active in demanding at least the right, if not the control, in the development of continuing education programs are in-house groups (for example, hospitals in the case of medicine; school districts in in-service training for teachers in major urban areas), purveyors of correspondence study (such as publishers in professional fields), and private enterprise organizations, particularly those that have significant amounts of funds to divert to philanthropic ends for purposes of tax deduction.

Considering first the appropriate role of institutions of higher education, a reasonable approach currently seems to begin with the concept that they cannot expect to be the sole selectors of (1) criteria for courses and curricula in continuing education for the professions and (2) criteria for the earning of credit or noncredit units, certificates, or other forms of award on completion of these programs. If they did expect to run the whole operation, they would be on a collision course with the professional associations and other continuing education "consumers" bent on developing their own criteria—not only for programs and awards, but even for the selection of institutions they will accept as program providers. Corbally (1976, p. 10) emphasized that "whatever the pressures or stimuli, higher education must not claim to be the sole chosen instrument to respond and to overcome. Too many of our current problems can be traced to our willingness to overrespond, to overstate our capacity to solve problems, to claim sole jurisdiction. . . . We must join in mandates with care and with caution." So it seems valid to concede to the professional associations the essential control in setting standards for continuing education for the professions. Colleges and universities, however, should be involved in the standards setting and must be the primary implementing agency. They are in the business of education—chartered in the field. The wealth of talent and knowledge in professional school faculties, together with the experience of continuing education divisions in the diverse means of delivering educational programs, is essential to the planning, development, and presentation of these programs for professionals. Only through their special expertise can the maximum dissemination of both new research knowledge and professional experiential knowledge be achieved for the enlightenment of all members of the professions.

Some important cautions are in order. First, it is crucial that the various institutions of higher education work together, in state or regional groups. The idea of competition among them must be abandoned. Only in dedicated, joint effort can they assure their own effective role in service to the professional world, and through it to all the people.

Second, any remaining fossilization from the past must be cleared away. The more rigid structures of study in undergraduate and graduate settings are not appropriate to continuing education in the rapidly changing present. Flexible sequential certificate programs can concentrate on a highly specialized area of emerging knowledge, coordinated with immediate statewide or regional professional needs.

Third, institutions of higher education working together must study both their states' laws regarding continuing education for the professions and their state's commissions, boards, or other regulatory agencies that exist to enforce them.

Fourth, all interested institutions of higher education must develop close contact with the faculties of the great centers of professional learning within their state, to ascertain what continuing educators as a group can provide of unique significance that could not be provided by the professional associations. One example would be the multiprofession approach mentioned earlier, which only a major university or a group of institutions can offer. With such background development, educators can come to the professional associations with a plan, whether for individual conferences, certificate programs, or other forms of sequential study.

Fifth, all institutions of higher education that have not already done so should investigate the Continuing Education Unit (CEU). This noncredit unit has been established by a national task force as a means of recording, accumulating, and transferring units of noncredit study, such as professional or paraprofessional continuing education. Some professions have accepted it with enthusiasm. Others regard it as a questionable, even dangerous, concept because it recognizes time spent in learning rather than what has been learned.

Sixth, the highest quality in continuing education programs for the professions must be achieved. This involves a multifaceted approach. The best balance must be struck between the amount of content that needs to be presented and the time limitations that forever plague the pressured professional. Further, the best balance must be maintained between the theoretical and the experiential or applied. Another important factor is accurate market assessment, whether of already existing markets for a proposed program or of a latent market that could be developed. Emphasis should be given, too, to providing high-quality information about programs to the audience they are designed to serve. That is, any promotional material must accurately reflect the program's content, the instructional methods, and the bases for performance evaluation, to provide learners a clear idea of what to expect before they enroll.

As to the faculties selected for continuing education programs for the professions, they must be of a very special breed. They must not only meet standards of quality as high as those for degree-program faculty but be flexible as well. To provide access equally to the academic learning resources of the university and the experiential learning resources of the community, as well as to provide the most effective instruction, both research faculty members and practitioners should participate.

Finally, performance evaluation is an essential factor of any quality program—and that means evaluating not just the learner's performance but the performance of the programs and the instructors themselves in achieving the desired ends. Unfortunately, evaluation still presents one of the greatest difficulties in the whole arena of continuing education for the professions. The fact is that no universally accepted basis exists regarding criteria, methods, or approved authority in the field of evaluation, which appropriately leads into discussion of the second approach to continuing education for the professions.

Periodic Redetermination of Competence. The proponents of periodic redetermination of competence, demonstrated by examination, performance evaluation, or other agreed-on means of measurement, argue that mandated formal continuing education, though it may achieve results in some cases, is just as likely to fail. Such failure could occur whenever the program's content is not effectively planned, an instructor is less than excellent, or the individual professional as a student does not adequately participate in the program. In short, mandated continuing education, on the basis of some standard number of units or hours in a given time period, can range in quality. It might mean nothing more than sitting on a chair a sufficient number of times to qualify. Only if effective means of evaluation can be applied is it possible to determine the educational results of the number of hours. And, say the proponents of this approach, if effective ways of assessing knowledge and competence exist, only such evaluation itself is meaningful, and how individual professionals acquire the mandated knowledge and competence is a matter of their individual choice.

The basic proposal, although there are a number of variants, calls for regular, periodic reevaluation of theoretical knowledge based on recent research, of general background knowledge and of the professional's ability to apply such knowledge in actual practice. The three major problems in this approach, though presumably not insurmountable, pose great difficulties of implementation. These consist of determining (1) what agency shall establish criteria for evaluation, (2) in what setting competence evaluation can take place, and (3) what formats evaluation should take.

1. The whole controversy about control—educational institution versus professional association versus funding source versus ultimate consumer—arises again here, with each constituency wanting its share of input. Although diverse programs are under way, featuring various combinations of these constituent ingredients, no overall pattern has yet been established.

2. In some professions the setting problem is not too hard to solve. For example, great medical centers offer facilities for observing the individual professional in practice, as well as for direct personal contact between observer and observed and for access to computerized processing of responses to printed survey instruments. In some other professions, however, less defined or less extensive settings for evaluation exist, and the question of where observation of practice can occur and who shall serve in the role of observer becomes more difficult to answer.

3. The format issue is somewhat related to the preceding question, since the format can either determine or be determined by the available setting. It is generally accepted that some form of written examination must be included and that some means of observing the professional in actual practice must occur. How to administer the latter component for the hundreds of thousands of

professionals who would be scheduled for reevaluation each year is a problem of extraordinary dimensions.

What all this indicates is that the concept of periodic re-evaluation as a means of assuring competence carries with it monu-mental problems that have only begun to be dealt with. Houle (1976, p. 126) called this "the center of our concerns." After listing the variety of activities currently most frequently mandated with the aim of improving professional performance, he stated: "At this time we seem to have nothing better than these activities to satisfy our [adult educators'] own concerns or those of consumers and social policy groups, such as legislatures. . . . The center of our concerns, therefore, must be the creation of forms of assessment which measure or are probably correlated with what both pro-fessionals and the general society demand to know: How well does every licensed or certified practitioner maintain an alert, continuing performance of his or her duties in as effective a fashion as the current knowledge base permits? To the extent that there is any deficiency in that performance, how can it be remedied?" Indeed, the breadth of the problems is undoubtedly one factor that has led to the already widespread acceptance of the first-mentioned ap-proach—that is, the mere accumulating of a mandated quantity of continuing education without qualitative assessment of the results.

With "quantity" education not really satisfactory and with "quality evaluation" very difficult to implement, there remains a third approach.

Self-Guided Study. This approach relies on the individual's own sense of responsibility to the profession and the clients as well as on his own survival instincts, to assure that up-to-date knowledge and competence are maintained. The proponents of this method make a very good case indeed. Mandated formal continuing educa-tion, they contend, has a tendency to achieve reverse effects. By being forced to attend courses which may or may not be personally valuable in content or presentation and may or may not be con-veniently scheduled or located, the practitioner is often turned off rather than turned on. At the same time, they also contend, no really effective way of judging competence on any broad basis has been established. And, most important of all, the proponents contend, really dedicated professionals will voluntarily give their time, effort, and whole selves to attaining the best possible fulfillment of their particular unique talents, which only they understand and assess.

Seldon (1976, p. 5) made a compelling case for this viewpoint: "Despite all regulations and requirements that may be imposed, the greatest force for continuing education is the desire and motivation of individuals for self-improvement, broader knowledge, and expanded competence. . . . It is my great concern that we may overlook too readily the values of self-motivation, professional pride, and individual commitment for service to society, as we hastily embrace the concept of mandatory continuing education for the professions." Hence, the key to it all, say the advocates of individual responsibility, is motivation. The motivated professional needs no mandated push into continuing education. The nonmotivated will probably go through the formal motions of enrolling and paying fees, and perhaps even take the requisite number of units or hours, but will do so with the least possible effort or personal involvement.

Who Shall Control Licensure and Relicensure?

In this area many rules and regulations and the agencies for enforcing them are of course in existence. The process of licensure has long been accepted, is largely in the jurisdiction of individual states, and is primarily controlled by the professions. Regulatory boards and commissions established by the states are most often controlled by the very professions they were established to regulate. Only quite recently has there been a strong move, emerging partly from state and governmental sources but primarily from consumers either individually or through consumer organizations, to include anywhere from one or two to an actual majority of nonprofessional members on commissions and boards regulating licensure and relicensure. In California, for example, with the exception of those bodies regulating accountants and professionals in the health fields, all boards and commissions now are required to have a majority of nonprofessional members. In support of the legislation which effected this requirement, Governor Edmund G. Brown, Jr., in his State of the State address on January 7, 1976, called for "opening up the professional and licensed occupations by increasing public accountability within their governing boards. It is time to eliminate arbitrary restrictions that serve more to create a monopoly and protect the profession from the people rather than the reverse." As of March 1977, some sixty public members had been appointed by Brown to various California licensing agencies—and the University of California had begun planning programs for these new public members to give them the extensive information they need to be effective.

As Hill (1975) pointed out, continuing education statutes in a number of states have been held invalid principally because they delegate authority to the professional society. He cited the case of the Podiatry Society of New York in which the society claimed that its continuing education programs automatically qualified under the law. In striking down this interpretation, "the court held that 'while private professional societies may . . . make recommendations to the state boards and the Department of Education in matters affecting their professions, . . . the interpretation urged by petitioner would result in an unconstitutional delegation of governmental powers to a private corporation representing the interests of the members of the petitioner society' " (p. 5). Professional associations in other states, however, continue to maintain full control.

The matter of licensure and relicensure is inseparably bound up with the issue dealt with earlier under the second approach to professional continuing education—that is, the matter of establishing control over, criteria for, and approaches to programs. Licensure has largely been based on obtaining degrees and passing established state board examinations; hence, licensure remains a relatively cut-and-dried affair. Relicensure, however, is a completely new issue, and what must be determined is whether it shall be based on mandated credit units, or on continuing education units reflecting hours of instruction, or on some as yet not fully developed methods for reevaluating knowledge and competence.

The problem is further complicated by the diversity among states. In some, for instance, licensure is not required for practice in certain professions, particularly in certain categories of engineering. Diversity exists also with respect to the accreditation of study for licensure and relicensure: some professions accredit program providers, others do not. Pearson (1975, pp. 2, 14), discussing the variance in continuing education requirements from state to state for the certification of certified public accountants, emphasized that "diversity is not in the profession's best interests." He warned that "while so far the problems arising from the differences in . . . laws and regulations are mainly administrative and/or potential in nature, . . . I would suggest steps be taken to eliminate the differences while there is still time and before there are a few 'horror' stories about CPAs who lost their license or permits because of the differences."

In a number of states, legislative bodies have already moved to establish not only authority but extensive criteria for relicensure in a variety of professions. Donnelly (1976) provided a detailed report of data on many professions licensed in the Commonwealth of Massachusetts, including the date first licensed, the number of practitioners currently licensed, the requirements for licensing and relicensing, the status of continuing education, and other related information.

It might be added that at least one state moved too quickly regarding continuing education, to its subsequent regret. The Michigan legislature found that it had rushed into a mandated program of relicensure based on number of hours of study and that this approach proved to be inadequate in accomplishing the desired objectives. As reported by Geake (1976), Michigan has moved to revise its program via a very different but very promising concept, that is, an initial examination to identify the areas where a professional's knowledge and skills are weakest, where behavior needs to be modified. With this knowledge, continuing education can be required to meet specific educational needs, and the professional is likely to have real interest in the process. The final step is to "assess the effectiveness of the process by means of peer review and practice audits" (p. 15). The arbitrariness of relicensure based on hours of exposure to instruction is thus replaced by relicensure based on specific accomplishment.

Because of the variations in the extent and type of regulations and regulatory agencies from state to state and profession to profession, and because of the massive amounts of federal money now going into health care, transportation, legal services, urban planning, and other professional service areas, the question is being widely discussed whether the federal government will order more standardization of requirements on a nationwide basis, both for continuing education and for the relicensure to which it leads. Indications of some moves in that direction are already apparent in recent publications of the U.S. Department of Health, Education and Welfare. One HEW document (Subcommittee on Public Health Service, 1976) concerning the proposed credentialing of practitioners in the health fields recommended such elements as national certification, national standards, and various national directives to states on how and when they should license and relicense.

Beyond this, there arises also the question of the role of the courts. With constitutionality being challenged increasingly in every aspect of life, the ultimate consumer is demanding to know whether it is constitutional for states to mandate hours of continuing education for relicensure without guaranteeing performance change. At the same time, professionals are asking whether it is constitutional to require them to study if they are not offered the opportunity first to demonstrate competence. As such constitutionality questions proliferate, public awareness advances concomitantly and the public begins to question every aspect of professional life as it serves the entire U.S. society. This consideration of the professionals' obligation to society leads to a wholly new aspect of continuing education, that is, the ethical issues involved in the education of a professional.

Loss of Trust in Professionals

Because of the now vast role of professionals in making decisions about public policy and because of the extensive control they wield over the lives of Americans, people are increasingly demanding that responsibility be commensurate with power. Public concern over whether a sense of responsibility exists among professionals is evident and growing. The latest polls on the degree to which the people "trust" or "have confidence in" this or that group serving the public, ranging through all levels of government and all the professions, illustrate the point. It is useless to quote current percentages, as they are invalidated almost as soon as quoted, but the extent of the loss of confidence is staggering! Without necessarily agreeing with any given explanation for this situation, I believe it is important to cite the issues and questions being raised, because if adult educators are to be fully responsible to their particular profession and hence to the public, they must study the ways in which they may have contributed to the loss of trust and the ways they might seek to help rebuild the core of responsible service, the only foundation on which a return of trust can be based. Some of these issues—malpractice, professional attitudes toward clients, economic and racial privilege and discrimination, public accountability, problems of the professionals, and the institutionalization of Amercan society—and related pertinent matters are dealt with in the following sections.

Malpractice. The issue of malpractice in medicine is already a problem of massive scope. Lawsuits against physicians and surgeons, as well as against hospitals and their staffs, abound. The charges concern wrong diagnosis; overtreatment and undertreatment as well as wrong treatment; carelessness in the prescription or administration of drugs; carelessness in administering anesthesia; surgical error; the application (or withdrawal) of life support; mixups in the identification of X-rays or other laboratory tests and, in some cases, even reports on tests never actually performed; and a host of other errors.

An adjunct issue is that of "covering up" for colleagues in the medical profession. If, as some observers claim, several thousand physicians and surgeons are either incompetent or addicted to some substance, the public wonders why only a handful of licenses to practice are rescinded in any given year. Although the records indicate that approximately two-thirds of medical malpractice suits are resolved in favor of the doctor or hospital in the case, the public also is questioning whether interprofessional collusion may exist in such resolutions. A climax of sorts was reached in California in late 1976 when information surfaced leading to charges of gross neglect and even willful mistreatment of more than one hundred patients in the state's mental hospitals.

Although medicine has come under the most fire to date, the field of education is also feeling the impact of malpractice suits, most of which involve educational programs that allegedly misrepresented the employment placement opportunities of students who completed the programs. In fairness, we should certainly note that the disproportionate number of suits in the medical profession probably stems from its more direct relationship to life and health and death.

Professional Attitudes Toward Clients. An issue related to the malpractice problem is the growing discontent among consumers regarding their inability to reach the professionals on whom they have come to depend. The professionals are said to take an assembly line approach and to be cold, condescending, disinterested, impersonal, and even angry. Clients allege that their queries are brushed aside as not worth answering or irrelevant—or are totally ignored. Behavior of this nature has been noted in the health sciences, in law, religion, and education, and in other professions.

Economic and Racial Privilege and Discrimination. It is a sad reality that despite affirmative action and other antidiscrimination programs, barriers remain around the professions in America today. The professions are "white man's land." With few exceptions, they remain a privileged bastion inaccessible to blacks, Mexican-Americans, and other ethnic minorities. Antidiscrimination admissions programs at state universities have provided for a certain proportion of minority applicants to be accepted for graduate professional study, even though their eligibility on the basis of grades, while acceptable for admissions purposes, may be lower than that of some white applicants who are turned down. However, accusations of reverse discrimination from these white applicants have been frequent, culminating in the well-known "Bakke case."

Compounding racial discrimination is the problem of the long-term, excessive cost of professional study, since ethnic minorities are often also the economically disadvantaged. Economic access to training and licensing is available to the poor only through years of sacrifice, whereas the sons and daughters of the well-to-do are free to devote their entire effort to the field of study.

In addition, questions are being raised about whether access to the professions is being limited intentionally to foster short-supply conditions which permit their members to demand accelerating increases in professional fees. With licensure and even admission to study still largely controlled by the professions themselves, the field of professional practice is fenced with heavy-duty chain-link, and the professionals are today clearly making hay in that field. Burke (1976) contended that the engineer's work is currently guided mainly by his employer's profit needs, even if the resulting product or process proves wasteful or socially harmful. Peters (1976, p. 5) decried medical costs so high as to deprive many citizens of adequate care and called for placing the whole system of health care under public control. Citing "the doctor who thinks $75,000 a year is his divine right—indeed, a bare minimum from which he should advance to ever-higher fiscal heights," Peters insisted that "those who control whether we live or die must be under our control. We already control soldiers, policemen, firemen—every group with a life-protecting function except doctors. It's time to end that exception."

Public Accountability. The public accountability issue has to do with the matter of licensure and relicensure discussed earlier. Recapping briefly: the essential question is whether state licensing commissions, boards, and other such agencies actually protect the consumer or the licensee. As mentioned previously, extensive governmental pressures as well as consumer pressures resulted in all licensing and regulations boards under California's Department of Consumer Affairs—except those in the healing arts and in accounting (a rather substantial "exception")—being required to have a majority of nonprofessional members.

Problems of the Professional. Some of the reasons for consumer revolt against the professions clearly stem from actual malpractice based on incompetence, drug use, and other factors that seemingly should qualify as bases for dismissal from practice. However, in the heat of criticism, it is all too easy to forget the tremendously dedicated work of hundreds of thousands of professionals who have devoted their lives to the public good. Moreover, it is all too easy to fail to consider the pressures under which the individual professional works today, some of which were delineated in the opening pages of this chapter. Karl Menninger provided some enlightenment on this subject in an address quoted by Nelson (1976b). Although speaking to a group of high-level executives, Menninger referred to both businessmen and other professionals. He characterized them as sharing a tragic weakness: the tendency to think of themselves as high-powered pieces of machinery rather than as "human need systems" and, as a result, to think they need help from no one because they are the font of all knowledge. They see themselves as persons who give advice and help to others but do not need it themselves. Menninger spoke of the resultant deterioration in their human values and the destruction of their family relationships. He cited the Menninger Foundation's efforts to conduct educational programs on human behavior to help such persons, who come to them with the "appalling" statement that "they have no one even to talk to." One of the worst aspects of the problem, according to Menninger, is that many never become aware of the fallacy of their thinking.

Maslach, as reported by Stix (1976, pp. 1–2), presented still another critical aspect of professional life, particularly in the "helping professions." Maslach identified an ailment she termed "emotional burnout" and classified it as a "common afflication among health and social service workers, as well as law enforcement personnel, who often fail to recognize its existence." The problem is especially acute among those public servants who deal with hopelessly unresolvable situations. Many, unable to cope with the stresses of their work, solve the problem by "distancing" themselves from their clients, making the latter more object-like and less human. In brief, the end result is often anger; they shout at and condemn those they are appointed to serve or refer to them with jargon terms, such as "he's a coronary," or "my case load," a "delusional syndrome," or "the poor." The distressed workers then turn on themselves, condemning themselves as inadequate. In such condition, they can do little to help either themselves or their clients.

Institutionalization of American Society. Underlying the issues in any given profession, or even the broader issues of the professional world against the people it serves, is a far more severe kind of social syndrome. For whatever reasons and with whatever initial validity, we have become an institutionalized society, our people dependent to an inordinate degree (even for the decisions of their daily lives) not only on the professions but on the whole superstructure of all-controlling government, with its myriad professions. No one has put the picture in a more succinct nutshell than Ivan Illich, the controversial historian-educator who in recent years has thoroughly shaken up two of the most traditionally revered professions—medicine and education. "Medicine," said Illich (Illich and Verne, 1975, p. 22), "has made life the subject of medical care; education makes existence the subject of a study course." Further, as quoted by Nelson, 1976a, p. 35), Illich stated: " 'Progress' has turned pain, illness, and death from a personal challenge into a problem for experts, and health from a sometimes harsh, sometimes pleasant experience into a property measured and protected by doctors." And again, regarding education, "the institutionalization of permanent (that is, continuing) education gathers together and formalizes a whole set of informal activities, tags the educational label on to a whole set of spontaneous gestures and behavior patterns." Illich did not blame evil doctors and educators for having usurped power. Rather, he held that the fault lies with "social addiction to the management of life." Speaking in the same vein, Lewis (1976) called too much dependency on the professional a "drug rather than a stimulus" for the client being served.

A prevalent feeling about our professionalized society among the young people who drop out of college either before or after earning the baccalaureate, because they see no reality for themselves in the degree-related career road, might be summarized in these words from Henry Miller's *Tropic of Capricorn* (1975, p. 300): "Even if there were a job for me to fill, I couldn't accept it, because what I needed was not work but a life more abundant. I couldn't waste time being a teacher, a lawyer, a physician, a politician or anything else that society has to offer. It was easier to accept menial jobs because it left my mind free."

"What shall we then say to these things?" (St. Paul, Epistle to the Romans, 8:31), to this gathering storm of questions and issues?

The Future Questioned

This chapter has dealt with some of the concrete issues in continuing education for the professions. Still another point should be raised: whether adult educators have a responsibility far beyond mere professional education for professionals. Is there, for example, a need for expansion through continuing education divisions nationwide of the concept proposed by Menninger—that is, educational programs on human behavior for those involved in professional service? Is there a concomitant, need, say, for education for non-professional people in the deep ethical and philosophical questions of professional practice, in the limits of professional knowledge? Do adult educators focus too much on providing opportunities to earn "a scrap of paper," whether certificate, license, or whatever, at the expense of assessing the critical needs of the people—the humans—that make up the membership of America's professional associations? Finally, do continuing education specialists "continually educate" their own ranks with sufficient effectiveness? Is involvement in the practice of continuing education empirically sufficient as experiential learning?

In view of the immense territory of learning and the over-burdening problems of the professionals' needs to accumulate knowledge, it is incumbent upon adult educators to give very serious study to these questions and issues, to the new directions in which the profession of education might seek to serve itself and its colleagues in the professional world. Perhaps there may still be a way to rebuild the lost trust through dedication and service in the professions to the people of America. Perhaps there is yet "a way—to get back home."

Chapter Six

Human Resource Development for Managers

Leonard Nadler

Managers play pivotal roles in any organization. Good ones contribute greatly to the organization's success, while dissatisfied ones can contaminate it and help to cause its demise. Similarly, any organizational change requires the cooperation of the managers, who often have the power to sabotage the proposal if they do not like it. Thus, to have satisfied, effective managers, organizations are increasingly giving them opportunities for training, education, and development.

Definitions

In organizations in the United States, just who the managers are is sometimes hard to determine from their titles. In many

82

industrialized countries outside the U.S., the specific titles used immediately identify the level of the individual within the hierarchy, and from one company to another, these designations are consistent. But since no comparable agreement on titles exists here, managers must be identified in terms of their function. Thus in the literature on management and in this chapter, the manager is defined as a supervisor of supervisors, or, to put it another way, as an individual who does not supervise other employees who are not supervisors. The highest managerial position is usually that of chief executive officer (CEO). In some organizations the CEO, and perhaps even those reporting to the CEO, are considered executives rather than managers. However, we need not make that distinction, which is variable, in discussing human resource development (HRD) programs for managers.

Since 1970, the term *human resource development* (HRD) has gained acceptance as the broad heading for learning activities provided by organizations for both employees and non-employees (Nadler, 1970). Under this umbrella organizations offer learning experiences related to (1) the current job of the individual; (2) a different, but identified job; and (3) the possible directions of the organization and society. These three types differ in how they are designed, in the expectations of the learner and the sponsor, in the responsibilities of the providing organization, and in the way they are evaluated. So it is important to distinguish them clearly, and to that end I have labeled them as follows:

> Present-job learning = Training
> Different-job learning = Education
> Future-directions learning = Development

To the degree that these distinctions are not made, the possibility is lessened that mutual expectations will be met or that individual needs will be fulfilled. Nevertheless, distinctions do not mean hierarchies, and educators should avoid a tendency to consider "education" better than "training." Actually, each term describes a different kind of learning activity designed for different managers and for different purposes.

Internal Programs

Often an organization itself provides the human resource development instead of sending its managers outside for their learning. When the organization has an HRD unit, and most large organizations do, its staff members either do the teaching themselves or it provides money to hire other instructors from outside.

Learning Needs. Although training programs for managers are as susceptible to current fads as are those for any other group of employees, most often they are responses to specified needs. For instance, a class is established to help managers having difficulty with written communication, as evidenced by their memorandums, reports, and correspondence. Or changes in procedures, product lines, or company policies require managers to receive training so they can cope effectively. Other needs derive from the constant changes of society, which put more pressure on the managerial level than on any other level in the organization. One example of how organizations work to identify the training needs of their managers is provided by Exxon Corporation, International Business Machines Corporation, and others, which have developed a system for maintaining an inventory of what managers do.

Needs for education programs, as distinguished from the preceding training programs, arise for several reasons. One is that too often individuals are elevated to the managerial ranks without sufficient prior education. Such programs are particularly important for first-line supervisors who are promoted and who do not appreciate the vastly different behavior expected of them as managers. Education programs are even needed by persons recruited from outside to fill managerial posts. Recent graduates of university management-education programs have usually considered management only from a general, theoretical viewpoint, because universities cannot focus on the specific managerial behavior needed in a particular organization. After they are hired, therefore, they must relate their broad learning to the norms of their new employer, and this is where management education makes its contribution. A third reason for internal education programs is to prepare managers for both upward and lateral movement. Once a person enters the managerial ranks, he is expected not only to be successful but also to rise to higher levels of management. And generally the larger the organization, the more levels there are to adapt to, and the more education programs are needed. Similarly, larger organizations often have many branches or subsidiaries. A manager may have been concerned with the domestic side of the organization's operations and then be assigned to the international side. Or a manager may move from one part of the organization to another or even from one part of the U.S. to another. When the national economy is depressed, internal movement slows, but never is it entirely absent, and thus education programs are always necessary.

When we come to development programs for managers, it is difficult to be specific. Development, as contrasted with education and training, focuses on the future and long-range planning, both of which should be important to organizations. So one would suppose many such programs have been created. But this is not the case. Although there has been much talk about the future, and even some action—the *Wall Street Journal* reported that some organizations have hired futurists—and although one important task of managers, particularly as they reach the higher levels, is acknowledged to be long-range planning, generally speaking it is not easy to identify development needs. And thus the current shortage of sound development programs for managers.

Another difficulty is that development programs are much harder to evaluate than training and education programs and offer no direct return to the organization. They are not reflected on the "bottom line," that is, the last line on the profit-and-loss statement. Yet despite this difficulty, organizations that have used development programs feel the results were useful. One major international textile firm, for instance, has a policy of sending selected managers overseas for short periods of time, usually three months. The manager selected is one who is neither currently involved in international operations nor expected to fill an international operations position. The manager may be accompanied by his family. During that three-month assignment, the manager is attached to one of the company's foreign branches but only for such support as exchanging money, getting medical help, obtaining housing, and getting some orientation to the country. The overseas office or factory is specifically advised that the manager is not to do any work while on this assignment. Rather, the purpose is to expose him to different cultural norms and to new experiences. This company reports that managers who have been through this developmental experience return with broader perspectives and tend to be more open to accepting new norms.

As development programs are not related to a person's current job or to a future job, organizations tend either to shy away from them or to conduct such programs without identifying them as developmental. As one company officer put it, "I would not want to have to justify the management development activities to our stockholders. They might see it as an extra fringe benefit for managers or just a junket. So, we do have management development, in addition to management training and education, but we don't show it as a line item in our reporting system."

Regular Programs. Human resources development programs for managers tend to be repeated at specified intervals. Announcements of regular management programs being offered by large organizations are much like college catalogs. This format is not necessarily a handicap, since the probable participants usually are college graduates and therefore are comfortable with this type of announcement. It also suggests that some needs of managers are as apparent as those of a student body, whose members are constantly changing and who therefore need the same programs over and over. Given the mobility of managers, the same programs can be offered periodically and will reach new managers each time. In addition, regular programs meet individual needs at different times. A manager may not see the necessity of a particular regular program the first few times it is offered but subsequently finds he has a learning need that can be satisfied by participating in it.

Almost all regular management progarms include material on human relations, unions, working with groups, Theory X/Theory Y (McGregor, 1960), and motivation theories, particularly those of Maslow (1968) and Herzberg (1966). Though much of this subject matter is similar to that presented by college management education programs, it frequently is coupled with in-house experiences and applications. Thus some core material is assumed to be needed by every manager. Most programs include something on planning, coordination, and similar generally accepted management functions. In recent years, as some of this more traditional material has been criticized for being neither meaningful nor helpful, some efforts have been made to reexamine the core content. But the practice has been to retain the core and add new materials to it.

Special Programs. Special programs are designed and offered for a particular need that has arisen. And even though some of these later become part of the regular offerings of the HRD unit, they are listed initially as special items. Quite often such activities have occurred in response to federal legislation and regulations. For example, when the Civil Rights Act, which established the Equal Employment Opportunity Commission (EEOC), was passed in 1964, few organizations understood the impact of the legislation in the work place. At that time the Act was thought to be concerned only with blacks not having to move to the rear of the bus and being able to share public accommodations with whites. The Civil Rights Act was considered merely a social gesture to one minority group, despite the obvious fact that the name of the Equal Employment Opportunity Commission, which was to enforce the Act, included the word *employment.* Those organizations that had alert HRD units at that time began to design management concerned with equal employment opportunity. In some organizations these are still considered special programs that are offered only when the organization is confronted with the need for some kind of affirmative action plan or is under attack from a particular minority group. But since the passage of the Equal Employment Opportunity Act of 1972, which expanded the responsibilities and authority of the EEOC, the trend has been for more organizations to include this subject as a regular part of their usual management training and education programs.

Organizations that contract with the government of the United States also must contend with the Office of Federal Contract Compliance, which oversees the equal employment opportunity programs of government contractors. As new and different federal agencies implement laws governing equal employment opportunity, special programs are designed for managers to learn about the Office and what is required to comply with the Equal Employment Opportunity Act. Still another example is the Occupational Safety and Health Act (OSHA), which requires extensive training programs so that managers may recognize the changes that must be

made in their organizational policies and practices to meet requirements. At some point this too might become a regular program, but
for the most part it is still considered special.

Other stimuli for special programs come from internal
changes to which a learning experience is an appropriate response
and from general societal situations. Following Watergate, for example, organizations began exploring the need for training programs
in managerial ethics. When one organization found, after an
exhaustive survey within the industry, that there were no existing
ethics programs, it invested large sums of money to develop its own
program. At this writing, managerial ethics is still considered a
special program but is being offered so frequently that it is slowly
moving into the regular category.

Instructional Resources. The HRD staff usually does most
of the teaching in management programs. In many organizations
these people, in addition to being adult educators; are expected to
be fully conversant with management science and behavioral science
and to be competent to instruct in all three areas. In other cases,
since large organizations tend to rotate employees, even those with
some specialities, some or all of the people in an HRD unit are
identified not with adult learning but with some other profession,
frequently that of general management. Such HRD staff members
often do not feel comfortable teaching management programs. Thus
if most of the staff are professional adult educators, this resource
can be extremely helpful.

The HRD unit also may call on experienced managers who
are not part of the unit but who, with a little preparation and support by the HRD staff, are capable of conducting learning experiences related to management, and can be made available for brief
periods. Using managers in this way is effective—benefits accrue
from having managers train managers (peer-mediated learning)
and from having managers educate future managers (role modeling). But since managerial time is expensive, using a manager as an
instructor must be weighed against other alternatives. One is to use
what public school people call "team teaching," wherein the bulk
of the course is taught by a person who is not a manager (usually
from the HRD unit), but at prearranged times managers are called

in as resource persons, who share experiences and lend validity to the content.

Quite a few internal programs are conducted by persons from outside the organization. These resource people have a wide range of affiliations, from higher education institutions to private companies, both profit and nonprofit. Such people usually have generally known, well-identified specialities, and the HRD unit contracts with them to provide part or all of a program. The instruction is given either at the organization's facility or at a special facility leased or owned by the organization for HRD activities. Many outside resource persons specialize in providing HRD programs for managers, and some have a "product," in that they provide a fairly fixed program. This statement is not to be construed as negative criticism. The HRD unit purchasing such a program will at least have some notion of what to expect and can check with prior purchasers about its effectiveness. Such programs have a wide variety of subject matter, including problem solving, relationships, managerial leadership styles, and the motivation of subordinates.

Locations and Methods. Although no specific data exist on the location of most management HRD programs, they are likely to be conducted in a classroom. As might be expected, the classrooms for some of these management-level programs are rather elaborate, with a wide array of sophisticated supporting facilities and equipment. And since some of these facilities are not exclusively for managers, their range of classrooms and equipment is also rather broad. The teaching techniques used are similar to those of higher education programs, particularly MBA programs. Some organizations, for example, rely quite heavily on the case method.

Another common strategy, job rotation, is also controversial. Although it is or can be particularly useful in management education, it has only limited value for training and development. And too often it is used primarily to improve production rather than to teach. To be used most effectively, job rotation should have clear learning objectives and a well-defined process of periodic evaluation, so that the focus remains on the learning. Job rotation is a major part of management intern programs for new employees, who are selected right after they graduate with bachelor's degrees or, more often, master's degrees. And herein lies a problem with job-rotation intern programs: after spending most of their lives in school, the interns want to be productive, to begin using what they have learned, instead of continuing as learners for two more years. Until this conflict is reconciled, it is unlikely that management interns will be satisfied or that organizations will receive the highest returns on their investment in the program. Appropriate methods that consider the interests of both the employees and the organization need to be developed if the effectiveness of such intern programs is to improve.

Indeed, improved strategies are needed in all HRD programs for managers, especially since the time a manager spends in a learning situation is expensive. One method being explored is self-instruction. When the organization has its own computer or ready access to computer terminals, the instructor may use them. Computers are more successful in programs related to knowledge than in those related to attitudes, skills, or interacting with people. The latter may become more likely objectives, however, as some refinements in computer technology appear to be moving in that direction.

In group instruction, a frequently used strategy is simulation; that is, the learner is involved in a life-like learning situation and has an opportunity to test new knowledge and behavior acquired at earlier sessions. One might question why simulation is needed in a training program, since the learners are currently managers and can go back to the job to apply the new learning. The answer is that the learners can try out new approaches and ways of acting with little risk to the organization and to themselves. The simulation encourages the kinds of high-risk behavior that are desirable in learning situations. Since the focus in management education is on preparing learners for jobs they have not yet had or for tasks they have never done, simulation allows them to rehearse before actually going on the job. This experience also can make learners feel comfortable and can provide some direct feedback on their ability to apply new learning in situations as real as possible without risking punishment for mistakes.

Another interesting strategy is the formation of learning communities, composed of individuals who gather to learn informally. Such groups, without instructors or organized curricula, illustrate one kind of self-directed learning. For example, given the proliferation of books in the management field, few managers can keep up to date on all of them. So some managers meet together from time to time and share brief book reviews. No deep discussion occurs, since not everybody has read the book, but the gatherings do allow the members to exchange ideas and become familiar with books as they are published. The meetings also can serve to stimulate a particular member to obtain a book and read it.

One group of managers in a large midwestern city meets once a week for breakfast. They all work for the same organization, in the same facility, but they are physically separated. Although they meet in staff meetings and at other organizationally directed activities, they felt the need for a less formal and continuing relationship. So they arranged to meet and just sit and talk about their insights into management. There are no instructor and no ground rules—just a continuing, informal relationship. When queried, they were able to point to several examples of learning from each other.

External Programs

Despite the high cost, it is culturally acceptable for managers to go outside their organizations for learning experiences. In many organizations the HRD units provide internal programs only for employees below the middle-management level. Once employees become middle managers, they are expected to participate in external HRD programs. All expenses are absorbed by the organization, sometimes including those of the learner's spouse. Some organizations, depending on how their HRD units are staffed, prefer to meet most of the HRD needs of their managers—at all levels—outside the organization, because maintaining the internal resources for such a program can be extremely expensive.

Using external programs has both advantages and limitations. One limitation is that the organization has less control over the instructional resources and strategies of outside programs. Moreover, most such programs attract a mixture of learners: some are there for training, some for education, and others for development. As a result, they all have different objectives, levels of experience, and frames of reference. Thus it is unlikely that any one program will meet all the needs of the various participants. One frequent advantage, however, is that these external programs very often enjoy a prestige that may be important to the self-image of the manager and the organization. In addition, these programs, which are grouped under higher education offerings and public seminars, promote cross-fertilization among managers from different organizations.

Higher Education Programs. Almost any college or university that has a school of business offers either full-time or part-time programs for managers. These may be regular programs, open to all regularly enrolled students. Some organizations offer their managers "school-leave" opportunities, whereby the managers are assigned to return to the campus as full-time students. This leave may be for a particular course, a group of courses, or an advanced degree in the field of management. Most often, however, the higher education offerings are noncredit, nondegree programs conducted either on campus or off campus at facilities such as Columbia University's Arden House and George Washington University's Arlie House. Designed to appeal to as large a group of managers as possible, the programs cover general management topics, such as the use of survey research within an organization or the newest thinking on organizational behavior. The instructors generally are regular faculty members from the sponsoring institution, although not uncommonly professors appear on programs offered by a university other than their own. Some universities offer programs and services that an organization can contract for and conduct internally. Such contract programs, however, are not a major activity.

Community colleges that offer management programs are finding a ready market for them, particularly among small organizations lacking HRD units. Given the nature of two-year colleges, they tend to have fewer big names in the management field and therefore are less attractive to some of the larger organizations. However, as managers retire but still seek stimulation and part-time work, they are becoming a valuable resource for community colleges. These second careerists have the validity of having been successful in their own communities and are of particular interest to managers of small businesses.

Public Seminars. The largest category of external programs is public seminars presented by private organizations, both profit and nonprofit, to anybody who wishes to attend. Higher education institutions offer the same kinds of opportunities, but here we are considering those public seminars with no college or university affiliation. Probably the largest number of public seminars for managers is given by the American Management Association. Periodically, the Association issues a voluminous catalog listing its various courses in different parts of the U.S., as well as in foreign locations.

A wide range of organizations offers public seminars, and some have established reputations in the field that facilitate their identification as appropriate external resources. Many small organizations offer public seminars, too, and as may be expected, these vary in quality. Some depend on a particular individual or a small group of individuals as resource people. So one can make some guesses about their probable outcomes on the basis of the reputations of these resource people. Other programs do not utilize resource people who have established reputations, but they do produce attractive brochures to attract clientele. Some of these programs are excellent; others are a decided waste of money. Currently, there are no commonly accepted objective criteria for evaluating public seminars. Some agencies that offer public seminars are trying to establish ways of guaranteeing to the client that, as a result of employees' attending them, some kind of identifiable benefit will accrue. For some management programs, particularly those focusing on training, this approach is highly desirable.

Public seminars tend to use many of the same teaching techniques discussed earlier, except for job rotation, which obviously is not feasible. Since public seminars often use copyrighted exercises and instrumentation, managers who take back materials to their organizations should take care to avoid violating the copyright while sharing the results.

Individual and Organizational Growth

So far, the programs I have been discussing have been explicitly or implicitly for individual managers. In fact, for years the emphasis in HRD programs was on helping or changing the behavior of individuals, on the premise that what they learned would be carried over into the work place. But toward the end of the 1950s and certainly in the early 1960s, this premise was challenged, as it became increasingly apparent that putting managers through learning programs did not produce the desired changes in either individual or organizational performance. For instance, follow-up studies of the participants in some of the early laboratory sensitivity programs, which highlighted the notion that behavior could be modified as a result of attending laboratory sessions (particularly under the sponsorship of the National Training Laboratory—see Watson's chapter in this book for more information on these sessions), revealed that when the participants returned to their jobs, the new learning did not produce new behavior.

One reason for this finding may have been that some loss of learning is inevitable in the "transfer of training" (Thorndike and others, 1928), that is, in the movement from the learning situation to the time or place of application. But this long-known principle of learning was not a sufficient explanation; nor could the expected loss be compensated for in HRD programs by overtraining, a method that sometimes works in the case of technical instruction. A more profound reason was that the returning learner/managers immediately confronted the large, unchanged organization, with its established norms and many employees who had not had a similar learning experience. In this sense, the managers were somewhat like criminals—if I may make a perhaps odious comparison—who participate in a rehabilitation program, then return to the community, where surrounded by the same old attitudes and norms (as well as fear and rejection in this case) they quickly revert to the behavior that brought about the trouble in the first place. Research on recidivism showed this to be the typical pattern. Similarly, managers found it difficult to maintain and apply their new learning or behavior in the old setting.

The answer, apparently, was to try to change the job environment, the organization, instead of the individual. Thus the organizational development movement came into being. This movement called for the training of individuals in working groups in the natural work setting since, ideally, such an environment would encourage lasting change—in contrast to the case where an individual took a course outside the work place. This new emphasis certainly offered some benefits, but it also produced an unfortunate dichotomy: organizations thought they had to choose between individual development and organizational development. We now know, however, that this is not an either/or situation but a complex combination. There are times when individual change should be the objective, just as organizational change is an appropriate goal in other cases. Generally both objectives need to be considered, and both need to be built into the plans for the learning experience. Such planning avoids the possibility of learning without change, which can be as useless as change without learning.

Additional Resources

Management HRD is a constantly changing arena. During the 1950s the emphasis was on human relations. In the 1960s it moved toward technology. The 1970s have witnessed a return to some aspects of human relations but with more emphasis on performance than on understanding concepts. The 1980 picture is still unclear. A number of source materials can provide some assistance in keeping up with these changes. Some aspects of management development programs are discussed in the *Handbook of Training and Development* of the American Society for Training and Development (Craig, 1977) and in Patten (1971). Those who are interested in the manager in the public sector might consult Byers (1970). On the international side, examples of management programs conducted by companies in Europe are provided by Frank (1974). There are differences within Europe, and certainly these are compounded when one looks at management programs in various parts of the world (Taylor and Lippitt, 1975). Some useful periodicals are the *Training and Development Journal* and *Training: The Magazine of Human Resource Development,* which feature articles on management HRD. Occasional articles also can be found in such publications as the *Harvard Business Review, Personnel,* and the *Personnel Journal.*

The Future

Human resources are a growing concern in the work place. This concern is taking form in a variety of activities related to improving the quality of work life. The focus is on identifying ways to help managers have more control over their work life. One developing trend is *flexitime,* or allowing managers to set their own hours within each working day as long as they work a set number of hours a week. This is not a new approach; managers have always done this, and usually worked more than the standard forty hours. The acceptance of flexitime, however, recognizes the actual pattern of work behavior. Growing out of this are *flexiday* and *flexiweek*. Other types of work schedule being experimented with are tied much more to productivity than to the number of hours worked. This flexible approach to work also includes a sabbatical, a practice well know in universities but only occasionally used in the work place. The increasing complexity of work and the rapidity of change are contributing to a need for sabbaticals (*fleximonths*) for managers as one way of providing additional growth. Such experiences tend to be classified as development rather than as training or education.

The change in the age structure of the population indicates that until 1990 more younger people will become managers than had entered the managerial ranks earlier. Thus, we will need to know more about where these younger managers have come from and their life experiences on their way into the work force (Nadler, 1971).

The bottom line—profit and loss—is still very important, despite the appearance of more humanistic trends in the work situation. Efforts are being made to couple behavioral science with accounting through a concept called human resource accounting (Caplan and Landekich, 1974). There is still much more to be done, however, to make this concept acceptable and workable.

Technology can always be expected to influence the work of the manager, but some of the new technologies have less to do with production and more to do with providing learning opportunities. Computer-assisted instruction (Silvern, 1970) is not new, but home computers are. They are already available, and their price has decreased so much that almost every home can easily be equipped with its own computer. Not only will Johnny have opportunities to learn at home through this means, but so will his father, who is a manager. The software is slowly being developed for learning programs for managers. Thus human resource development for managers promises to be one of the most innovative and challenging areas for adult educators for the future.

Chapter Seven

Adult Basic Education and English as a Second Language: A Critique

Ann P. Drennan

Programs of adult basic education (ABE) and English for speakers of other languages (ESOL) in the United States have long been important elements in the field of adult education. In this chapter, the objectives of ABE/ESOL programs, program design, and staffing are followed by a discussion of when and where programs are held. Attention then is focused on the role of the teaching staff in their relationships with and guidance of students. The final sections have to do with funding sources, some suggestions on writing proposals for demonstration project funding, and the current status of evaluation of ABE/ESOL programs. The chapter ends with some projections for the future of ABE/ESOL. The statements made herein indicate what experience has shown about ABE/ESOL programs and their probable future course in the U.S.A.

Rationales

The twentieth century has produced several popular and changing rationales for ABE/ESOL, rationales that tend to be based on major social needs rather than on any student's needs at a particular time. An effect of this tendency is to subordinate the individual interests and motivations of learners who require varying amounts and kinds of instruction to goals that are often poorly defined or faddish. Program goals in ABE/ESOL have varied with national fashions in education and the interests of frequently changing commissioners of education. Consider, for example, "Right-to-Read," "Career Education," and "Competency-Based Education"— all laudible and needed concepts, all requiring retooling of programs, materials, teachers, and students, and all the hobby horses of individual, short-tenured U.S. commissioners of education. Thus while institutions offering ABE programs have always had as their basic purpose the development of English language and computational skills in American adults, they have also had to react not only to educational fashions but to changing political and economic climates.

Since the sixties, a dominant theme in ABE/ESOL programs has been vocational preparation, because adult educators have tended to believe that the disparate scales of living in this country originate in income differences. And such differences have been viewed as preventable or alterable through vocational or academic education. In other words, the demonstrated correlation between years of schooling and income often is considered to indicate a causal relationship—education increases income—and thus ABE programs must be directed toward helping individuals enter or be upgraded in the labor market. This rationale has several flaws, however. For one thing, length of vocational training may not enjoy the same high correlation with income that academic education has. Moreover, little has been made of the fact that education is a consumer item as much as a producer of income; and the higher the consumer's income, the more education he or she participates in. So the known correlation between schooling and income may actually indicate the opposite causal relationship—income causes education.

A third weakness of the vocational rationale is that the equation is too simple. It ignores the sociological factors that govern who gets what jobs. In a society incapable of supplying enough jobs for everyone interested in working, these factors seem not to have been explored deeply by either adult educators or funders of adult educaton. In an economic sense the ABE/ESOL graduate who replaces the less-educated worker does not yield social profit; adult education programs often accomplish their goal of rendering graduates employable at the expense of already employed nongraduates. Thus the net gain to society at large is questionable. Only if graduates are truly more productive workers than non-graduates can one say that a social or economic gain has accrued. However, certain elements in U.S. business still automatically judge the high school graduate as the superior candidate for employment, regardless of the applicant's functioning skills. Graduates thus gain personally, and the unemployed nongraduates become a new clientele for adult education programs; as a recruitment method, this is of dubious merit!

The final argument against the vocational rationale is related to the first one. Even though many adults with limited basic skills who enroll in ABE programs probably are gambling on the purported causal relationship between education and income, economists state that the relationship between adult education and increased income has only the slimmest of documentation nationally. It is difficult to point to data which prove that a decade of remedial adult education programs has lessened the rate of either functional illiteracy among the undereducated adult public or their unemployment—in real numbers or percentages.

Another rationale for ABE/ESOL is that every adult has a basic human right to skills in communication and computation. Thus society should not expect to accrue benefits from ABE/ESOL but should see itself as having a responsibility to its members. However, human rights in the arena of ABE/ESOL do not find ready dollar-and-cents support in Congress. This lack of an effective level of support is probably partly due to pervasive coercive measures, such as certain recruiting and enrollment-maintenance strategies, currently required to obtain and to keep ABE students. Members of the intended audience often indicate that they do not see literacy and education as human rights but more as onerous tasks for which they have dubious skills and which in their view yields a dubious return.

A third rationale is that educating parents will improve the future of their children—often cited as the second-generation effect of ABE/ESOL. Several studies have shown a correlation betweeen certain characteristics of the home and the academic and eventual economic achievement of the second generation (Coleman, 1966; Thorndike, 1973). This correlation usually is defined as the relationship between social class and achievement. Of course, social class is defined in part by the educational attainment of the father or the head of the household. But sociologists tend to rule out the effect of social class on the achievement of the second generation. The general stance that social class influences are beyond educators' interpretation needs much closer scrutiny. A study conducted by Wang (1975) in Malaysia showed that the comparative impact of the family and the school depends on how stratified the society is. Among highly stratified Indians, children's achievement was determined by the home environment. Among unstratified tribal Malays, the schools determined achievement, and among the moderately stratified Chinese, both home and school had an influence. Children's achievement also could depend on the education of the parents. This is a rationale for ABE/ESOL that needs much more research. The few studies that exist indicate that ABE/ESOL has a dramatic impact on the second generation (Appalachian Adult Education Center, 1972; McDonald, 1975).

The final rationale, presented by some individuals who have local responsibility for developing ABE/ESOL programs, is that teaching "unmotivated" adults to read—that is, developing word-attack or word-calling skills in resistant adults—is simply Good; no other purpose for such programs is required. This view has so limited ABE/ESOL in some locales as to make those programs almost inoperable. Conversely, the expectations of various strata of legislative personnel that ABE/ESOL, with or without a vocational skills component, should result in profound individual, social, and economic changes in the absence of other reforms in society is probably even more stultifying to reasonable ABE/ESOL program development than the "literacy-is-a-certain-grade-level" school of thought.

Public ABE/ESOL programs are operating in most parts of the nation, but amid the flurries of changes and pressures, this broad availability does not indicate whether or not specific programs are effective either personally or socially. Whatever the rationale—human rights, vocational development, second-generation influences, or Good—periodic review of a program's purpose by concerned public officials, as well as by program staffs and current students, seems to be essential.

Developing Communication and Other Skills

Despite the differing educational rationales, ABE and ESOL programs have a common base in their attempts but they differ in other ways. ABE has a more limited clientele in terms of educational level, to develop communication skills, being aimed at under-educated adults—here defined as those with less than a high school education. And adult basic education usually aims not only at developing competence with printed English but also computational skills. Other coping skills are often added as well. In contrast, the main emphasis in ESOL is on teaching conversational skills—a response to the needs of the non-English-speaking peoples, who frequently cannot get work because they cannot converse. In Illinois, for example, the "vast majority of ESOL students are between eighteen and twenty-nine and are well educated, having completed high school in another country, but are underemployed" (Bilingual Education Service Center, 1976, p. 24). So conversational skills are considered the most pressing need for everyday life by most ESOL program designers. Often reading skills are assumed to have been mastered in the native tongue and to be transferable to English. Because of this stress on conversational skills, until recently the training of ESOL teachers did not include courses on teaching reading. Now, however, reading and writing are receiving increased emphasis.

Communication skill—the ability to express oneself and understand others in oral and written modes—seems to be the most useful goal of ABE/ESOL. In contrast to communication skill, literacy so often is defined in terms of the basic ability to translate printed symbols into sound that it has almost lost its usefulness as a concept on which to base educational goals. Surely a major aim of ABE/ESOL in the United States is the ability to understand many kinds of printed English, regardless of whether this understanding requires thinking, reading, or vocabulary skills (skills often not included in definitions of literacy).

Understanding the print encountered in everyday life is a problem for all Americans because of the diverse writing styles in print media, which can be termed "written dialects." But understanding is particularly difficult for new English speakers and for Americans who do not regularly use standard English. All groups, national or international, have their own vocabularies and usages. Age, profession, geographic area, and ethnic group affect usage. Speakers of specialized sub-English also tailor their language to their peer groups through deletion of connecting concepts assumed to be known to their communication group. So part of developing communication in English is obviously the development of varied concepts, since one cannot read with understanding concepts that one does not have in one's mind.

Another common element of ABE programs has been the attempt to achieve what are called "adult performance levels" (Northcutt, 1976) or coping skills. Proponents of the inclusion of APL or coping skills as an objective recognize that when adults lack well-developed communications and computational skills, which more educated adults have acquired through exposure to print, they also tend to lack other important abilities and knowledge. The adult-performance-level (APL) concept is also welcomed by some adult educators because an emphasis on adult tasks requiring several skills breaks away from childhood learning sequences and the accompanying grade-level terminology. Such terminology is based on the grades in which children are most frequently taught certain skills, not necessarily when they learn them. Fundamentally, however, this terminology refers to the sequence of skills—which skill usually is a precondition for learning which other skill? Only in the case of truly insensitive adult educators ("You can only read like an eight-year-old") is grade-level terminology not useful. Although some regard this terminology as meaningless and irrelevant to adult education, I believe it provides a handy measurement of educational progress by sequencing skills as well as by providing both a method of organizing instructional materials and a language about them.

The APL idea is a part of the recent trend toward competency-based education; and like any trend, it is capable of abuse.

This concept may lead to setting only modest educational goals, such as so-called literacy, thereby severely limiting the educational development of "off-time" individuals (those who did not learn basic skills at socially dictated elementary school ages). For the questions must be asked, Who decides what are the minimum adult performance levels? Should it be the researchers of a national study? Federal, state, or local legislators? Civil servants? Education officials such as local school administrators? Members of professional organizations? Individuals? Some combination of the above? (Murphy and Cohen, 1974). Many ABE/ESOL programs in the United States have reported success in teaching coping skills combined with more generalized communication and computation skills. Such a curriculum may aid the individual in handling the present and may influence the future.

Clientele

The stereotyped ABE adult learner is poor, possibly intellectually subnormal, and defeatist. The stereotyped adult ESOL student is well educated but malfunctioning economically because of a language barrier. Actually, it is neither meaningful nor possible to describe ABE/ESOL learners as a class. Some learners, actual or potential, are millionaires. Their affluence has caused their standards of living and tastes to be upper middle class. Other potential learners have given up completely; they have redefined all their problems as facts of life without resolution, to be avoided rather than to become informed about. Often the reason for the latter to enroll is survival: somehow their limited incomes are threatened if they do not.

Four main categories of learners can be drawn from the array of individual learners in the ABE/ESOL programs.

Group I: Those who can achieve with any type of instruction—group or individual—and who have transportation and child care, the time for regular attendance, and the ego strength to persevere. They also can respond to mass communication.

Group II: Those whose work schedules limit the time when they can study. Individualized instruction, which does not involve missing content owing to absence from class sessions, is necessary for this group.

Group III: Those who believe in the efficacy of education but have hindrances to enrollment, such as difficulties with child care and transportation. This group probably needs counseling services and some financial help as well as individualized instruction.

Group IV: Those who cannot or will not arrive at ABE/ESOL programs on their own but will respond to home instruction. To leave home instruction out of ABE/ESOL program services is to exclude a significant proportion of high-priority potential adult learners (Hayes, 1973).

The following are thumbnail sketches of some of my students over the years, many of whom were taught at the same time. None fits the stereotype.

1. A thirty-year-old black man, steadily employed as a custodian, was considered retarded as a child and dropped out of school after the fifth grade with no skills. He lives with his mother and tries to control a truant younger brother. Initially a nonreader, he is learning to read, type, compute, and write shorthand. He also takes boxing lessons. For years his schedule four days a week has consisted of rising at 4:30 A.M. to go to work and returning home from adult education classes at 11:30 P.M.

2. A twenty-seven-year-old Jamaican woman, married to an American, has a nurse's helper diploma but works in a coffee shop. She had little education in her rural upbringing and came to the program reading at the ninth-grade level and computing poorly. She wants to train to be a nurse.

3. A thirty-three-year-old white man, steadily employed in a civil service position, owns a new car and a motorcycle, lives in a nice bachelor apartment, and goes to luxury ski resorts for vacations. He initially was at the fifth-grade reading level, despite his high school diploma, and could not pass a job-upgrading examination. He is particularly interested in philosophy and nutrition.

4. A sixteen-year-old black man, a junior high school dropout on probation for purse-snatching and for possession of marijuana, lives at home with his mother and stepfather, who send him away from time to time to a deprived rural environment when he displeases them. A bright young man, he was reading at the second-grade level. He is the shadow of his white male teacher.

5. A twenty-four-year-old white woman, who is so shy and

silent she seems catatonic at times, has never worked for hire or had a date. She was a promising student as a child, double-promoted twice before she dropped out in the ninth grade because of shame about her welfare status. She has good mathematics skills, loves reading, and wanted—and achieved—a GED, "just because." Still she has no plans for future employment and squats with her mother in an abandoned house. They subsist on thirty-seven dollars a month in food stamps and a ton of coal a year from the county.

6. A Portuguese woman in her fifties, single, and a professional housekeeper, was one of nineteen children in a poor family; she nevertheless had a sound eighth-grade education in Portugal. Although she is bright, she has great difficulty learning English. She is most disapproving of the younger ABE/ESOL students, especially those of nonwhite backgrounds. She works in affluent homes and might be said to be "cultured" in her tastes.

7. A black man, near retirement as a driver for an institution, was a nonreader. He and his wife own their home and have reared several successful children. He is afraid to face his retirement years unable to read the newspaper. He suffers from hypertension, and his medication often makes him so foggy it is hard for him to concentrate. He is erratic in attendance and appears to suffer from mood swings. He often attends ballets and concerts.

8. A thirty-year-old paraplegic from the Vietnam War with low skill levels who barely managed to get accepted by the service. His rehabilitation worker was trying to restore his interest in self-employment but first had to find home teachers for him.

9. A young, married, white mother of eight children lives in one room on a subsistence income, too proud to accept welfare. Her beautiful, bright children could not speak when they started school; she kept them quiet so she "wouldn't go crazy with the noise in this room." She learned to read so she could help her children and work a little for hire. She probably will continue to have a baby a year because she does not believe in putting "foreign objects" (pills or other birth control devices) in her body.

10. A seventy-five-year-old woman from Mexico is in and out of the hospital and initially was illiterate in Spanish and had no English. She lives with her married daughter and wants to learn to read the Bible—in English. Her family works and she is very

lonely. In her gratitude she showers her home teacher with home-made presents of food and clothing.

11. A forty-three-year-old black woman was removed from school in the seventh grade by her father (who had had two years of college), because others at her junior high school were violent toward her. Her husband is an alcoholic and abusive. She lives in run-down public housing. She has advanced rheumatoid arthritis which immobilizes her in damp weather; so she frequently misses class. Her only son, a very bright twelve-year-old for whom she has great hopes, is becoming unmanageable at home and at school. Her burning intellectual curiosity causes her to read widely and to watch public television.

12. A sixty-seven-year-old Vietnamese woman is not only totally illiterate in her native language but also innumerate. She had no English and no grasp of sound-symbol relationships. She is bereft of her extended family and home in her native country and con-fused in her new country. Catholic Charities is supporting her for the time being. A married elder son, who brought her out of Viet-nam, was a medical doctor. He has failed the medical language examination three times and is distraught. He studies day and night and cannot be very supportive of his mother.

Given the wide range of needs and personalities which qualify persons for ABE/ESOL, one has difficulty developing a coherent program rationale or clear objectives. Yet the important truth is that the ABE/ESOL programs can successfully respond to this variety, as long as the teachers and planners recognize that whatever the experience, education, and interests of the adult learners may be, family, health, transportation, and employment problems are likely to interrupt their learning from time to time.

Objectives

All common knowledge could be included in an ABE/ESOL curriculum, so eager are many adult minds when finally gaining access to printed language. However, few programs have the re-sources to provide services from zero to the Ph.D. The process of limiting possible offerings thus begins the process of objective setting.

The urge to be all things to all people results in diffuse and unproductive programs, which often recruit large numbers of aspiring learners but serve only a few. The others leave without mastering the desired skills. At the same time, very limited objectives also severely limit program participants. Such restriction is particularly hazardous because a characteristic of many ABE/ESOL participants, especially those in ABE, is an initial tendency to set their personal objectives lower than necessary, given their potential in terms of intelligence, energy, and time. Stated ABE/ESOL objectives need to include the possibility of advanced levels of mastery, either within a given program or through articulation with other nearby programs.

Within the limits of feasible offerings for a particular program, each larger objective needs to be broken down into a series of learning events or behavioral objectives. Staffs need to know precisely what subskills are to be offered by the program, in approximately what order, and which materials teach each subskill. This knowledge needs to be communicated to the learner in an easily comprehended form.

Like overall rationales, objectives need frequent review. Important questions are these: What is the maximum range of learning sequences this program can honestly offer? Are these the most useful sequences to our students and to this geographic area? Do the skills in which we offer instruction truly fit our particular students? A parallel question which usually arises at this point is: Are we recruiting the students whose needs fit the charge for which this program was developed?

Objectives are set with each student and include the development of general basic skills and of those coping skills most urgently needed to meet that individual's immediate need or life problems. Including a time limit in each behavioral objective permits periodic assessment of progress and grants adult learners more active control over their educational life. Learners can decide when and if to finish a segment and can make considered judgments about the use of their personal time for study, leisure, and other responsibilities.

Program Design

Most ABE/ESOL learners and teachers report that learning is enhanced in small groups and in one-to-one instruction. Although studies of the optimum number of students per teacher almost invariably have shown that the achievement of the majority is not affected by class size, one recent study suggests that "disadvantaged" learners may indeed need small-group or individual instruction or both (Summers and Wolfe, 1976).

According to Teaching English to Speakers of Other Languages, a national professional organization with an adult education section, ESOL programs often consist solely or largely of group instruction, particularly when the development of conversational skills takes up 80 to 90 percent of the instruction time. In contrast, an unpublished 1972–1974 study of ABE programs by the Basic Education and Reading Committee of the International Reading Association found that most ABE programs gradually turn to individualized teaching, regardless of the program design they began with. A chief contribution of individualization to basic skills development is that it allows individual progress, despite the interruptions in instruction that plague adult education endeavors. Individualization also enables the teachers to adjust to the diversity among their students, who typically begin at very different levels of skill and who learn at different speeds. In very large programs, learners operating at the same level can be grouped, although such groups need constant reassessment because of their members' varying rates of learning. A third, less recognized, contribution of individualization is that it limits the learner's and the teacher's stress. Additionally, one-to-one sessions tend to build learners' self-reliance and ability to learn independently.

The term *individualization* usually refers to a diagnostic and prescriptive teaching approach in which an individual's skills are assessed and a program is designed to start where the student is in each subskill and to provide the appropriate learning experiences, accompanied by personal encouragement. Individualization usually requires much self-directed study, although a learning prescription may include small-group instruction on specific subjects. *One-to-one instruction*, in comparison, means one teacher teaching one student. The observation that one-to-one instruction seems essential for the progress of beginning adult readers has led to the development of volunteer literacy councils all over the world.

According to Pidgeon (1976), between 59 and 70 percent of adult beginning readers could profit from individualized instruction. The rest, if carefully grouped so no one is "in over his head" or waiting for others to catch up, can progress satisfactorily in groups. About 30 to 50 percent of those needing individualization will require varying amounts of one-to-one tutoring up through at least the third or fourth reading level, the intensity of this tutoring depending on the degree of past educational damage the learners have suffered and how this experience has affected their belief in their powers of learning. Sometimes the learner profits from both receiving tutoring and studying in a regular program. For others this dual teaching is not necessary.

Staff

Ideally, ABE/ESOL teachers are selected on the basis of (1) their interest in and ability to relate to adults who have few literacy skills and varying cultural styles; (2) their past experience in teaching both basic skills and adults; and (3) their training and certification. Seniority in the public school system and financial need are never educationally defensible criteria for selection. Although adult learners tend to be exceedingly sensitive to the personality of their teacher and quick to feel demeaned, teachers with quite varying personalities seem to function productively in ABE/ESOL programs. Whether the teacher is formal and authoritarian, or informal and warm, as long as adult learners are treated in a dignified manner, most will stay and learn in the program. Teachers trained for traditional elementary schools sometimes find the transition to teaching adults difficult because of the need to develop a collegial relationship with fellow adults who also happen to be students. Still, elementary school teachers often have valuable training in how to develop specific skills. Special education teachers, too, seem to derive teaching skills from their training which are particularly useful for ABE/ESOL.

Some of the most important personnel in a program are the clerical workers and receptionists. Since these staff members represent the program in most initial contacts, they must be carefully selected and trained. If the preponderance of the adults served by the program have a common language, such as Spanish or Korean, the telephone should be manned by people competent in that language. Curt behavior, making people wait, hostility, lost messages that force students to keep calling back, and constant appointment changes are all common failings of adult education programs that can be partially avoided by providing special training for the front-office staff.

Many programs both here and abroad have found that carefully trained volunteer tutors and paid paraprofessional teachers often are as productive as professional instructors in teaching beginning-level skills. However, their effectiveness often declines sharply when the learner reaches the third- or fourth-grade level. The Southeastern Ohio ABE program has successfully employed trained paraprofessional teachers with no college background to give one-to-one home instruction, from beginning reading through high-school-equivalency training. One indication of the success of this program is the fact that for several years every student in the Southeast Ohio program who has taken the GED examination has passed it.

In addition to an understanding of the learner, the most beneficial knowledge base for the ABE teacher seems to include a sound grasp of the sequence of reading and mathematics skills, a knowledge of various ways to assess the development of specific skills, a large repertoire of exercises to teach each subskill, and acquaintance with methods for helping students cope with other problems. This last element, the capacity to teach coping skills, increases both the immediate and the long-term utility of the learner's developing abilities.

Whatever the experiences and training of the staff, the program manager leaves nothing to chance, providing preservice and continual in-service training for all staff members, professional or otherwise. These sessions are only productive, however, if they are substantive rather than administrative; that is, they should deal with how to teach and counsel, not with which reporting form to use.

In deciding what proportion of professional, paraprofessional, and volunteer teachers to recruit and hire, the program manager must consider first of all the educational levels of the potential learners. I contend that every effort—far more effort than is employed in most American communities—needs to be expended to reach and teach those persons who have the least skills. However, these students require much attention. The use of volunteer tutors for beginning readers can expand the available ABE/ESOL services at a relatively low cost. Whether or not the program permits dual enrollment, that is, allows the student to have both classroom instruction and tutoring, true one-to-one instruction is labor-intensive and can be costly. Where volunteer tutoring organizations exist, they can be relied on heavily, with certain provisos: the ABE/ESOL program manager has some say about the recruitment and training of the tutors, there is a conscientious volunteer or paid coordinator, and the adult learner is considered by himself, by the tutor, and by the program staff as an enrollee in the ABE or ESOL program. If there are no volunteer tutoring programs in the community, the program manager might encourage their development through such institutions as churches or professional sororities and fraternities. Since truly one-to-one instruction is expensive but important to beginning instruction, volunteer efforts provide about the only alternative if students are to be taught rather than allowed to become discouraged and drop out.

Materials and Methods

The chief rule of thumb for selecting ABE/ESOL materials is that no one set of workbooks or one teaching method suits any student all the time or even all the students some of the time. Despite the time and cost involved in developing them, alternatives are needed. Far too many programs invest in a few series of workbooks and feel that the expense of additional materials is unwarranted. Adult learners need more reinforcement of certain skills than can be found in even three or four series (and which skill needs additional attention is an idiosyncratic matter). Obviously the program needs a resource center which houses, in "findable order," reinforcement exercises developed by the staff. Teachers can be trained and encouraged to accumulate these important additional materials on their own. For instance, discarded public school materials that do not have childish texts or illustrations can be taken apart, filed according to the type and level of skill they pertain to, and used in nonconsumable fashion. Word games, for those adult learners who do not seem to feel demeaned by them, can be filed by skill. Lists of real objects and of suggested field trips and field experiences (such as using a bus directory to go to a strange, unfamiliar part of the city) can be filed by coping skill. Life-related materials with teaching sequences also can be filed, either by basic skill or by coping skill, although to file by the latter tends to make for a more diffuse program in which teachers can unwittingly call on students to apply unlearned basic skills (Shaw and Roark, 1977).

The current interest in adult performance levels has engendered a need for a wide range of materials related to coping skills. To help meet this need, the program would do well to enlist the cooperation of the local public library system. Increasingly, public librarians are helping ABE/ESOL programs find easily understood printed and nonprinted materials on pressing problems of life. Since many librarians count success by how many users actually come into the library building, it is a good idea, in a spirit of cooperation as well as of service to students, to introduce ABE/ESOL students to the use of the library and to arrange borrowing privileges for them. Such an arrangement benefits the students, the library, and the ABE/ESOL program and makes a lifelong resource available to the students.

The adult's first encounter with the program requires reasonably skillful orchestration by program personnel. To illustrate: ideally, the initial contact will be friendly and businesslike; the structure of the program will be clearly and simply stated and repeated in various ways during the initial interview. The interviewer will make certain that the adult knows exactly what is offered, has a candid approximation of the time it will require, and understands what will be expected of him as a student. Initially, too, the interviewer will try to find out why the person is there, although usually the interviewee will not divulge such information until he feels more at ease. Extreme care will be taken not to violate the new enrollee's privacy. Any forms to be filled out or questions to be answered will be preceded by the explanation that the information is helpful in serving the enrollee and keeping the program funded but that the person is not obligated to respond to any inquiry he does not choose to answer.

Although it may seem redundant, any testing of the enrollees' coping skills needs to be preceded by testing of their basic skills levels, because many of the available coping-skills materials are written on or above the fifth-grade level. Presenting such material to a person with very poor skills, who in the past has only been punished by tests, can ensure a threatening experience. The beginning diagnoses of enrollees almost have to be conducted individually. Diagnostic techniques include both informal and standardized reading tests, oral or silent, and paper-and-pencil mathematics tests. Initial group testing, used to decide which level of a standardized test to give and administered on the basis of years of schooling, simply eliminates most beginning readers. They either walk out on the test or do not return to hear the scores. An interview and a test, or an interview and informal testing followed by standardized testing, are necessary to design instruction that fits the enrollee and to monitor program success.

Two arguments against initial testing are presented by many adult educators: it is too costly in terms of staff time and test prices, and it frightens the potential learner away. Yet almost all expenses for test materials can be eliminated by using combinations of oral tests (for beginning readers), such as the Gray Oral Standardized Paragraphs with comprehension check combined with the Slosson Vocabulary Test and the Dolch List; informal reading inventories which a staff member can design and share with his colleagues; and informal mathematics surveys, among others. Usually, enrollees who are sensitive to test situations can be put at ease if teachers point out that they need to know what the student already knows so that the program will not waste the student's time in reteaching and that this is not a "test" in terms of receiving a judgment or being able to "flunk" it. Alternatively, an informal series such as O'Donnell's (1974) can establish an instructional level based on the enrollee's needs, and formal and more complete testing can be postponed to the third month of instruction, by which time the learner usually feels more comfortable and less threatened and has relearned previously known skills.

During the initial interviews it is most useful to ask the enrollees how they learn best—that is, through their eyes, ears, fingers (writing), or some combination of the three. The Niagara Falls (New York) Learning Center uses cognitive-style mapping to determine which sensory mode and which setting are most comfortable for each enrollee, since some people do not know which sense is most efficient for them. The interview also determines what the enrollee infers from different forms of information, that is, how best to explain things to him (Franciosa, 1974). Generally speaking, the multisensory approach has always been effective—using all working senses to reinforce learning. In fact, tutoring programs that stress oral reading should consider oral skills as only a reinforcement of silent reading.

When instructing some ABE learners in beginning reading, teachers should use a logical system for associating sounds and written symbols, such as the system of diacritical markings. One speculation about why some adults do not learn to read is that their exceedingly logical minds cannot handle the illogic of the English language. The logic which serves them well in many areas of their lives only brings defeat after defeat in learning to read—so they withdraw (Pidgeon, 1976). Pidgeon further reported that after successfully associating sounds and symbols accurately through the use of such approaches as the initial teaching alphabet, adults find it easier to switch over to traditional orthography.

In teaching ESOL in the United States, one faces at least three unresolved questions: Should adult learners who are illiterate in their native tongue be taught literacy first in their own tongue and then be taught English? Should those who are literate and illiterate in the native tongues be taught together? Should foreign languages, including English, be taught aloud in pattern practice or silently as a reading task?

On the basis of some reported data, first rendering adults literate in their own languages appears to be feasible. It seems absurd and time-consuming to attempt to teach people new concepts and a new language simultaneously. The public adult education program in Brownsville, Texas, teaches literacy in Spanish and expands the students' vocabularies with respect to such pertinent subjects as health and child care. The students then learn the same content in English. McDonald (1975) reported startling time savings in gaining English literacy by this method. A 1965 adult education special demonstration project among Spanish speakers in New York City produced the same results, as well as an unexpected side benefit: elimination of accent (Mangano, 1970). Most urban and some rural ESOL programs, however, teach persons who all speak the same languages and cannot hope to foster own-language literacy. In well-funded programs, native-speaking tutors using beginning reading materials in the learners' native tongues could work with the learners on own-language literacy at the same time that the learners are taking English in class.

When literate and illiterate adults are taught English together, it is important that a significant proportion of the time be set aside for reading development, particularly for those illiterate in their own tongues. In this learning situation, conversation can take a back seat, since some ESOL authorities maintain that picking up conversational skills is a matter of ear and that some learners with no native literacy may have a better ear for English than do their Ph.D. classmates.

Some programs, such as the Albany, New York, Learning Center, are experimenting with silent materials. In doing so, they are deviating from the oral-first-and-foremost mode of language teaching, which became dominant as a result of teaching foreign languages to intelligence agents and military technical assistants in World War II. That approach has had to be modified to meet the long-term living requirements of American immigrants, who needed to learn their new language more thoroughly than did wartime agents.

Scheduling

Adults' lives seldom can be arranged as children's are to facilitate traditional schooling; so ABE/ESOL programs need to be as flexible as possible in terms of both scheduling and location. This adaptability will determine to a great degree their exclusivity or availability to potential learners. In this respect, an adaptation of McFann's model (1970) for adult education programs could be useful. According to McFann, mastery learning is possible only when either program variables (place, teacher, methods, materials, and sequence of teaching) are fixed and time is individualized or both program variables and time are individualized. Since adult learners begin at different levels and learn at different rates, the time factor in learning is crucial.

Most ABE/ESOL programs are offered in the evening, even though at that time adults are tired, have transportation and child-care problems, and may even have work-schedule conflicts because of swing shifts, overtime, or evening work. In these days of declining enrollment by young people, virtually no attempt has been made to develop daytime adult programs in elementary and secondary schools; such a move would increase the average daily attendance of these schools—the basis on which many are funded—and also improve services both to adults and to their children. If parts of some teachers' time were assigned to teaching adults during the day, all would benefit. Institutions of higher education have made some attempts to adapt to an adult market in the interest of their own survival. But considering the attacks the school systems of the 1970s have sustained over the "Johnnies who cannot read," it is odd that the fact that Johnny's parents cannot read receives so little critical attention and response.

Another time-related problem is the shortness of the instruction period. Most ABE/ESOL programs are offered on a limited number of evenings or, in far too many cases, only once a week—or the student attends only once a week. This arrangement persists despite studies of New York's large public ABE/ESOL population showing that the optimum amount of instruction and study for rapid and dependable progress is nine to twelve hours a week, divided into at least two sessions. Less than a minimum of six hours of instruction and study per week was found to make for very uncertain, if any, gains. More than twelve hours a week statistically did not yield further achievement gains (Bureau of Basic Continuing Education, 1967). Although students can profitably spend some time on carefully structured homework, in many instances, especially in rural areas, programs for basic skills development die aborning because they offer too little instructional time.

Learners who will need prolonged study because they began with particularly poor skills should be encouraged to come into and out of the program as their lives allow but to be persistent during each learning period. It is frequent reinforcement that yields improved skills.

Physical Facilities

Many programs are offered in existing, centralized facilities —schools, community college buildings, churches, jails, offices. Such centralization often makes sense by efficiently using these existing facilities rather than establishing new ones nearer to the students, but it may not make sense in terms of the students' needs, especially in rural areas. The cost of transportation to work, food, and medical care can consume the poor rural family's annual income (Survey Research Center, 1975), leaving nothing extra for getting to the ABE class. Schools, colleges, and other program sponsors can be more responsive to such difficulties by viewing themselves as a mobile unit offering teaching services where there is an audience, rather than as buildings in which people work and to which people must come to study. Community colleges, for example, could offer extension classes to the shy or geographically removed. When Toledo, Ohio, evening schools were closed because of the energy shortage, ABE programs were moved to branch libraries that were open in the evening. This adaptation yielded a felicitous combination of materials and staff.

Prison adult education programs sometimes are attached to school districts. This, too, is a felicitous arrangement, because when former inmates are referred to programs near their homes, the files on them that are forwarded to the new program reveal only their association with the school district. Thus their privacy is protected; nowhere do the files show that these adult students had been in prison. Many ABE/ESOL volunteer agencies use branch libraries, schools, churches, union halls, private homes, and other locations, such as offices, as places in which to tutor. In some locales, these agencies are fighting for local or other funding to keep office facilities open longer hours or, at the very least, to install an answering service.

Social Reinforcement

It is an axiom among adult educators that adult learners need some socialization to facilitate learning, but social reinforcement can be a problem in ABE, especially with beginners in the program who feel uncomfortable exposing their poor skills. Although ABE learners are not atypical adults, they have come to feel they are, because in this country we unconsciously teach youngsters who have not learned to read by the end of their seventh year to make damaging judgments about themselves. They see themselves as "dumb, stupid, a freak." The more profound the reading problem, the more shameful it is likely to be viewed by the individual, and this stigma carries over into adulthood. Thus plans for social reinforcement for ABE learners probably require more sensitivity on the part of the staff than is necessary for any other group of adult learners. Some may avoid any interaction with fellow students. These people usually end up in one-to-one teaching situations, preferring to share their imagined ignominy only with the teacher who may be able to remedy it. Still, even self-directed learners occasionally break out of their privacy to find reinforcement (Tough, 1971). The ESOL students, of course, seldom suffer from such feelings. And in most programs they get a great deal of social interaction while developing conversational skills, especially if oral pattern practice is regularly employed.

Social reinforcement can be encouraged by occasionally calling some students together in a small or large group to teach a single concept that most seem to need. Or a purely social time with refreshments and entertainment can be set aside. Incorporating social reinforcement with appropriate instruction usually reaches more students than do recreational occasions, which some students shun.

Staff-Student Relationships

The relationship of the staff members and students can be a collegial one. The master-subordinate and mothering roles of the classroom teacher and the social worker are inappropriate here. Since one purpose of ABE/ESOL is to encourage adult learners to be more independent in their public life, it is most unproductive to allow or to encourage learners' dependence on their teachers. A good way to build their self-sufficiency is to remind students frequently that they learn through their own diligence and brainpower: "Look how far you've come. You couldn't do that last week. Good!" Although most people, including ABE/ESOL teachers, respond positively to gratitude, teachers must keep in mind that no one can make another learn. The appropriate response to effusive expressions of gratitude or gifts is a vehement "I can't put anything into your head. You did it all yourself." Such a response contributes to the adult learners' sense of independence and recognizes their power and self-sufficiency.

Teachers can also help by being candid about what the learning process requires. Some educational principles, such as the need for reinforcement of learning (no drill, no skill) and the concept of learning plateaus, should be shared with adult learners. By these means students can be made as aware as possible of why the teachers are prescribing learning sequences, and the teachers themselves should know enough about the needed sequence of skills to explain it. This awareness of the learning steps can allay discouragement and can help adult learners assume responsibility comfortably for their learning. In a multilingual ESOL program, however, such explanations pose a problem. If the ESOL program concentrates on English and the learners are mostly literate in another tongue, it is worthwhile to have a simple explanation of some fundamental learning concepts translated for those learners to read.

In addition to being honest about the learning process, teachers will also need to show some candor and openness in the personal realm, since the majority of adult learners arrive at the ABE/ESOL program door with many energy-draining, unresolved problems that tend to interfere with their regular attendance and learning. If the program staff are serious about teaching basic skills, they cannot help but become involved in teaching how to find information and to resolve personal problems. Individual teachers and administrators need to adopt their own styles in this regard, however. Many professionals feel too shy, too uncomfortable in personal relationships, or too inadequate to deal with a particular problem of a given student. And there are acceptable limits beyond which ABE/ESOL personnel should not go. Neither domineering nor mothering or fathering is appropriate. Again, care should be taken to be supportive without usurping the learner's independence.

Staff members who are confronted with students' personal woes might take note of a recent study showing that people deal with life's problems in four stages: a worry stage in which individuals feel they lack control over the situation; a problem stage in which they know what they want to do but some obstacle or barrier stands in the way; a comprehending stage in which people want to understand or comprehend something; and a decision stage in which a choice must be made (Dervin, Zweizig, Banister, and others, 1976). Dervin and her colleagues (1977) also found that professionals usually can handle the comprehending and the decision stages reasonably well but are stymied or actively resentful when dealing with the worry stage, which may require a shoulder to cry on and no more, and the problem stage, which may require time on the part of the problem owner and no action on the part of the professional.

This discussion of the personal relationships between teachers and students brings us to the subject of counseling and guidance, a sore spot in ABE/ESOL. Although a few big-city programs and fewer centralized rural programs can provide counselors, those provided seldom have been trained to counsel barely literate adults. Thus, the ABE/ESOL teachers bear the major burden in counseling, partly because of the inadequate funding of the program and partly because the students come to know and trust their teachers and are more likely to confide in them. A study at the University of Texas in the late 1960s showed that it was almost always the ABE/ESOL teacher who had to provide whatever counseling was offered, while "guidance counselors" did testing, that is, student diagnosis and program evaluation (Barron, 1969).

What does one do when one's students are distracted by personal concerns or crises and cannot learn—or perhaps cannot even show up for the needed amount of instruction? The paraprofessionals in the Southeastern Ohio home study program found that although instruction starts immediately, it usually takes about three months of problem-solving assistance to clear away major unresolved situations in the new students' lives which distract them from learning and keep them from settling down to serious study (Appalachian Adult Education Center, 1972). But program staff often expect serious study on the part of their students from day two, at least. Thus, adjusting one's academic expectations to the realities of the need to provide counseling so that achievement can occur is an important change of behavior on the part of adult educators.

Nevertheless, as little ABE/ESOL program time as possible should be used in responding to students' personal problems. Teachers should try whenever they can to refer students to the proper helping agency. Many localities have information-and-referral centers or consumer agencies that can be helpful. In these cases the teachers' familiarity with other sources of assistance proves to be an asset to adult learners.

Community Relationships

Relationships between ABE/ESOL and other adult education services are desirable, too. Since the level of proficiency needed to "pass" ABE (which varies from seventh-grade level to ninth-grade level in all skills) is not sufficient for comfortable functioning in most parts of the United States, especially in the urban areas, ABE/ESOL programs would benefit by being combined with high school equivalency programs, Comprehensive Employment and Training Act activities, guidance, welfare education, and similar programs that too often operate in isolation because they are administered separately by local and federal governments. If money, staffs, and most especially students were integrated in a coherent program, the learners would have many choices of content and mastery levels without the frustrations of applications and waiting lists.

If the local political climate is not conducive to coordinating programs, the next best approach would be to establish strong, formal ties among program administrators, counselors, and (if possible) teachers, so that as learners need or want amplifications of the ABE/GED curriculum, these can be arranged without months of waiting or endless paperwork. If all else fails, the conscientious teacher and the administrator informally need to search out information about all other available programs to enable them to make effective referrals when their learners are ready for more advanced or different programs. Making information about the ABE/ESOL program available to all other agencies in the area increases the number of people these agencies send to ABE/ESOL in return.

Paying for the Program

In the late 1960s the public was inclined to pay for ABE/ESOL programs, but a decade later there was virtually no further momentum. Only the habit of past support has kept programs alive, and increases in support have barely kept pace with inflation. Moreover, some persons have made serious attempts to lift the financial burden of adult education off the public's shoulders by redefining the literacy rate in the nation through increasingly simplistic and uninformed census-taking methods, so that literacy does not seem to exist (Coles, 1976).

Those public and private ABE/ESOL programs that still offer the time and the diverse services needed to ensure the learners' growth and that seem to have a future are those that have combined money from several sources. One source is too narrow a financial base to provide adequate and secure ongoing ABE/ESOL services. Administrators need to acknowledge the stresses and frustrations involved in dealing with many public offices and get on with fund consolidation. Administrators also need to ask the following questions with respect to each possible source: What is the fundamental purpose of the ABE/ESOL program for which we are seeking support? Does this source show promise of furthering that purpose, or will retooling the program to meet the source's requirements actually reduce instruction time significantly? Are the effort and money spent on developing the proposal and reporting on it going to yield a significant return or simply take time and money from the program?

When administrators do obtain money from demonstration and other discretionary (usually federal) funds, it often is not used in the manner originally intended. The intent of administrators is to support their programs. The intent of the Congress in setting up the funds is to support experimental programs that can devise novel solutions to common ABE/ESOL problems for the benefit of like programs. But the adequate demonstration project requires much more retooling of the program, paperwork, and reporting than the average ABE or ESOL staff cares to do. Because of the extra work involved, administrators should have the consent of the majority of their staff members before applying for such money and should discuss the proposed project with students through the student council or advisory group.

Paramount to receiving support for a demonstration project is the writing of an adequate proposal. Some timely suggestions are offered here. (1) Know why the money is available—what the law says, in the case of federal sources, or what the philosophy and goals of the private source are; spell out precisely but briefly how one's organization can meet these goals. (2) Study the language of the proposal guidelines carefully and use it in writing the proposal; in this way you will be speaking to the proposal readers in their own vocabulary. (3) For some reason, most organizations issue at least two discrepant sets of guidelines. Especially if the funds are federal, look at and follow the *Federal Register*—then make any additions according to the administering office's guidelines. (4) Pick out all the required parts of the proposal, restate them as questions, and answer them briefly and clearly in terms of your program plans, with projected figures, not bland generalizations. (5) Be certain to include a well thought-out evaluation. Specify, for instance, what data must be collected before the project and the evaluation begin. Scrutinize each of the projected objectives to be sure that the evaluation scheme will assess all of them. (6) Despite pleas and demands for brevity on the part of funding agencies (who, after all, have to read them), include all the material possible about past accomplishments—your program's track record. Also, staff resumés can be necessary and persuasive. Spare the paper where you can. (7) Get tentative commitments from as many of the potential staff members, consultants, and sites as possible and explain clearly how the others will be selected or recuited. Include letters of agreement from those committed. (8) Do your homework. Know what other programs have done allied work; cite them, and describe whether the information on them is available in printed or oral form; then distinguish what you are doing from past efforts. (9) Define the extent of the ABE/ESOL problems and potential in the geographical area where the project is to be undertaken. Never assume the proposal reviewers know the size and depth of the problem, regionally or nationally. (10) Include a detailed table of contents and number all pages. Proposal readers usually have a rating scale; they must be able to locate with ease the sections to be rated. (11) Be sure to include all compliance forms. (12) Include a schedule of activities and events so that the projected chronology is apparent. (13) Include letters of support from community and national agencies. (14) Be sure the abstract does not exceed the total number of words requested; if no abstract is called for, write an executive summary and place it immediately after the table of contents. (15) Use the budget forms, but include a narrative breakdown (and justifications of possibly questionable items) for each line item. Be sure that every aspect of your plan of action is reflected in your budget. The list of do's and don't's in proposal writing is endless. The foregoing are offered to help proposal writers well on their way.

Evaluation

The unreported and unassessed program will have a difficult time finding continuing support. If money and time allow, several reports aimed at different audiences should be prepared. Administrators usually desire logistical information answering the following questions: How was the program paid for? How many students were there for how long? How were staff members selected? How were staff members trained and supervised? What recruitment procedures were effective? "On-the-firing-line" teachers want descriptions of students and answers to such questions as these: What parts of what materials were successful with students having what disabilities? What counseling problems arose and how were they resolved? Local, state, and federal decision makers want to know the social and economic impact of the programs, the differences that this expenditure of public money made in an occupational sense. University faculty members want to know about program design and statistics; the reporting demands of higher education vary from those of most other audiences. Administrators of ABE and ESOL programs have neither given nearly as much attention to these groups of decision makers as they should have nor used enough imagination in their reporting.

Evaluating students and assessing programs can be two very different and sometimes conflicting activities. Data from reading inventories, criterion checks, and commercial surveys that identify strengths and weaknesses in skills and keep track of programs cannot be applied easily to program description and assessment. The standardized tests that can be used to compare programs or a program from year to year may not reveal what the individual student has learned. Or they may be so generalized that the development of specific skills is not detectable. The weakness of standardized tests is the assumption that all students need to know only what is on the test. Otherwise, there would be no justification for comparing programs or individual students on the basis of those particular results. It is nonsense, however, to suppose that all men and women, rural and urban, of any occupation, and of any age or ethnic background need to know the same concepts—even specific reading concepts.

I maintain that despite the obvious need for accountability and the thriving modern business of evaluation, the state of the art of evaluating social science programs is primitive—a mere fledgling stepchild of research in the "hard" sciences and of virtually no objective use. For example, although few ABE/ESOL staff members ever mention to the recipients-students that a program goal is to get them off welfare, and the program may offer training only in basic skills, a plethora of ABE/ESOL programs use numbers-off-welfare data to judge their success. This is not valid evaluation. Equally invalid are the number registered to vote and voting, the number employed and upgraded on jobs, the number attending PTA meetings, the number reading the newspaper, the number with new library borrowing privileges, and so forth. To judge an educational program mainly on covert criteria is absurd. Only if the student is aware of these program intents and if a sequence of skills for each intent has been taught can the program be held accountable for such results. This is not to say that ABE/ESOL never yields employment or increased citizenship activity or that these results should not be reported. They are important, but they are side effects. To use an example from another field of education, one of the outstanding benefits found in studies of Head Start is the increased health of the participants because of increased exposure to medical care. Should Head Start be judged an educational success because of the greater physical well-being of its participants, or is this a fortunate side effect?

Another fallacy of modern ABE/ESOL evaluation is that two to three grade levels are considered a good gain in short-term ABE/ESOL programs. Many job-training programs operate ABE/ESOL sequences in isolation from other programs for only twenty-seven or thirty-six weeks a year. If the participants were total nonreaders, or even reading at the fourth-grade level, two years of growth would simply not be sufficient to yield a satisfactory terminal level. The participants' expectations for an improved standard of living have risen, but the development of their usable skills to effect improvement has not kept pace. A more useful program strategy would be to place the training-program graduates in jobs, if possible, and at the same time place them in continuing ABE/ESOL programs at the appropriate level. Since nonacademic print in this nation generally is at the tenth-grade readability level, mastery at the tenth- to eleventh-grade level is an important minimum goal. Using "average years of achievement gain" as a criterion of success is more a paper-shuffling procedure than a means of educational evaluation, because this method does not indicate the absolute (and most relevant to adult life) level of achievement. Significant program goals and instruction must have some connection with the realities of adult life.

How, then, to evaluate programs? First, the goals of the program, either written or understood, are reviewed by a group of laymen and adult learners. There is no point in assessing progress toward goals if the goals themselves are not suitable. Next, the population of adult learners is examined. Are most of the actual students those for whom the program was originally intended? From the middle 1960s into the late 1970s, the answer increasingly has been no. Adults functioning at the ninth-grade level and above, or who have had that much schooling, whatever their functioning level, are much easier to recruit, take less time to teach, demand less staff time for productive instruction, and yield greater returns to the program in terms of the number who pass the high-school-equivalency test. The staff members will need to decide whether they care to live with this goal displacement or desire to correct the imbalance through intensive personal recruitment and the adoption of teaching techniques that will ensure progress and program continuation rather than discouragement and dropouts. Many ESOL programs will not admit persons who are illiterate in their own language, although a strong case could be made that they should have the first priority as a target audience.

The hierarchy of behavioral objectives is next examined. Do they aim at clear stages of competence? Next, the activities that are meant to encourage the accomplishment of each objective are delineated. The question is, do the activities logically follow from the goals and objectives? Once input has been examined—goals, adult learners, and activities—results need to be assessed. To examine endings one must examine beginnings. At the beginning of each program year, an attempt should be made to define where the program is so that a comparison can be made at the end of the year. Similarly, prechecks and postchecks of learners' functioning levels are made; the key is not to be simplistic in that checking.

One problem for every administrator is the time-consuming paperwork involved in tracking each adult learner. Some of this paperwork could be done by individual learners as they advance through the program. The teaching staff needs to be free to help in making the judgment about what information is important for the whole program to collect. After the decisions are made, however, administrators should demand compliance from individual staff members. Unfortunately, some of the best teachers are hopelessly inept in keeping up with their paperwork, and some of those most conscientious, in terms of paperwork, are unproductive as teachers. The staff members who can both produce and record good information are pearls without price.

One largely neglected part of ABE/ESOL programs is follow-up. It is difficult for ABE/ESOL teachers to assess their own part in the life changes of adult learners which may also have been influenced by more advanced programs. However, adults themselves report changes in their functioning which they attribute to the ABE/ESOL program. The pressing question "Does ABE/ESOL really make any difference in anyone's life?" must be answered to many persons' satisfaction if services are to continue. The public must be satisfied, to ensure monetary support; the adult learners must be satisfied, to prevent dropouts; the staff must be satisfied, to prevent high staff turnover. Therefore, the systematic collection and collation of vignettes, which tell so much about the program's impact, and the systematic follow-up of former learners who did and did not reach ABE/ESOL mastery are important. The returns from education are often only identifiable some months after a student leaves a program. Only follow-up procedures can tap such effects. Moreover, if the ABE/ESOL program is really lacking in some aspect, the former participant, now at some distance from the program, can be its most valid assessor.

A significant movement against the human services in the United States threatens to sweep away all programs for actual or potential welfare recipients and others. Taxpayers revolts are not specific. Basic education for adults, having risen and fallen at least twice during the twentieth century, will disappear altogether if adult educators do not gain the attention, compassion, and cooperation of the community. If programs of adult basic education and English for speakers of other languages are to receive sufficient support to continue through the 1980s, they will need to become much more efficient, and currently scattered exemplary practices will have to become the accepted methods of program operation.

Chapter Eight

Education for Economic and Social Development

Violet M. Malone
W. L. Flowers, Jr.

Although addressed through a variety of programs, the goals of economic self-sufficiency and social development for all American citizens have still to be achieved. In the 1970 U.S. census, thirty million adults with less than a high school education were reported to be unemployed, and twelve million adults were reported to have annual incomes below the officially defined poverty level. In 1975 the Department of Labor records showed that 7.5 percent of the adult population was unemployed and 12.5 percent was in the low-income category. These disadvantaged adults were unable to become part of the economic and social mainstream which is prescribed by the norms and standards of the larger society—those who are in that mainstream (Yetman and Steele, 1971). The enormity of the educational task necessary to help these disadvantaged adults into the center of society, the dwindling resources available with which to perform the task, and the larger society's doubts about the wisdom of investing in some past and current programs form the bases for this chapter.

Although the term *mainstreaming* is today used almost exclusively to denote the practice of putting handicapped children in regular classrooms, it has had other meanings over the years (Good, 1974). As used here, it refers to developing and employing various educational processes and programs to help economically and socially disadvantaged adults develop the abilities they need to become productive, self-directed individuals within the larger society (National Association of Education, Professions, Development, 1976). Education as a means for providing disadvantaged adults with access to the good life is intertwined with the economic system of this nation. In the United States an investment of education is viewed as a means of helping individuals achieve economic self-sufficiency and as a vehicle for fostering their social development. It is regarded as an investment in human capital (Johns and others, 1970). The goal of economic self-sufficiency is related to the expectations that investment in education should result in some tangible economic return for the society.

Adult educators have played and should continue to play an important role in influencing the form, function, and scope of programs aimed at mainstreaming adults. In the past, adult educators have helped to shape legislation, identify client groups, assess their needs and interests, develop long-range goals and plans, design and implement learning experiences, and monitor the resulting education system. However, their impact on the problems of the disadvantaged has been limited because they have not always been effective in impressing the larger society with the value of these programs. Mainstreaming poses two major questions for adult educators: To what extent can we or should we use education in our efforts to overcome the economic and social inadequacies of disadvantaged adults, and how should the results of mainstreaming efforts be evaluated?

The Principle of Reciprocity

Reciprocity refers to gainful return on an investment; it is not a "one-for-one" return—that would represent a replacement of the amount invested. Rather, the term refers to a basic proposition in American society: for goods or services rendered, a multiplied return is expected. In the educational system and in the world of work, the principle refers to financial, physical, and human resources as inputs to the system for the maintenance and development (education) of individuals who, as human capital, will multiply the returns (output) on the investments. Educational services are a primary example of economic reciprocity: the returns on the educational investment are expected to exceed the value of the monetary investment. Thus these inputs have two social purposes: to maintain members of the society and to enhance their development. Those subsidized through public social services are being maintained by the larger society. Among this group are some unemployable individuals whom society does not expect to develop and whom it is therefore willing to support because it has the philosophical ideals of compassion and justice (Bishop, 1977). But also included in this subsidized group at present are some young and able-bodied persons with a right-to-maintenance mentality. Their lack of motivation to work conflicts with the generally held capitalistic values of society; those in the work force voice strong objections to having their tax dollars used to support people who can work but do not wish to. Furthermore, the rising costs of maintaining both the unemployable and employable are causing great public concern. Can the capitalistic system survive this increasing drain on its resources? It seems apparent that some limits must be placed on society's willingness to maintain and develop individual members of society. Therefore, action to reduce the number of nonproductive individuals as quickly as possible has become a major economic and social imperative, with particular emphasis on mainstreaming those whom society believes can be developed.

Since adult education programs are more closely related to the world of work than are other education programs, the principle of reciprocity is most relevant to them. Thus the effectiveness of programs for economic and social development (mainstreaming) will continue to be measured by how much they multiply the return on society's investment in them. And yet educators frequently ignore this principle, in spite of its application to their enterprise (Hills, 1976). Perhaps partly because of their failure to heed this principle, the observable return on public investment in education has declined for several decades while expenditures for educational services have risen sharply. One consequence has been the development by the private sector of educational programs thought to be economically productive. A number of adult education programs and physical facilities have been established independently of traditional educational institutions. Examples are educational programs created by such businesses as the Xerox Corporation, General Motors, and International Business Machines, as well as by the military (Somers, 1968).

How resources are divided between maintenance programs and development programs varies according to social expectations and to the economic health of the society. The costs and benefits of each are carefully considered by funding agencies. Educational programs producing marginal economic or social benefits are less able to acquire resources. Thus, a maximum output in terms of human productivity for each unit of input is the ultimate goal of educational efforts (Warner, 1975).

Student financial aid programs mirror the operation of this evaluation system. Generally, through fellowships, subsidies, scholarships, or grants, relatively high levels of financial support are provided for those in the mainstream who, through being educated, have the potential for providing a high economic return to society. For example, witness the number of dollars society invests in the maintenance and development of medical students. But a potential or demonstrated return is not the only determiner of where the money goes. Society's values and status system also are significant elements. Even though evidence of the return has not always been available or easy to measure, society has always provided comparatively high levels of postsecondary scholarship support for young adults who do well academically. However, for the manually skilled young adult who studies to be a carpenter, mason, clerk, typist, seamstress, or mechanic, similar extended postsecondary scholarship support is rarely provided (O'Toole, 1975). Furthermore, higher levels of economic support are provided for the few in graduate programs than for the many in undergraduate studies. And students in some fields are subsidized for longer periods than those in others. The more highly educated generally also have a higher economic value. Vocational education, in contrast, continues to be regarded as less prestigious and less valuable than academic education and, consequently, is given less support.

Historical Perspectives

Concern about helping disadvantaged adults through economic and social development is deeply rooted in United States history and is nourished by the ideals of the greater good, compassion, and justice (Young and Myers, 1967). Mainstreaming, however, has stemmed more often from the latter two ideals than from the ideal of the greater good. It is with these three ideals in mind that we explore the origins, purposes, and successes or failures of several early efforts at mainstreaming.

In the early history of the nation, circuit riders and mobile pioneer schoolteachers brought religion, news, and education to many isolated frontiersmen and their families. At that time, the economic and social development of those isolated individuals and groups was not a major social issue, because the provision of goods and services was localized and the norms for social development were easily identified and transmitted. As the population increased and the effective distances between people and places were reduced through the improved communication and transportation systems that accompanied industrialization, the need for new knowledge and skills became a growing social concern. It was at this time that the need for education, in particular, came to be related to the economic and social development of the individual and of the nation.

In 1892 Booker T. Washington at Tuskegee Institute in Alabama developed and implemented a mobile educational program for farmers (Work, 1936). Shortly thereafter, Seaman Knapp performed his excellent demonstration work among farmers in Texas. These efforts, along with the Farmers Institutes—initiated by Cornell University and later dispersed throughout the East and the Middle East—sought to help farmers adopt agricultural practices that would stimulate their economic growth through increased production. The programs were successful largely because farmers came to view the new technology as useful and workable. However, common economic and social needs did not always mean common responses by the educational structure. Society had isolated individuals according to race; and education, being a child of society, developed differently for each group. The first annual Negro Farmers Conference, for example, grew out of Booker T. Washington's efforts to educate farm families within Alabama communities. This endeavor followed the establishment of the Negro land-grant institutions in 1890, almost thirty years after the establishment of the white land-grant institutions in 1862 (Campbell, 1936).

The land-grant institutions were developed in response to the educational needs of both the agrarian element and the embryonic but rapidly growing industrialized sector, which were not being served by existing institutions. These institutions, referred to as "people's colleges," provided instructional programs at the collegiate level in agriculture and mechanic arts, concentrating in the beginning on rural youth. They received a big boost in 1887 from the Hatch Act, the primary purpose of which was to provide land-grant institutions with the much-needed resources to carry out research on agriculture and related subjects.

The Cooperative Extension Service. The subsequent rapid discovery and accumulation of research-based knowledge related to agriculture and rural living, coupled with some pressing problems being faced by the rural population, led to the passage of the Smith-Lever Act in 1914, which established the Cooperative Extension Service as an integral part of the land-grant institutions and of the U.S. Department of Agriculture. Its creation represented the third leg of the tripartite structure of the people's colleges: collegiate instruction, research, and extension services. The extension function was to provide these institutions with the capacity to disseminate research findings to, and encourage their application by, persons who were not enrolled in regular degree programs and who resided on farms and in small communities and towns. The mission was and is to tackle problems of agriculture, home and family living, youth development, and community development. Thus, the land-grant universities, with their three functions, constituted a major early attempt to facilitate the movement of working people into the mainstream of American society.

The early educational efforts of the Extension Service included providing farmers with the knowledge and understanding needed to increase farm production, creating informal educational programs for the young, and working with homemakers for the betterment of the family environment through home economics (Harrill, 1967). Family participation in Cooperative Extension Service (CES) programs has continued to play an important role in the transmission of information from the land-grant institution to the local level. The intent of the CES today, as from its beginnings, is to improve the quality of life through educational programs that are cooperatively supported by federal, state, and local revenues. A cadre of subject-matter specialists based at the land-grant institutions continually transmits research findings to county extension agents, who use this information to help citizens in satisfying their local needs and interests. Local lay groups help to determine the scope of their county extension programs.

One reason for the success of CES programs in mainstreaming rural Americans has been a concern for keeping the public aware of the value of agriculture to society. Although current census data show a major decline in the number of families actively engaged in farming, public acceptance of the importance of agriculture to the nation's welfare has helped farmers and their families maintain a significant role in decision making that affects the economy of the United States and other nations. A second reason for Cooperative Extension's success is its flexibility in adapting to the changing needs and interests of diverse client groups. Although the subject matter remains essentially the same for rural and urban consumers, new delivery systems have been devised to accommodate the economically and socially disadvantaged in metropolitan areas.

As an example, in the late 1960s the Cooperative Extension Service launched a major educational effort, now called the Expanded Food and Nutrition Educational Program (EFNEP), to provide low-income urban and rural families with the knowledge, skills, and attitudes necessary to improve their health through adopting improved nutrition practices. The program employs indigenous paraprofessionals, called program assistants, who translate technical knowledge concerning food and nutrition into practices that are appropriate for the cultural, social, and economic environment of the participants. The level of funding for EFNEP has fluctuated with the economy, even though it has been successful.

Other CES programs aimed at helping local citizens solve their community, economic, and social problems are the Community Resource Development and Small Farmer programs. Designed to meet the needs of a specific clientele, each program uses local paraprofessional staffs whenever possible.

Americanization. Education is a tool that has been used by the government for many years to assist in mainstreaming persons whose cultural backgrounds and language differ from those of the majority. The influx of immigrants, particularly during the industrial revolution, gave rise to "Americanization" classes designed to help equip immigrants to move into the center of American life (Fisher, 1967). Americanization programs, still successful with immigrant adults, offer new language skills and an understanding of the American "way of life," both of which are welcomed by participants. The economic and social gains achieved both by these individuals and by society as a result of their personal gains are evident.

Community Action Programs. During the 1960s, several programs, initiated at the federal level and put into operation locally, were developed to help adults in economically disadvantaged areas to improve the quality of their lives (Fisher, 1967). The programs were designed to meet the needs of local citizens by first of all having them find out what they needed, establishing pertinent programs, and then evaluating those efforts. These various programs, subsumed under the umbrella term *Community Action Programs,* were administered by the Office of Economic Opportunity of the Department of Health, Education, and Welfare and were operated by local community action agencies. Through the social action process, groups of local citizens applied for federal money to conduct economic, political, and social programs ostensibly for the benefit of the community.

Community action agencies were a product of the 1964 manpower act called the Economic Opportunity Act (EOA). The EOA offered special work and training programs for disadvantaged adults whose characteristics "severely handicapped . . . [their] ability to secure or retain self-sustaining jobs" (Employment and Training Administration, 1975, Part I, p. 6). One of the successful aspects of the program actually formed the basis for one of its failures. Citizens' involvement in programs that affected their way of life was critical to the programs' success. But even though participation was high, most participants lacked the appropriate knowledge and skills to effect changes through a community organization, and community action programs floundered in the absence of leadership. Lack of coordination among community agencies also resulted in considerable duplication of effort. Yet such programs as Operation Mainstream for older workers, the Neighborhood Youth Corps, and the New Careers and Public Careers programs served for a time to alleviate some of the barriers to economic progress.

Cost-effectiveness studies on many of the EOA programs showed varying results, none of which met the expectations of either the local organizers or the federal funding agencies (Fisher, 1967). The economic return on their investments was a basic concern of both groups in measuring the worth of the programs, while social development among the participants remained an intangible outcome of appreciably less concern (Gans, 1971).

Other manpower planning legislation enacted before 1964 and aimed at reducing unemployment through training consisted of the 1961 Area Redevelopment Act (ARA) and the 1962 Manpower Development and Training Act (MDTA). The ARA provided federal money to help unemployed persons who lived in economically depressed areas to qualify for self-sustaining employment. The goal was to provide a labor base that would attract new business enterprises to the area and thereby stimulate the local economy (Somers, 1968). The limitations of the ARA were reduced by the MDTA, which was aimed at assisting experienced workers to find jobs and offering money through the Departments of Labor and Health, Education, and Welfare to provide classroom and on-the-job training "to deal with structured unemployment problems which were believed to result from rapid technological change—automation" (Employment and Training Administration, 1975, Part I, p. 4). In this program, state employment agencies identified the skills in demand, and state vocational education agencies arranged for trainers and certified the training institutions. Nonetheless, duplication of services remained a major problem until the Cooperative Area Manpower Planning System and the Concentrated Employment Program were developed in the late 1960s.

With declining unemployment, the emphasis in the MDTA program shifted to include disadvantaged adults who faced additional obstacles to self-supporting employment, over and above a lack of technical knowledge and skills. Unfortunately, however, the program's administrative guidelines neither identified those obstacles nor suggested ways to overcome them. Another shift took place in the distribution of the money: now half went to the private sector for on-the-job training programs. The MDTA program was successful to the degree that some participants did develop technical job skills and became employed. But others remained unemployed and continued to be subsidized by federal and state dollars (Mangum, 1967). Thus these latter adults remained outside the economic and social mainstream.

Between 1964 and 1971, two other manpower acts were funded—the 1967 Work Incentive Program (WIN) and the 1971 Emergency Employment Act. The WIN program aimed to assist employable recipients of Aid to Families with Dependent Children (AFDC) to join the economic mainstream, since the rising costs of welfare and unemployment programs were consuming the resources which otherwise would have been available for the production of goods and services. The elimination of barriers to employment for the AFDC recipients was listed as a goal; however, interagency and intraagency policies and procedures, combined with the government agencies' relations with the private sector, severely limited the intended outcomes of the WIN program (Ehrenberg and Hewlelt, 1976). The Emergency Employment Act was designed to provide transitional employment in public service programs for the underemployed and the unemployed. Job creation was a major emphasis, and training and manpower services were limited to programs intended to develop the competence the recipient needed to qualify for a new job. The target group included "Vietnam-era veterans, former manpower program enrollees, youth and older workers, migrants, persons with disadvantaged backgrounds, and those displaced by technological change or shifts in federal expenditure patterns" (Employment and Training Administration, 1975, p. 7). The reform of state and local civil service systems was among the program goals because these systems were viewed as barriers to the employment of the target groups. Individual programs under this

Act achieved some success (Fisher, 1976), but generally the endeavor failed to meet its intended goals largely because a large bureaucratic system was not able to coordinate efforts so that the cost-benefit ratio would be acceptable to the funding groups. Likewise, mainstreaming through employment did not occur for many program participants, and their nonproductivity continued to be viewed as an obstacle to the development of the nation (Hauser, 1968).

The dissatisfaction voiced over the results of manpower-training programs over a ten-year period led to the development of a comprehensive manpower program to accomplish the stated goals of providing training, employment, and services to economically disadvantaged adults and to lead them to self-sufficient, unsubsidized employment. The compromise legislation—the seven-section Comprehensive Employment Training Act (CETA)—was finally approved and funded in 1973 (Employment and Training Administration, 1975). A decentralized manpower system paid for by the federal government and operated by state and local "prime sponsors," CETA offers training, counseling, testing, and job placement for several categories of persons. The Act provides for the inclusion of activities deemed successful in previous programs: local planning groups, local implementation, the creation of public-service jobs, and youth employment, as well as classroom and on-the-job training. However, CETA programs were to be judged on how much they reduced the target areas' unemployment rate and increased the participation of the private sector in providing unsubsidized employment to persons in the target groups. Employment was expected to provide the program participants with the self-sufficiency needed to enter and remain in the mainstream of society. If CETA programs are evaluated on the basis of these criteria, they have not been effective in mainstreaming adults (Employment and Training Administration, 1975). Evaluators have cited causes but have admitted that the existing barriers could be eliminated in time by allowing for some stabilization in current guidelines and by minor modifications at the level of implementation. Four reasons for program ineffectiveness have been cited: (1) the prime sponsors' inability to operate a comprehensive program, (2) the abbreviated start-up time, which limited planning for implementation,

(3) the planning councils' lack of understanding of their role and inability to translate economic and social needs into education programs, and (4) disparities between the definition of need as intended in the legislation and as interpreted by the prime sponsors.

The impact of CETA is unknown at this time. Despite the billions of dollars which have been spent through this act, no definitive evaluation of its effectiveness has been made. Those assessments that have been undertaken used indirect measures that are incapable of demonstrating whether or to what extent this program has accomplished its stated objectives.

The Cooperative Extension Service, Americanization classes, and Community Action Programs were developed in response to the economic and, to a lesser degree, social needs of individuals and the society. These endeavors were designed to provide job skills to the unemployed and underemployed as quickly as possible. Sponsors of the programs supported the point of view that an individual's economic self-sufficiency contributes to the economic development social growth, and maintenance of the society. The intended outcomes of these programs, however, have not yet been achieved.

Obstacles to Mainstreaming

The obstacles to the mainstreaming of the disadvantaged through economic and social development appear to be built into the structure of American society. Part of the problem rests in the value systems of that society, which supports education primarily as an investment in human capital, expecting increased economic benefits as a return on investment (Freeman, 1977). Therefore, cost-benefit ratios in education continue to be debated. Another obstacle is that the increasing amount of tax dollars being spent to maintain disadvantaged individuals in a variety of subsidized programs, such as CETA, has led to questions whether the outlay of those dollars is in fact providing those being subsidized with the means for the good life (Ribich, 1970). The maintenance of certain of the disadvantaged without an expected return can be tolerated until times of economic crisis call for the mobilization of a vast number of human resources to develop goods and services (Carnegie Commission on Higher Education, 1937b).

A less obvious but still potent barrier lies in the differing concepts of maintenance and development held by the general society and by the disadvantaged. Their perceptions of the appropriate means and ends for the economic and social development of the disadvantaged are not the same. These differences in perception, which may be attributed to educational and environmental differences, are a source of conflict between the users of the resources— the subsidized—and the producers and providers of those resources (Malone, 1973). Each group questions the motives of the other, and actions to change the current system often become misdirected. Most often, the results of this conflict are educational programs in which the goals of neither the maintained group nor the larger society are achieved (Barlyn and Schein, 1976).

In investigating the effects of these differing perceptions on efforts to mainstream disadvantaged adults, we found few pertinent studies in education, probably because perceptions related to the economic and social development of individuals are difficult to identify under controlled conditions. However, studies in anthropology (Leibow, 1967; Schensul, Paredes, and Peeto, 1968), community development (Bishop, 1967; Cassell, 1970), and social psychology (Etzioni, 1976; Miller, 1964) provide some evidence to support the idea that varying perceptions influence the effectiveness of mainstreaming efforts.

Through the process of negotiation, the views of both groups might become more congruent, and environmental and educational barriers might thereby be lowered. A willingness to make adjustments in what each group would accept as reciprocal behavior would help provide the maintained group with a framework for establishing goals congruent with those of the larger society. Society in turn might modify some of its expectations of the disadvantaged (Lester, 1969). The degree to which congruent perceptions develop will depend on the degree to which educational programs can be designed and implemented to help both groups improve the quality of their lives (Wethey, 1974).

In some parts of society, obstacles to mainstreaming exist because of ignorance or discrimination based on ethnic origin, income, and sex. Although efforts have been made to remove such obstacles through legislative mandates, the implementation of laws sometimes raises additional barriers. The content and the delivery systems of the resulting education programs often are considered irrelevant and are rejected by the intended participants.

As long as society views economic self-sufficiency as a major goal of the system, sees the individuals in the system as human capital, and considers outlays for education as investments in this capital which are expected to produce a return, mainstreaming efforts for the disadvantaged will continue to fluctuate with prevailing economic and social conditions, which affect the availability and accessibility of resources for both groups. (Rothman, 1970).

New Approaches

Educational programs for mainstreaming disadvantaged adults should have a high priority in the allocation of economic resources in the United States. And they should not be based, as past efforts were, on an economic model that gave only limited consideration to the social-development part of mainstreaming (Welch, 1975). If the maintained group is to be assisted by means of education, new approaches need to be developed that take into consideration the cognitive style of the adult learner, the teaching style of the adult educator, and the teaching-learning interaction. Moreover, these three elements should be screened through the economic, social, and political philosophies which affect both learner and teacher. Such programs also should take a developmental instead of a remedial approach.

Recommended, too, is a learner-oriented curriculum (Cross, 1975) in which the learner has opportunities to participate in learning events that (1) provide a knowledge of the social system and the decision-making skills to cope with it, (2) provide opportunities to risk and to practice new behavior in a less stressful environment before that behavior is used in the larger society, and (3) provide for goal attainment, supported by services offered through interinstitutional and intrainstitutional systems. In addition, appropriate monitoring structures need to be built into each program to provide for the accountability expected by the providers and the users of the resources.

Ingham (1973a, 1973b) reported on a successful program

that encompassed the three aspects of the learner-centered curriculum suggested later by Cross (1975) as a developmental approach to mainstreaming. The program combined simulation and on-the-job experiences for undereducated adults who were employed in nonacademic positions at a university. Its objectives were to upgrade job skills and to provide supportive services to sustain the employees' job stability. In the first six months on the job, employees were assigned fulltime to specific jobs on the basis of an inventory of their skills and interests. A portion of each work day was spent in the computer-assisted instruction laboratory. The laboratory sessions included experience with a computer programmed for the special skills and knowledge needed by the individual. Small-group guidance sessions were provided twice a week in which participants could, by role-playing, act out some of the concerns they had about their jobs and the social situations that affected their job stability. Skills in group decision making were practiced. In addition, participants had access to and used community services that were coordinated through the university. As an example, employees with health problems could be referred to the employee medical service or to the Department of Vocational Rehabilitation for such items as eyeglasses. They also could use the credit union and other university services. Working with the employees' supervisors, the program staff assessed each participant's progress toward achieving adaptive skills, environmental skills, and cognitive skills. The program, a self-paced and self-directed learning experience, resulted in increased job stability and job satisfaction for both the employees and their supervisors. None of the participants was subsidized. The costs of the program were shared by state agencies, the private sector, and federal agencies—the computer-assisted instruction laboratory received a federal grant to develop the individualized lessons. Other institutions have adopted this program in their efforts to reduce the high cost of job turnover. Currently, an attempt is being made to transfer this small program's success to the larger community through a Learning Resource Counseling Center.

Volunteerism is another means by which the disadvantaged can acquire the abilities they need to negotiate the social system. This approach may be especially reasonable, since research findings suggest that altruism is more prevalent among low-income groups than among other income groups (Rotter, 1966). One of the deterrents to volunteerism among the economically disadvantaged learners—the out-of-pocket expenses—could be subsidized. The attractiveness of volunteering would be further enhanced if properly managed volunteer experiences were equated with paid experiences. In this way volunteer credits could be accumulated by the learners and used as acceptable experiences for transfer to the labor market. Of course this arrangement may require society to adopt new values concerning volunteerism.

Full-time schooling as a means of mainstreaming does not appeal to the majority of adults. Therefore, another approach would be to develop an educational system and programs that would permit adult learners to enter and leave institutions without penalty whenever they felt their educational needs had been met. This freedom would necessitate a support system that would help participants assess their needs and determine ways through which those requirements could be satisfied by the educational process. To implement this idea, adult educators would need to consider flexible scheduling as well as varying teaching-learning strategies (Carkhuff, 1969), the social intervention process (Havelock, 1970), and microteaching (Cross, 1976), among other possibilities. This system also might include an approach used by military educators, that is, sending personnel at company cost to that facility which is best equipped to provide them with the needed knowledge or skills. Duplication of service thus would be eliminated, and the staffs of the facilities would be free to concentrate on developing specialized knowledge and skills.

If designing learning opportunities that enable disadvantaged adults to move into the mainstream is an important societal goal, then adult educators will have to learn how to develop programs that maximize individual learning that is pertinent to the current economic situation and structure. The rate of learning, life situation, and learning style of the individual are to be considered if in-class programs are to become useful to learners in mastering real-life challenges. Furthermore, if a specific kind of behavior is to be produced in an individual, adult educators will need to consider that its occurrence will be determined "not only by the nature or importance of goals or reinforcement, but also by the person's anticipation or expectancy that these goals will occur" (Rotter, 1966, p. 16). Adult learners modify their individual goals in light of the economic and social situations with which they must cope.

Challenges and Future Perspectives

At this point we have established that education for the economic and social development of all citizens remains an imperative for action and support by our society. This society has willingly developed and maintained educational programs for mainstreaming those who are economically and socially disadvantaged. However, having reviewed the outcome of some past efforts and having applied the principle of reciprocity, the public has expressed alarm about the lack of return on its investment. The outlay of dollars by the public sector for the education of subsidized groups remains high, and the value of the investment continues to be measured on the basis of how frequently those subsidized individuals enter mainstreaming programs and how frequently they leave those programs for unsubsidized employment. In marketplace terms, educational programs are viewed as successful if the participants convert the educational input into productive work output. We found little evidence that investigators consider social development in calculating the return on money allocated for mainstreaming.

Thus athough attempts at mainstreaming have historically focused on both the economic and social development of individuals, success has been judged solely in terms of an economic index. When the programs have presented subject matter relevant to the learners' needs, they have had moderate success. Sometimes they have failed because certain groups of potential learners experience obstacles to their access. Moreover, those obstacles—economic, social, environmental, and procedural—are perceived differently by members of the maintained groups and by society at large. Efforts to modify those perceptions may be more important to encouraging participation than any attempts to deal with the obstacles directly.

In the future new approaches to mainstreaming should probably involve both the private and the public sector in joint, but nonduplicating, efforts to provide the subsidized group with the competence needed for economic self-sufficiency and social development. We also recommend volunteer work, flexible scheduling of educational activities, and varied teaching-learning strategies.

Adult educators can contribute to mainstreaming in three areas: graduate education, staff development, and community development. At the graduate level, adult education professors could develop programs to give students a strong affective and cognitive understanding of the nature and characteristics of those not in the mainstream. Graduate students could also be provided with an opportunity to acquire the interpersonal skills needed to work with the disadvantaged—skills that can be acquired only through first-hand experiences. In addition, adult educators could increase their efforts to work with both the public and the private sector in designing staff-development programs that focus on ways to aid in mainstreaming disadvantaged adults. In the area of community development, adult educators can direct their efforts to becoming change agents in the social and economic systems on the local, state, and national levels.

Finally, adult educators should seek the leadership role in the restructuring and operation of those mainstreaming programs that currently are meeting with little success. Although adult educators cannot totally divest themselves of the failures of many of these programs, the leaders of many unsuccessful programs were political appointees who had neither adequate knowledge nor adequate skills in adult education. Adult educators face the challenge to demonstrate their ability to direct successful mainstreaming programs and establish their credibility in the eyes of the decision makers so that increased resources will be provided to support well-designed and well-conducted programs of social as well as economic development for disadvantaged Americans.

Chapter Nine

Education for Handicapped Adults

Thomas R. Shworles
Paul H. Wang

The large and diverse "handicapped" population in the United States contains a sizeable number of adults who have sufficient interest and ability to use adult education to improve their lives. They are many, and they are becoming more visible and militant in demanding learning opportunities. But before we can discuss such issues as establishing nationwide access and providing pertinent programs, we must first consider just who these people are and what their number is.

Definitions and Estimates

In clarifying the definitional issue, Garrett (1976) spoke of impairment, functional limitations, disability, and handicapped.

According to him, *impairment* refers to a defect caused by disease, accident, or abnormal birth; it may or may not lead to functional limitations. *Functional limitations* are restrictions or losses of one's capacity to do such physical or mental activities as walking, lifting, dressing, thinking, or attending school. *Disability* is the inability to perform a certain social role, such as homemaker, worker, or student. Looking at disability from the point of view of work capacity, Garrett defined the term as a limitation on the kind or amount of work (or housework) one can do, a limitation resulting from a chronic health condition or impairment that lasts for six months or longer. Lastly he stated that the word *handicapped* is often used as a synonym for disabled. Nagi (1977) presented a more detailed discussion of these terms, pointing out the differences between organismic functioning and social functioning. The former he arranged in four categories—physical, emotional, intellectual, and sensory; the latter term refers to functioning in "social roles."

The concept of being handicapped is rapidly changing. Previously, it was viewed as a state of impairment. Now it is considered a state resulting from interaction between the disabled person and the physical and social environment. This emphasis on the environment's impact was reflected in the following definition established by the Chicago Planning Council on Aging (1976, p. 55): "A handicapped person is one who has a physical, mental, or emotional impairment or disability which together with the existing physical environment and prevailing social conditions substantially limits that person's major life activities." Definitions reflecting this new awareness of the influence of the environment in determining "handicappedness" are becoming more common. Even legal briefs find this type of definition useful: "It is these physical and social obstacles which cause the primary difficulty in the integration of disabled persons into the mainstream of society, not something inherent in the disabilities themselves" (National Center for Law and the Handicapped, 1977, p. 29).

The foregoing definitions reflect a new understanding of the cause of the handicapped condition and a shift of emphasis concerning how to serve the disabled (Shworles, 1977). The old medical model whereby the disabled had to be changed to meet the community's demands and needs is constrasted to the new view, in which the community and the social institutions must be changed to meet the needs of the disabled. These changes represent a significant evolution. But more is demanded by some members of this group. One improvement, suggested by Gentile (1975), might be to replace the negative label *disabled* with *handicapped*.

Unfortunately, the statistical data available to describe this population suffer from a lack of precision largely because of the problems of definition. But our uncertainty regarding the actual characteristics of the "handicapped" portion of the adult population does not obscure the fact that these adults are present in sufficient numbers to be of interest to adult educators. By the most conservative estimate, four to six times as many adults as children are handicapped. The largest estimate of handicapped individuals comes from the U.S. Department of Labor—45 million. Although 35 million were considered capable of doing some kind of work, only 7 percent were employed (Kopecky, 1977). If one accepts the estimate that there are 7 million handicapped children of school age (in addition to 1 million of preschool age), then one may generally conclude that at least 35 million persons may be handicapped adults (Council for Exceptional Children, 1977). Garrett (1976) estimated that there were 23.3 million noninstitutionalized disabled persons aged eighteen to sixty-four in 1975 (4.2 million were "most severely disabled," 3.9 million were "severely disabled," and 15.2 million were "partially disabled"). And on the basis of the 1970 census, Nagi (1977) estimated that 4.9 million persons between the ages eighteen and sixty-four could perform only limited work roles and activities.

LeBlanc (1973) presented his data by type of disability. He estimated the total afflicted with multiple sclerosis in the United States to be 250,000; muscular distrophy, 200,000 (135,000 children); cerebral palsy, 600,000; and legal blindness, 450,000. LeBlanc further estimated that 2.3 million persons were limited in mobility owing to arthritis and rheumatism but not institutionalized, 300,000 had spine bifida, 340,000 were afflicted with hemiplegia or hemiparesis, between 125,000 and 200,000 were paraplegics, and 38,000 were quadriplegics. More recently, Brubeck

(1976) estimated that about 2 million disabled persons in this nation were homebound, whereas Salisbury (1977) gave a much lower figure, 1.35 million.

With respect to mental and emotional disabilities, we find the following statistics. One commonly used estimate is that 3 percent of the U.S. population is mentally retarded. Using this figure, Bilovsky and Matson (1977) listed 5.4 million as retarded. Among them, Krause (1976) described 300,000 as severely and profoundly retarded. Estimates concerning the number of persons disabled by emotional disorders have varied widely, depending on the definitions used. It has been estimated that 85 percent of that population was suffering from a psychiatric or psychological disorder. In Chicago alone, 3 of every 1,000 residents were institutionalized for emotional disabilities (Srole, 1962; Levy and Rowity, 1973).

Obviously, estimates of the proportion of handicapped persons in the United States vary significantly. The editor of the *Journal of American Rehabilitation* went so far as to say that there were no complete and accurate data on "who are the handicapped" and "what are their needs." And Nagi adds (1977, p. 32), "In addition to data about the handicapped being imprecise and incomplete, studies relevant to the handicapped have differed in definition of terms, making comparisons between studies and extrapolation of data very limited." Nevertheless, Nagi estimates that from 10 to 20 percent of the total population is handicapped.

Thus educators of handicapped adults will be concerned with the greater portion of 10 to 20 percent of the population. In seeking to help these people, educators will have to go beyond labels that indicate only physical impairment. To understand the real meaning of a handicapping condition and to design effective educational programs, adult educators must be aware of how an impaired person's life is influenced by social and other environmental variables—his economic level, community, and family resources; whether he has one or several impairments; and whether he has been homebound or institutionalized a long time. Educators will need to know what architectural and social barriers preclude the impaired person's physical, social, educational, and vocational mobility. When these configurations are assessed, adult educators will know whether they are in touch with handicapped adults, how handicapped they are, what their educational needs are, how much those needs differ from the needs of nonhandicapped adults, and what to do as educators.

Justification, Philosophy, and Criteria

To deny the opportunity of education to handicapped adults in this postindustrial society, where the emphasis is on white-collar and knowledge-based jobs, is to deny them access to typical means of livelihood. Not only does education lead to a satisfying level of living, but for many handicapped persons it is the only avenue to independence (Smittkamp, 1972). To overcome stereotypes, handicapped persons often must prove competence beyond a doubt, and so they need more education and credentials than others to compete for jobs (Weintraub, 1974). Inflation too has its negative impact on handicapped adults, many of whom are already penalized by the extra costs associated with their condition (Newman, 1974). Thus, it is important to improve the work-related skills and alternatives of handicapped adults through vocational, continuing, and higher education.

Further justification for expanded programs of all three kinds derives from the fact that vocational rehabilitation facilities are failing to meet the educational needs of the handicapped. Severely handicapped persons have the potential for far more education and training than can be provided by existing rehabilitation programs. Other handicapped adults are potential continuing education students. Twenty-five percent of the graduates of state-federal vocational rehabilitation programs are under age twenty and seeking education (Skelley, 1975). Persons with less severe handicaps also are more likely to become the responsibility of the educational system than of the traditional rehabilitation network. A recent national study indicated that a large but highly motivated group of handicapped persons was unemployed but capable of improving their lives through education (Nagi, 1977). And finally, the Bureau of Education for the Handicapped (1975) predicted that of the approximately 2.5 million handicapped youth who would leave school within the next four years, only 21 percent would be either fully employed or involved in college, 40 percent (1 million) would be underemployed and living at a subsistence level, 8 percent would be idle much of the time, 26 percent (650,000) would be unemployed and on welfare, and 3 percent would be totally dependent and institutionalized. Clearly, a substantial portion would or should be looking to adult education for improvement in their lives.

Lifelong training is becoming a reality. Soon there will be a federal commitment to the idea that education does not stop after high school and is not restricted to the "halls of higher education" (Kirkwood Community College, 1976). Handicapped adults increasingly perceive themselves as having an equal right to society's benefits. Therefore, there is no reason to think that only a few handicapped adults will want to participate in lifelong learning experiences.

If for no other reasons, educators' concern for handicapped adults would be justified by new and far-reaching federal laws. Justice Louis D. Brandeis observed that government, for better or for worse, is a teacher to society and that society will imitate what it learns from the government (National Center for Law and the Handicapped, 1977). Three laws in particular, which can only be touched on here, will be influencing adult educators for many decades. Signed by the president in late 1976, the Education for All Handicapped Children Act (Public Law 94–142) assures that all handicapped children will have available to them a free and appropriate education. Although this Act has the greatest impact on primary and secondary educators, it undoubtedly will also set the pace and will create substantial expectations for follow-through education at the postsecondary level. Section 504 of the Rehabilitation Act of 1973 requires that all educational institutions (1) become readily usable, (2) make reasonable modifications to ensure full educational opportunity, and (3) provide auxiliary aides to ensure full participation of handicapped persons. In the words of the secretary of health, education, and welfare, (Califano, 1977): "In many cases this regulation calls for dramatic changes in the action and attitudes of institutions and individuals who are recipients of HEW funds. . . . It opens a new era of civil rights in America." Certain features of the Educational Amendments of

1976 (Public Law 94–982) will change already existing vocational programs for handicapped adults. Not only are the amendments in conformity with Section 504 of the Rehabilitation Act of 1973, regarding access and mainstreaming for the handicapped, but most importantly they will expand the financial base for vocational education programs for handicapped persons under Part B, set-aside funds.

A philosophy regarding handicapped adults and their education could be worked out by taking the concept of normalization and by drawing from the handicapped-rights movement and from teaching materials which deal with the self-image of handicapped persons. "Normalization" was introduced in the United States by Nirje and then promoted by Wolfensburger (1974, p. 27), who cited Nirje's normalization principle as making "available to the mentally retarded patterns and conditions of everyday life which are as close as possible to the norms and patterns of the mainstream of society." Wolfensburger (p. 28) then redefined the principle of normalization as the "utilization of means which are as culturally normative as possible, in order to establish and/or maintain personal behaviors and characteristics which are as culturally normative as possible." Here, Wolfensburger implied that inasmuch as nonhandicapped persons need normal environments in which to grow, so too do handicapped persons. Wolfensburger (p. 28) went one step further by indicating that norms of human behavior are culturally determined, and therefore to establish and maintain culturally normative behavior in a person, one had best use means that are culturally normative. Thus, normalization calls for the integration of disabled persons into the community rather than their isolation in training, education, and employment. It likewise implies that what most needs changing is not the disabled but the society which rejects them as part of the community.

Two implications of this philosophy for education are apparent. First, more disabled persons who are traditionally clients of rehabilitation networks will become students of regular educational systems. Second, to make educational environments more growth facilitating for handicapped adults, schools will need to adapt programs, policies, procedures, and physical facilities.

Assertiveness on many fronts is becoming a trademark of the

"new handicapped generation." They no longer see education, rehabilitation, and the use of other public resources as a gratuity. They see themselves more and more with equal rights to the same environments that enrich the lives of nonhandicapped persons. Some handicapped adults are so aware of the benefits of equal access to educational programs that they insist on being involved in the planning, implementation, design, and operation of the educational programs that serve them. Evidence of this new assertiveness is abundant; indeed, it is sufficiently universal to be considered not as a fad but as a permanent cultural change (Shworles, 1977).

Information from investigations of "negative imaging" of the handicapped is another factor that can be used to develop an underlying philosophy for the education of adult handicapped persons. This term refers to the general public's negative perceptions of the handicapped as generally dependent, nonassertive, ill, and always requiring special services—perceptions resulting from the way public media and some programs serving the handicapped have unwittingly portrayed them. One consequence of this view is that members of the public may feel they have little in common with handicapped persons and thus will not support efforts to mainstream them.

Guidelines for developing adult education programs for the handicapped are implied in the normalization philosophy. Important among such guidelines are the following: (1) The public's perception of handicapped persons will be more positive if handicapped adults are seen participating in regular educational programs; (2) the sense of having things in common with others arises not from the handicap but from experiences shared with nonhandicapped students, such as the need for financial aid and counseling and common educational, vocational, social, or recreational goals; (3) handicapped adults should be allowed to enter educational programs without going through a special registration procedure and without being detoured by a single-entry program; (4) handicapped adults must be basically responsible for their own educational decisions and must have the right to make some mistakes on their own; (5) programs for the adult handicapped must constantly reexamine their priorities and activities to assure that they serve the consumers and the public and not merely themselves; and (6) as major allies of the normalization of handicapped adults, educational programs should divest themselves of all processes belonging conventionally to the rehabilitation network.

Some Current Approaches

Some representative programs that characterize the direction of education for adult handicapped persons are described in the following paragraphs. They are examined with respect to the populations they serve, the courses they offer, and the delivery systems they use. We have not evaluated these programs in terms of their efficiency, cost-effectiveness, administrative features, or relative importance; nor have we attempted here to address all these concerns. Nevertheless, we want to make very clear that these issues would have to be resolved before commitments could be made to program development.

The City Colleges of Chicago (CCC) Program. The CCC is a large, diverse, and geographically comprehensive system (seven two-year colleges; a major urban skills training institute; 400 "outposts"; and a college which coordinates education programs that have a citywide impact). At any one time in its regular school year, the CCC system serves more than 100,000 students, of whom approximately half are enrolled in continuing education, adult basic education (ABE), the high-school-equivalency (GED) program, or general education programs. Because of such varying student needs and equally diverse resources, CCC finds itself offering handicapped students a variety of educational programs. CCC's programs for handicapped adults are presented first not because they are considered superior to those outlined later but because they contain the elements to be found in most adult education programs for the handicapped—delivery systems ranging from unique to conventional; courses that are ordinary (job skills development) and atypical (survival skills development); and students having a wide range of handicaps, from the retarded to the severely physically handicapped who are homebound, to the psychiatrically handicapped and institutionalized, and finally to students with "commonplace" handicapping conditions.

No major effort is under way at CCC to develop special

courses for the handicapped adult. The system's primary purpose, through its Center for Program Development and the Handicapped, is (1) to promote its numerous educational resources among Chicago's 200,000 handicapped adults, (2) to integrate handicapped students as thoroughly as possible in all education and training programs, and (3) to provide support services—but only when appropriate—through its regular resource units, offices, and departments. For certain categories of physically handicapped persons who come to CCC already segregated and isolated, the school provides education where they are and begins a process whereby they will eventually have experiences more common to other students.

Through the Adult Learning Skills Program of its Chicago Urban Skills Institute, CCC conducts classes for more than 1,000 mentally retarded students at twenty-two sites. The classes are arranged in three categories: ABE (for improvement in reading, writing, and arithmetic), "Survival" ABE (for acquiring such skills as money counting, using city transportation, and telling time), and GED (preparation for the state-administered GED examination which is the means of earning a high-school-equivalency certificate). Students may register at no cost at any time during the year. In addition, CCC offers adult and continuing education programs through its Wright College to 152 mentally retarded students. Fourteen courses, taught at two sites, cover a broad spectrum of adult interests, such as arts and crafts, cooking, typing, educational counseling, and physical education for health. The system currently is implementing a coordinated plan through which more than 2,000 mentally retarded adults are being served through these courses. The general program mission is to help "normalize" these students' relations with their environment, to integrate them more completely into their communities.

More than 80 deaf students are enrolled in CCC adult education courses, and when a more cohesive operation gets under way, CCC intends to have over 200 deaf adults in courses in ABE; "Survival" ABE; GED; vocational, recreational, and career education; consumer education; and personal development. Among the other handicapped adults being served are more than 70 emotionally disabled and institutionalized adults who are enrolled in courses dealing with GED, ABE, and typing and business machine operation. Eighty-seven physically handicapped persons are studying the "Kentucky Series GED" that appears on Chicago's Public Broadcasting TV station. Twenty-seven of the more severely physically handicapped GED-TV students who are "tied" to their homes or institutions receive follow-up visits by an instructor. The less severely handicapped attend support classes located in Chicago public libraries along with scores of other nonhandicapped students. And the Illinois Division of Vocational Rehabilitation has enrolled 43 of its handicapped clients in a continuing education program for the improvement of general office skills.

Thirteen severely physically handicapped homebound adults are being trained as computer programmers and data-entry operators by means of video and audio cassettes, TV, and self-instruction modules. Attention is given not only to subject matter but to a socialization process whereby students ultimately will participate in the most normal instructional setting feasible. This training is part of a program for designing and testing an economical model that can be replicated using community colleges statewide for training and employing severely physically disabled adults in information-handling and -processing occupations.

Career education for the handicapped adult is an issue of paramount importance at CCC. Complex and persistent social forces steer the handicapped into narrow job pathways. Many handicapped persons are socialized by their families, peers, and even educators to view their range of choices as much more limited than that available to their more normal peers. But there is a growing national awareness concerning the need for career education that would lead more handicapped persons to vocational and social adulthood. In view of this perceived need, CCC enrolled fourteen students from the junior and senior classes of Chicago's high school for the handicapped in a career education course with emphasis on educational, vocational, and life planning. Also, CCC began offering citywide, beginning in the winter of 1977, a career education course for handicapped adults which, upon completion, will prepare the students to (1) seek jobs they previously did not consider open to them, (2) enroll in career education courses at CCC, (3) explore career opportunities with career education personnel, and (4) participate in other career education experiences such as work-study or cooperative education.

In the fall of each year, approximately 1,500 adults describe themselves as handicapped on a self-report form and register at CCC for an array of college courses that are different from the previously described programs. This fact supports my earlier observation that many and differently handicapped adults are both needing and seeking diverse educational experiences.

Seattle (Washington) Community College Program. The Program for the Blind at Seattle Community College provides in-service training for faculty and staff members, a student resource center, and a career search process. This last activity, which should be particularly interesting to adult educators, serves young blind adults who have little if any vocational skill or experience and who therefore need to sample jobs and get help from the professional staff in making a career choice. Blind students electing to enroll in this program are provided in their first academic quarter numerous on-site job samplings in careers of their choice, supplemented with industrial site explorations and samplings. Immediately following the first course, students are integrated in the full, regular college program. However, blind students are not required to enter the college programs by this route. Incidentally, this educational program for blind adults has effectively developed open attitudes among the sighted toward the capabilities of the blind.

Cuyahoga (Ohio) Community College Program. Certain courses at Cuyahoga Community College are broadcast live by special telephone equipment and color TV to hospitalized and homebound handicapped adults. This system also permits delayed color replay. Because of the telephone element, students are able to participate in class discussions and to benefit more directly from on-campus proceedings. During a recent nine-month period, 58 severely physically handicapped adults did regular college-level course work in English, medical technology, business, accounting, anthropology, and biology. Some of these students took basic skill courses in reading and arithmetic along with "mini-courses" designed to develop their skills in studying, outlining, listening, and note-taking. Three hospitals thus far have participated in the hookup, which includes audio-video microwave and cable tele-

vision. The program is supported by a grant from the Ohio Rehabilitation Services Commission and is considered to have far-
reaching consequences for the education of severely physically
handicapped adults.

*The Rehabilitation Services Administration and IBM Pro-
gram.* In conjunction with the Rehabilitation Services Administration of the Department of Health, Education, and Welfare, which
provided a "Project with Industries" grant, the International Business Machines Corporation formulated seven model programs at
different types of facilities around the country for the training and
employment of 75 to 100 severely physically impaired adults per
year in the highly competitive computer programming market.
Five of these programs are already in operation at the Center
for Independent Living, Berkeley, California; the Lake Shore Rehabilitation Facility, Birmingham, Alabama; the Woodrow Wilson
Rehabilitation Center, Fisherville, Virginia; the Easter-Seal Good-
will Industries Center, New Haven, Connecticut; and the University of Pennsylvania's Wharton School in Philadelphia. One of
the distinguishing features of this adult-education employment program at these five locations is the establishment of local groups of
computer science managers from industry who advise, provide
quality control for the education program, and assist in the job-
seeking process.

*Approaches Meeting the Aesthetic Needs of Handicapped
Adults.* Art education is a recognized means of general learning
and can be a vehicle for handicapped and nonhandicapped students
in improving their perceptual skills, increasing the quality and
quantity of their response to stimuli, improving their ability to
evaluate, and developing their capacity to generalize from responses
and perceptions. However, in spite of evidence showing a need for
such training, and despite research confirming the positive impact
of art on the handicapped and supportive statements by national
leaders, the literature reveals few programs that give art any importance. These few include the Theater of the Deaf and the
Gallaudet College drama and dance groups, which appear on TV,
tour the nation, and annually educate and entertain large numbers
of both handicapped and nonhandicapped persons. This lack of
attention to the role of art in the education of handicapped adults

as compared to the emphasis given to art in programs for handicapped children is paralleled by little information in the literature on vocational education for handicapped adults. Handicapped children still get the bulk of the attention from educators. But new laws, a growing national awareness, the emergence of advocacy organizations, and a reorientation of educators are forcing more attention to be paid to the education of handicapped adults.

We have made no attempt here to review these five programs from the standpoint of their cost-effectiveness, the degree to which they are managed by their "consumers," or how well they succeeded in getting their students into the mainstream. We presented them because they demonstrate that groups of handicapped adults eager for educational opportunities exist nationwide. They also show that educational materials relevant to the interests and aptitudes of these groups and to the manpower needs of the nation have been developed and are available.

Resources for Program Development

The program developer who is concerned with the education of adult handicapped persons must gather information and knowledge from diverse sources. It is not that handicapped adults are a complicated group with insurmountable problems; they are not a group at all. They are millions of American citizens of all socioeconomic levels in all corners of the nation. The degree to which their disabilities are handicapping depends in part on the varying conditions of their social and physical environments. They range from well prepared to ill prepared for lifelong education. They have divergent interests in and desires for education. Some want to be "mainstreamed" and "normalized," some are indifferent, and some seek security in isolation. Therefore a program developer needs to know something about population statistics, laws, techniques for removing physical and attitudinal barriers, pace setting, conference announcements and recommendations, model education programs, and sources of new information.

The Office for Handicapped Individuals. Situated within the Department of Health, Education, and Welfare, the Office for Handicapped Individuals has been trying to fill at least partially the data gap on handicapped persons. In cooperation with the National Center for Health Statistics, this office developed a supplemental questionnaire on impairments and disabilities that was administered in conjunction with the 1977 interview survey of the center. The supplement was intended to give greater insight, in more detail, into America's handicapped population than had been previously available. The questionnaire explored many characteristics and effects of handicapping conditions with families that had impaired members. For example, the impaired persons' ability to deal with education—including all types of training—was assessed.

The President's Committee on Mental Retardation. Many existing educational resources can be used effectively by adult educators concerned with retarded adults. The problem is for these educators to be aware of the past, present, and future of mental retardation in this nation. A massive report, prepared by the President's Committee on Mental Retardation, was submitted in the fall of 1976. The core volume, *Mental Retardation: Century of Decision,* examined issues and set national guidelines for the next quarter-century. The information, contained in several volumes, is presented in a convenient format and provides a quick way to become up to date and to devise a rationale for adult education programs (Cobb, 1976).

Resources Available to the Homebound and Institutionalized Handicapped Adult. Much concern has emerged for developing the potential of those who are homebound and institutionalized. A five-year national study described the characteristics and resources of this population, listed some successful educational programs, and ended on an optimistic note; all the information can be picked up and expanded by educators (Brubeck, 1976). Another resource is the National Rehabilitation Association's National Congress on the Rehabilitation of Homeland and Institutionalized Persons. Because the members of Congress are scattered throughout the country, it can be used locally by adult educators (Ozaki, 1977).

Center for Continuing Education, Gallaudet College. This Center in Washington, D.C., sponsors and otherwise supports approximately sixteen continuing education programs around the country for deaf adults in community colleges, vocational-technical institutes, rehabilitation facilities, and other settings. The Center also provides films, texts, pamphlets, and other materials to educators of deaf adults. Guidelines for developing continuing education programs are offered to interested educators. A free monthly newsletter is available on request.

Resources for Educating Minority Group Handicapped Adults. Handicapped adults who are part of ethnic minorities have unique problems. The following resources are recommended for educators who will deal with large groups of such persons. Issue papers prepared for the White House Conference on Handicapped Individuals addressed the unique problems of handicapped Asian Americans, black Americans, native Americans, and individuals with Spanish surnames. In addition, the Conference action plan, submitted to the president in October 1977, reflected the views of grass-roots consumers on the issue of handicapped minorities. The National Association of Non-White Rehabilitation Workers and the Mid-American Association of Educational Opportunity Program Personnel are groups that can lead interested educators to other resources and information (Wakabayashi and others, 1977).

The White House Conference on Handicapped Individuals. The passage of Public Law 93-516, "The Rehabilitation Act Amendments of 1974," authorized the White House Conference on Handicapped Individuals. The purpose of the Conference was to "develop recommendations and stimulate national assessment of problems and solutions to such problems facing individuals with handicaps." An estimated 2,500 persons attended the conference on May 23–27, 1977, in Washington, D.C. Some 3,500 issues were identified, many of which concern the education and training of the handicapped. On October 1, 1977, the Conference staff presented an implementation plan to the president and to Congress which suggested solutions to those issues. The report was intended for public distribution. The contents of the implementation plan could have a major impact on the design and implementation of programs for the handicapped for the next half-century. Educators also can avail themselves of "awareness papers" presented prior to the national conference, such as a thirty-five-page document dealing with educational opportunities for handicapped individuals (Council for Exceptional Children, 1977). But this paper's emphasis on children may make it disappointing to adult educators.

Before the national conference, every state was obligated by law to hold a statewide conference and from those proceedings to publish a "state book" discussing the issues and suggesting solutions. These state books—accurately reflecting the viewpoints of consumers, parents of handicapped persons, and providers of services—are rich sources of information concerning the educational needs of the handicapped. Copies can be obtained from each state's Governor's Committee on the Handicapped.

National Center for Law and the Handicapped. A joint project of the Department of Health, Education, and Welfare's Bureau of Education for the Handicapped and the Developmental Disabilities Office, the National Center for Law and the Handicapped publishes *Amicus,* a bimonthly which probably is the most readable, concise, current, and accurate accounting of legal issues pertaining to handicapped citizens. There is no subscription fee. Adult educators and program developers will find, for example, the history of "the handicapped civil rights act," as presented in the July 1976 issue, useful in interpreting their responsibilities regarding the mainstreaming of handicapped adult students. This law and the two mentioned earlier will have a profound impact on institutions and programs serving the educational needs of the handicapped adults. By reading *Amicus* regularly, adult educators can keep abreast of countless developments as educators, courts, and handicapped citizens interpret and implement the numerous aspects of these laws in many different settings.

National Arts and the Handicapped Information Service. The Education Facilities Laboratories, New York City, operates the National Arts and the Handicapped Information Service, which distributes information on such topics as funding services, architectural accessibility, conferences and events calendars, and sources of technical assistance, all related to the arts education of handicapped persons. This organization, like other significant resource groups, currently focuses its activities on handicapped children, but requests for service could lead to the compilation of information on adults. Such an agency as this also might be persuaded to direct its energies to the adult when public concern for the adult is expressed by readers of its public information publications. An overview article available from another source (Sjolund, 1976) provides perspectives and justifications for expanded arts education for handicapped persons.

The National Center on Education Media and Materials for the Handicapped. Based at Ohio State University, Columbus, the National Center on Educational Media and Materials for the Handicapped has developed a nationwide program to help increase and improve the education of the handicapped. Although its main concern is with children, its services can lead to resources pertaining to adults. The Center (1) distributes media kits; (2) provides information to teachers, parents, and other educators through a rapid computer-based retrieval system; (3) provides technical assistance to developers of instructional materials through publications and conferences; (4) serves as a clearinghouse of information by answering telephone calls and letters; and (5) operates a coordinated nationwide service system concerned with media-and-materials support services. Its newsletter, *Apropos,* is an excellent source from which to begin assessing these vast resources on behalf of the handicapped adult learner.

The Educational Resources Information Center. Operated by the National Institute of Education (Department of Health, Education, and Welfare), the ERIC clearinghouses around the country are repositories of information from libraries and information centers. In particular, the Clearinghouse on Adult and Career Education, the Clearinghouse on Handicapped and Gifted Children, and the Clearinghouse for Junior Colleges can provide information to educators of handicapped adults. For example, an Adult and Career Education pamphlet lists five current publications that deal with career education for deaf, physically handicapped, and mentally retarded students. This same clearinghouse also publishes a pamphlet listing nine publications on vocational education for the handicapped. The Clearinghouse on Adult and Career Education offers program descriptions, suggests course content, provides help in using the media, and presents research results, monographs, and bibliographies.

National Center for a Barrier-Free Environment. From its headquarters in Washington, D.C., the National Center for a Barrier-Free Environment provides materials, conducts meetings, and publishes a magazine dealing with access to all parts of the environment by handicapped persons. It will keep the educator apprised of laws, reports, programs, and meetings as they affect educational facilities and educational programs. The Center, for example, gives educators current information on the kinds of support services educational institutions are providing handicapped students as their responsibility under Section 504 of the Rehabilitation Act of 1973.

The Future

The future of adult education for handicapped persons has been implied throughout this chapter, as we presented justifications, outlined a philosophy, and recommended criteria for developing programs. In describing the status of such programs and the issues surrounding them, we have presented a picture of change. A summary of this chapter is therefore in fact a statement of the future: First, more precise local and national statistics will be available on the size of the handicapped population and on the characteristics of the handicapped. A continuing activity will be the interpretation of the meaning and applicability of federal laws to educational settings for the handicapped. The concept that environmental factors define the presence and extent of handicaps will become commonly accepted, and the negative imaging of handicapped persons attributable to educational service programs will be curbed. The use of all rehabilitation-style practices will decline in the education and training of the handicapped. And the unique problems of handicapped adults in minority groups will surface and be treated.

The nonassertive handicapped will be replaced by those seeking more active social roles, including the role of student, and the number of handicapped adults seeking education will rise significantly. The normalizing and mainstreaming of handicapped adults in regular educational courses will become general practice, and special classes for handicapped students will become fewer as more techniques are advanced for the integration of educable retarded adults in regular programs. The phenomenon of lifelong education will affect handicapped adults; optional introductory career education courses for handicapped adults which lead students to expanded educational, social, vocational, and recreational options will become commonplace. Finally, engineering techniques will be developed that will provide severely physically handicapped students with various means of meeting their classroom responsibilities, such as note taking, examinations, and the production of papers and reports.

In short, the world of handicapped adults will be altered significantly. Adult education could have a dramatic impact on the expansion of their opportunities.

Chapter Ten

Adult Education in Corrections

Sylvia G. McCollum

A chronology of prison education programs in the United States is difficult to establish. Some writers suggest that in the late eighteenth century, and continuing into the nineteenth, volunteers from various religious groups conducted religious services and classes in the hope that such instruction would prepare prisoners for a Christian, and therefore noncriminal, life. Literacy programs grew out of these efforts, since reading the Bible was an integral part of religious instruction. The prison chaplain and volunteer theological students served as instructors. Thus it appears that adult education in American prisons is as old as the prisons themselves.

Background

From their beginnings educational programs moved forward at different rates and in different ways, depending on the individual state and in many cases the individual institution. The federal prison system sometimes reflected developments initiated at the state level; at other times the federal system led the way. Commitment to education came relatively early from leaders of prison systems—in principle if not in fact. At the first meeting of the National Prison Association in 1870 (now the American Correctional Association), a "Declaration of Principles" provided strong, if somewhat melodramatic, support for education: "Education is a vital force in the reformation of fallen men and women. Its tendency is to quicken the intellect, inspire self-respect, excite to higher aims, and afford a helpful substitute for low and vicious amusements. Education is, therefore, a matter of primary importance in prisons, and should be carried to the utmost extent consistent with the other purposes of such institutions" (Committee for Revision of 1954 Manual, 1970, p. 541).

Correctional education leaders in the United States found support for their goals in pronouncements from international bodies. The first United Nations Congress on the Prevention of Crime and Treatment of Offenders meeting in Geneva, Switzerland, in 1955 adopted *Minimum Standards for the Treatment of Offenders,* which included a section on "Education and Recreation" urging that prisoners be provided educational, religious, recreational, and cultural activities. Stronger language was used for illiterates and young prisoners; in such cases, education was urged to be "compulsory." A far-sighted section, 77(c), strongly suggested that, "so far as practicable, the education of prisoners . . . be integrated with the educational system of the country so that after their release they may continue their education without difficulty." But despite these high-sounding words, genuine educational programs were not implemented for years and, indeed, are still lacking in many correctional institutions.

The current range and quality of educational and vocational programs offered and the rate of prisoner participation vary widely, from youth institutions devoted exclusively to education, to adult, long-term institutions in which education and training opportunities are marginal. Some institutions provide adult basic education (ABE) as well as classes at all elementary and secondary levels, including the opportunity to complete high-school-equivalency (GED) courses. In addition, most prisons offer some vocational training through on-the-job training, apprenticeship, or classroom and shop instruction. Postsecondary programs also are generally available. These programs, originally available only through correspondence courses and not as part of a degree program, have grown dramatically in recent years. Today, degree-earning programs are offered in many prisons and are provided in a wide variety of ways. "Study release" for college courses is a new concept that is just beginning to receive significant support in a few prison systems.

Current Status

Prisoners throughout the country share certain characteristics: they are generally poor, unskilled, and undereducated. Federal prisoners range in age from eighteen to seventy (the median is thirty), and a large majority are from an urban environment. Of all federal inmates, 36.1 percent are black, approximately 18.5 percent are of Hispanic origins, 1.6 percent are American Indians, and 43.8 percent are either Caucasian or of some other racial or ethnic group. The average sentence served is 19.3 months.

Educationally, prisoners range from those lacking basic literacy and occupational skills to those having graduate professional degrees. The average federal prisoner reads at the seventh-grade level and functions academically at the ninth-grade level. Most lack a legally marketable skill. Roughly 40 percent are high school graduates and 18 percent have been involved in higher education. Their intelligence levels (I.Q. scores) range from "low average" and below (only 13 percent) to "high average" and "superior" (37 percent). Fifty percent of federal prisoners fall into the "average" I.Q. range (91–110). Such variances in intelligence and in occupational and academic achievement are similar to those in the outside world and present a challenge to correctional adult educators as they strive to respond to the individual offender's educational needs.

Educational and Training Goals. In consideration of prisoners' needs, educational and occupational goals have been established by the federal prison system and similarly by many state and local systems. The guidelines generally provide that all inmates with the need and capacity should, during confinement, (1) complete an adult basic education program, (2) complete an adult secondary program, (3) acquire or improve an employable skill through one or more occupational education programs, (4) complete one or more postsecondary education activities, (5) complete one or more organized social education activities, or (6) complete one or more recommended recreational activities. These six goals are designed to meet specific needs for functional literacy, a high-school-equivalency certificate, marketable work skills, continuing education, personal growth experiences, and positive use of leisure time.

Programs. As the foregoing goals suggest, the educational and training programs that exist in varying degrees in most federal prisons, in some state prisons, and in few county jails are adult basic education, adult secondary education, postsecondary education, occupational education, social education, and recreation. Each of these programs is discussed in the following paragraphs. Adult basic education (ABE) is a remedial activity designed to provide sixth-grade-level reading, writing, and computation skills. Approximately one third of incarcerated offenders could benefit from an ABE program. In 1975 a little more than 10 percent of the average annual federal prison population successfully completed an ABE program (achieved the sixth-grade reading level) before release. Adult secondary education (ASE) consists of activities designed to help inmates complete a high school program. As in ABE, various modes of instruction are employed, with primary emphasis on self-paced study of programmed materials in learning centers and with peer tutors, if possible. During 1975 around 19 percent of federal prisoners completed an ASE program by earning GED certificates or regular high school diplomas.

Postsecondary education is provided for prisoners who have completed high school and wish to continue their education. To the extent that the desire, interest, and ability to succeed in college-level programs exist among offenders (and, as McCollum reported in 1975, there is evidence that these qualities are found in a rapidly growing proportion of the total population), institutions of higher education are used to provide such services. During 1975, approximately 3,000 federal prisoners completed over 9,000 college courses;

they earned 158 A.A. degrees, 19 bachelor's degrees, and 2 master's degrees. Payment for college courses depends on the individual prison's budget, the course a student desires to take, and the student's personal financial situation. In cases where the full tuition cost must be borne by the student, outside financial assistance is frequently sought. Prisoners are generally eligible to apply for financial assistance on the same basis as other students. Veterans' education benefits, Basic Education Opportunity Grants, Vocational Rehabilitation Program support, federally insured student loans, and private scholarships and grants are some of the sources available to an inmate involved in postsecondary study. The increase in the number of college courses completed in recent years reflects the growing proportion of inmates who have completed basic and secondary education before and during incarceration(s) and the availability of tuition grants and loans.

Occupational education is obviously designed to improve the employability of offenders—especially those without a significant employment history or salable skills—through a variety of activities including a general exploration of the world of work, formal vocational training, apprenticeship programs, on-the-job training in prison shops and prison industries, and work-release in the community. During 1975, 8,084 federal offenders completed various occupational programs in such areas as medical technology, auto mechanics, welding, pipefitting, dental technology, retailing, trucking, computer programming, business administration, and child care. The Bureau of Apprenticeship and Training of the Department of Labor registers approved prison-based apprenticeship programs that meet standards for various trades. Occupational education, however, is not offered solely for the purpose of getting inmates a job; it will allow them to practice specific skills which contribute to the development of a sense of self-worth and job satisfaction.

Social education is another major activity in which federal prisoners may participate and which contributes to a positive institutional environment. Education is focused here on helping inmates better understand themselves, develop realistic self-concepts, gain appropriate skills in interpersonal relationships, and cope with problems to be faced as consumers, family members, wage earners, and responsible citizens. During 1975, 5,303 prisoners completed programs with these aims, which are gaining a higher priority.

Recreation also is an important component. Physical fitness, opportunities to release tensions healthfully, and learning satisfying and productive ways to use leisure time contribute to an improved institutional climate. They also help the offender develop acceptable alternatives, interests, and skills that can be useful in the community at large after release.

Testing. Standardized tests are administered at many correctional institutions during the admissions and orientation periods. These exams are used as a part of efforts to provide effective educational counseling and placement. Specifically, the tests used in the federal system measure educational achievement, general ability, personality, attitudes, and occupational attitudes. The test results also are used to assist prisoners in developing personal programs for growth during imprisonment. The Scholastic Achievement Test (SAT), the Revised Beta Test, the General Aptitude Test (GATB), and the Minnesota Multiphasic Personality Inventory (MMPI) constitute the basic series of tests administered, with some exceptions, to all federal prisoners. Many state prisons and some local jails also administer these standardized tests, or similar tests designed to measure the same general characteristics. The SAT score is particularly important because it helps identify the approximate level at which an inmate who is interested in participating in educational programs should begin. If prisoners are experiencing excessive difficulty in their studies, the Beta ability-test scores may be consulted to determine whether too much is being required of them. Many occupational skills demand specific aptitudes, such as manual dexterity or visual perception; the GATB scores provide information on these characteristics. The MMPI provides an initial screening for personality disturbances in entering inmates. It is used only to give an indication of such behavior and some direction for further professional study.

In-House Programs. Approximately 95 percent of all education activity occurs inside the institutions. In an effort to provide positive motivation, many prison educational facilities have a pleasant appearance and a modern design, conducive to learning; and in many cases they provide up-to-date audiovisual materials and equipment. Others continue to offer only makeshift facilities, obsolete materials, and part-time instructors. In some cases volunteers from nearby communities provide an additional educational resource. Studies by the Rehabilitation Research Foundation (1971), and more recently by McCollum (1973), suggested that nontraditional learning procedures are most successful with prisoners, who are generally nontraditional students. Inmates who serve as tutors are sometimes used to increase personal student-teacher contact, especially at the ABE and ASE levels. Many programs maximize the use of individualized learning materials.

Community Resources. In-house education and training opportunities are strengthened by services provided by community educational institutions. Universities and two-year and four-year colleges provide both accredited academic courses and occupational instruction. Their courses may take place either inside or outside the institution, depending on the security level of the population housed at the particular facility. Study-release programs allow selected inmates to attend local educational institutions during the day and return to their respective correctional facilities at night.

Residential learning centers have been tried on a few campuses. Some, like that at the University of Minnesota, are outgrowths of earlier "Newgate" college programs funded by the Office of Economic Opportunity and evaluated by Marshall and others in 1973. Other such centers had their roots in the Office of Education's Teacher Corps programs. Two recent residential programs for offenders were initiated by the Bureau of Prisons—one on the campus of the University of California at Santa Barbara and the other at the University of Washington in Seattle. Prisoner students participate full time in university programs and live under supervised conditions at a residential center during their first year of incarceration.

Many correctional institutions enjoy a cooperative relationship with their nearby communities, involving their communities in different activities and inviting their participation in many special-interest groups that function within the facility. Excellent volunteer work is provided by community leaders who offer their services through such groups as Alcoholics Anonymous, Toastmasters, religious organizations, Jaycees, and athletic and recreational organizations. Periodically, these same individuals arrange for inmates to join them in the community for special programs sponsored by their respective organizations. Community agencies and volunteers of all sorts are indispensable to the provision of greater opportunites for incarcerated people. More detailed examinations of comprehensive efforts can be found in Ryan's analysis of correctional educational models (1972).

Offender Participation and Achievements. Accountability for educational programs is determined, in part, by the number of programs of each type that prisoners complete. Over the six fiscal years between 1970 and 1975, course completions in the federal system increased 143 percent, 118 percent, and 167 percent in adult basic education, adult secondary education, and occupational education, respectively. Greater increases were registered for social education, 366 percent; and for postsecondary education, a surprising 750 percent. Overall, course completions between 1970 and 1975 increased 245 percent. During the same five years the federal prison population increased approximately 11 percent—from 21,200 in 1970 to 23,500 in 1975 (Bureau of Prisons, 1976). Although much remains to be done (Education Commission of the States, 1976a, 1976b), there is no doubt that participation in education and training programs has increased significantly throughout most of the correctional systems, particularly since Ryan's collection of papers (1970) that described then-existing ABE programs and problems.

Special Programs. Several research studies indicated that no single prison program can have a conclusive effect on the behavior of prisoners after their release (Abt Associates, 1971; Lipton, Martinson, and Wilks, 1975; Pownall, 1969). Glasser (1974, 1975) suggested, however, that one is asking the wrong question if one tries to attribute particular outcomes to a particular part of a program. Job opportunities, the level of unemployment, the community to which prisoners return (including the climate of discrimination against ex-offenders), and other post-release factors also influence the ex-offenders' success or failure. In this regard, the family is a significant reference group, and working with the entire family to enhance post-release success is sometimes both desirable and feasible. Post-release behavior depends on many variables, of which education and training are only two. Thus it has not been possible to isolate the impact of particular prison educational programs on post-release "success." It is reasonable to expect, however, that the ability to read, write, and calculate, along with having a legal marketable skill, will contribute to positive behavior in the community (McCollum, 1977).

Visiting Room Programs—Children's Television Workshop. Cooperative arrangements with the Children's Television Workshop, producers of "Sesame Street," are one example of program efforts to influence inmates' attitudes. The visiting rooms of selected correctional facilities become the focus for involving children and other family members in activities designed to develop more positive relationships between inmates and their families. Such programs also provide occupational training for some prisoners who serve as child development associates under the supervision of accredited professional staff. In some cases college credit is provided for these associates. These and similar programs are described in *Education for Tomorrow* (Bureau of Prisons, 1976).

Artists-in-Residence—National Endowment for the Arts. In 1975 a pilot artist-in-residence project, cosponsored by the National Endowment for the Arts and the Bureau of Prisons, was initiated in three federal prisons—in Lompoc, California; Leavenworth, Kansas; and Tallahassee, Florida. These continuing programs are conducted by visual artists who specialize in oil paintings, watercolors, sketching, photography, and environmental sculpture. The artists, besides conducting prison art classes, work to involve nearby communities as resources for library materials, speakers, and other appropriate activities. Exchange exhibitions also are arranged between the prisons and universities, businesses, and museums. This arrangement affords a broad range of learning experiences for the prison art student and is a constructive forum for exposure between inmates and the community. The museums, art schools, and universities currently involved in these three projects are the Kansas City Art Institute, the Nelson Art Gallery, Kansas University Art Department, Florida State University, Florida A & M, and the University of California at Santa Barbara. Local artists from the East

Los Angeles area and the state art councils of Florida, Kansas, and California also are involved.

Critical Issues and Trends

Adult education and related programs have a firm foundation in prisons throughout the nation. However, some troublesome issues cut across all adult education programs in corrections. For instance, most adult education and related programs depend on obtaining part of the money that is allocated for administering the whole U.S. Department of Corrections. Education and training budgets thus frequently fluctuate with the philosophic views of the top incumbent administrators. As these opinions change, support for education and training programs likewise changes. As a result, programs often lack continuity, and new ones are difficult to initiate. The correctional school district emerged from these uncertainties and may stabilize program support in the future, at least in those jurisdictions that have embraced this delivery system.

Another matter arousing significant concern, described by Carlson (1976), is that major shifts are taking place in basic correctional philosophies. The medical model, within which offenders are presumed to be sick and are provided with treatment programs, is being replaced by a more realistic self-help approach, in which prisoners are encouraged to participate voluntarily in programs to accomplish goals which they believe to be desirable. Education and related programs within such a framework are viewed as what they really are, not as treatment for sick people. This more pragmatic approach may result in wider community understanding and acceptance of correctional education programs. Study release, volunteer tutors, the certification of programs through community educational institutions, the application of local as distinguished from out-of-county or out-of-state fee schedules, the facilitation of student grants and loans—these and a multitude of other educational opportunities and services depend on the assistance of individuals and groups in the community. In many places the assistance is there; in others it is not.

Despite lack of community support the prison education program limps along at a minimal level of performance. The basic program is provided in some way, however unsatisfactorily, even without community support. However, the basic program still continues in most locations. Correctional administrators cannot duplicate in prisons the "outside" educational world, and they have limited access to community-based resources. The physical plant, courses, teachers, and such auxiliary services as counseling and libraries inside correctional institutions do not meet minimum standards in many jurisdictions. The most encouraging sign is the increasing awareness of educators and others of the need for education. A detailed discussion of some of the major critical issues and trends follows.

Costs. In fiscal year 1975, 460 staff members were directly involved in administering and providing education and training services to federal prisoners. During that year, expenditures for these services in the federal prison system totaled approximately $11.4 million as compared to approximately $4 million ten years previously. Money for education and training in the federal system comes from two primary sources: earnings (profit) from Federal Prison Industries, Inc., and congressional appropriations. The cost of providing education and training services to state prisoners, who number approximately 250,000, probably exceeds $100 million per year. The 150,000 prisoners in local and county jails receive little if any educational services, but increased concern over this lack of programs will probably result in some future services and corresponding additional costs. Because of these and related problems, correctional educators are seeking more cost-effective delivery systems for education. The Correctional Economics Center of the American Bar Association, only recently established, has begun much-needed research into the cost of all correctional services, including education. A 1976 report by Singer and Wright began the analysis of the costs of correctional education.

Increased Use of Technology. It is highly unlikely that the use of emerging technology will increase in correctional education because of cost and other considerations. Dial-access videotape systems, computer-assisted instruction, and individualized multimedia programmed materials, packaged and delivered in many different ways, already are in use on a limited basis.

Not very long ago correctional educators were painfully

aware that while multimedia equipment was available, the software was in no way equal to the potential of the equipment. A very significant improvement has occurred in this respect, with such pioneer groups as the Manpower Education Institute and, more recently, the Kentucky Educational Television System, which developed an excellent GED audiovisual instructional program. Similarly, materials for social, occupational, and postsecondary education are available in a wide variety of multimedia formats. Until recently, bilingual instructional materials were very rare. Spanish versions of the GED and some occupational materials have been developed commercially and by individual instructors, but the lack of money to purchase equipment and instructional materials continues to be a problem. However, where support can be generated, good videotape recording equipment can be purchased and neat, almost people-proof, cassettes have replaced the difficult reel-to-reel tapes that frequently broke, tangled up, or somehow did not work when most needed. The emerging technology has made it possible for some of the new metropolitan correctional centers, for example, to provide education programs from a central station to different floors in the institution. There are still some problems with delays because of equipment malfunction, but certainly correctional educators are in a stronger position than ever before, in terms of equipment and instructional materials.

In the face of these developments, it will be important to maintain a balance between the use of equipment and person-to-person contacts. Human encounter will always be an important educational resource in correctional education, since personal contact has been found to be a motivating and positive force, particularly in working with nontraditional students.

Movement Toward Specialized Prisons. Increasing evidence indicates that it is not cost-effective to provide all educational programs at all correctional facilities. Within the constraints inherent in the need for security and other limitations, it may be possible to offer specialized education and training programs at designated correctional facilities. For example, one correctional facility might specialize in training for human service occupations and another in teaching the construction trades. Inmate students could, within appropriate limits, voluntarily select the programs they are interested in, and these selections could play a part in their institutional assignment, either for the period of training or longer.

Use of Contract Services. The growing emphasis on voluntary participation in programs, the development of educational and training programs that reflect emerging job opportunities, and the reality of the job market require flexibility and diversity in correctional education. A commitment to investments in expensive equipment and other traditional approaches reduce the administrator's ability to shift programs, as required. Correctional institutions have experimented with contracting for vocational and other kinds of education with nearby two-year colleges and vocational-technical schools in an effort to maintain flexibility and to provide the most up-to-date kinds of occupational training and education. These contact services provide a useful tool and may be more widely used in the future.

Educational Vouchers. Leiberg (1973) and Parker (1975) describe the Mutual Agreement Programs, initially supported as experimental demonstrations by the Department of Labor and administered by the American Correctional Association. These reports suggest that personal education-and-training vouchers may develop into significant correctional procedures. Arrangements among individual prisoners, institutions, and parole authorities whereby prisoners earn credits toward an education voucher that can be used either while incarcerated or after release are among the possibilities for the future.

School Districts. Another important development is the emergence of the prison school district, which began in the late 1960s. These school districts, which now exist in Texas, Connecticut, Illinois, New Jersey, Arkansas, and Ohio, function as separate delivery systems for correctional institutions in their respective states. They have their own boards of education, superintendents, and staff. In two states, New Jersey and Illinois, the school districts provide education through the second year of college. Virginia recently enacted legislation to adopt the school district concept, and at least six additional states have it under consideration.

Geographic Isolation of Institutions. Another critical problem in correctional education arises from the relative isolation of some institutions. Despite a recent trend toward locating new facilities either in or near urban centers, as well as the progressive urbanization of once-isolated rural areas, some correctional institutions are still far away from needed resources. In such cases correspondence courses and various audiovisual systems are welcome alternatives. But experience has demonstrated that students' initial motivation is not sustained and dropout rates are high when programs use correspondence courses and other kinds of individualized study that provide no contact with teachers.

Post-Release Linkages. In addition to solving the problems of cost and geographic isolation, educators need to devise new ways to strengthen the post-release connections between the student and a particular educational program. Ideally, the process should involve establishing contact with the admissions staff before the prisoner student's release and setting up specific procedural steps to ensure the enrollment of the student before, or very shortly after, he returns to the community in which the receiving educational institution is located. Considerable research evidence suggests that the first three months after release from prison are critical to the individual's adjustment to community life. There also is a direct correlation between the age of the released prisoner and the likelihood that he will get into further difficulties. These factors, among others, suggest that helping students establish post-release links with structured educational situations is an essential component of prison educational efforts.

Transferability of Earned Credits. During the course of serving their sentences, many prisoners transfer from one institution to another, sometimes within a state and sometimes between states in the federal system. The issue of the transferability of credits is therefore very important. The College-Level Examination Program (CLEP), among other arrangements, provides a strong foundation on which to build the general transferability of earned college credits. However, the transferability of credits between educational institutions remains a stumbling block in efforts to maintain the involvement of the prison student, particularly if the student's transfer takes place before a specific course is completed. This predicament has stimulated efforts by correctional educators to develop statewide consortia of postsecondary institutions for the interchangeability of college credits.

Prime Time for Education. Educators in the outside world

have to join with correctional administrators to discover ways to increase the number of day programs instead of relegating prison educational programs to the evening hours only. Education, as a program alternative, can be regarded as a reasonable competitor with prison industries, institutional maintenance, group counseling, and other types of institutional programs.

Physical Facilities. A lack of space and privacy to facilitate studying and the accomplishment of educational assignments can be a critical variable that affects the prisoner student's continuation in a program. Since most prisoners are housed in institutions designed for containment or punishment or both, rather than for educational programs, it takes considerable imagination and good will to provide positive learning environments.

Libraries and Education Aids. Libraries with readily available and appropriate books also are important. Some correctional institutions have met the need for a library creatively by using local mobile library units and interlibrary loan arrangements or by providing time for library work during study-release hours to complement prison library collections. Such special groups as the Association of American Publishers and the American Booksellers Association have donated reference and other books to prisons, and yet as LeDonne (1974) reported in her exhaustive study of prison libraries in the United States, the library situation in prisons remains poor. The use of tape recorders and typewriters is still viewed with suspicion by the staff of many correctional institutions. Members of the education community can make an important contribution in working with prisons, first, to develop an understanding of the need to use these machines in the educational process and, second, to assist in supervising the appropriate use of such mechanical aids by the students.

Challenges Ahead

The incarceration period can be used effectively for the education and training of prisoners. However, programs must be provided in nontraditional and creative ways if they are to attract and hold students. Adults are unlikely to respond positively to the same kinds of programs in which they have experienced failure earlier in the outside world. Additionally, the education and training offered in prisons are often perceived by the prisoners as "busy work" and part of the prison's loss-of-freedom punishment and therefore lacking in legitimacy. Overcoming these views is difficult, since correctional educators are part of the establishment, and they must meet the security and discipline requirements of a correctional facility. Despite this, or perhaps because of it, correctional educators in general have successfully established broad access to education and training opportunities for inmates. Access is by no means universal at this point, but it continues to broaden, and an increasing number of correctional administrators have accepted the practice of providing educational opportunities in prisons. More important, scarce dollars and staff members are increasingly committed to correctional education and training programs. Prison educational programs, nevertheless, suffer the same inherent limitations as education in general and often are criticized in much the same way as community-based educational programs.

Many critics of correctional education criticize it for not making up for all the deficiencies in the family, in the neighborhood, and in society in general. Correctional education can make a contribution to an individual's socialization, but it cannot be expected to compensate for the lifelong and complex economic, social, physical, and emotional disadvantages and disabilities of so many of the students who spend some time in prison. Despite all these considerations, correctional educators can and do make a significant contribution to helping inmates identify realistic goals and develop the necessary coping skills to achieve them.

The definition of adult education in correctional institutions is undergoing change. Adult education no longer is defined only in terms of basic literacy, GED preparation, or occupational education. Programs now include postsecondary education, social education, the visual and performing arts, physical education, and leisure-time and recreational programs. The change partially mirrors the expanding definition of adult education in the larger community. Correctional educators generally welcome this new and expanded definition.

Chapter Eleven

Perspectives on Education for Work

John K. Coster

Individual and societal goals are achieved through work, defined as the process of translating mental and physical effort into purposeful activity. Work, as an invention of man, increases in complexity as the complexity of society increases. Every society, regardless of its complexity, has defined its division of labor, established work roles and assigned values to them (Bates, 1968), and evolved a system for inducting youth into adult work roles and for maintaining adults as productive contributors to society (Benedict, 1934; Mead, 1955). In the following discussion of the role of public education in preparing persons for work, I consider first some historical perspectives and then look at contemporary trends and issues.

Historical Perspectives

In the United States, the responsibility for preparing people for work initially belonged to the family and the private sector of

183

the economy. The private sector provided training through guilds and apprenticeships (Barlow, 1967), as well as through institutions of higher education, such as Harvard, William and Mary, and Yale, which were established primarily to prepare men for professional work roles, such as the ministry. But with the establishment and expansion of public education, and with the transfer of ownership for the production of goods and services from the individually owned and family-owned unit to the corporate unit, the responsibility for preparing people for work was transferred largely to the public sector—to publicly financed educational institutions and government agencies.

The educational program most widely associated with preparation for work is known simply as vocational education. Educational aims and programs, including manual training and vocational programs, were expanding at the turn of the century, and a number of states soon enacted vocational education legislation. Indiana, for example, passed a state vocational education act in 1913 (Coster, 1964). But the major impetus for the shift from state to federal vocational education legislation came from the enactment of the Vocational Education Act of 1917, commonly referred to as the Smith-Hughes Vocational Education Act (Barlow, 1976). The controlling purpose of this Act was to fit persons for useful employment in agriculture, home economics, and industrial occupations. Programs offered pursuant to this and other federal vocational education acts expanded markedly from 1917 to 1976 (when the Educational Amendments of 1976 were passed) in terms of both the number of persons served and the range of occupations for which training was offered.

The Vocational Education Act of 1917 is historically significant for three major reasons. First, it marked the beginning of the use of federal money to support public education. Up to that point the commonly held belief was that since the Constitution omitted reference to public education, the responsibility for public education was delegated to the several states (Educational Policies Commission, 1939). The Act did not establish a separate educational system; indeed, it provided clearly that such education, supported in part with funds appropriated pursuant to the provisions of the Act, would be under public supervision and control. But it did set forth certain minimum conditions under which money could be spent, one of which was that it could be used only to support education for work programs of less than college grade (except for programs designed to educate teachers).

Second, the Smith-Hughes Act was the first federal act to provide funds for the support of adult education in the public schools. It was not, however, the first adult education act; the Cooperative Agriculture Extension Work Act, commonly known as the Smith-Lever Act of 1914, which established the Cooperative Extension Service of the Department of Agriculture in cooperation with each of the states, earned that distinction. The Smith-Hughes Act provided that federal money could be used to pay part of the costs of training and retraining adult workers, as long as provision for such activities was made part of the State Plan for Vocational Education in each state, an instrument of agreement between federal and state agencies for the expenditure of funds. In essence, Congress was serving notice in this Act that the federal government intended to move into areas of education in which the Congress found the need to be great, the response of the several states and school corporations limited, and the opportunities unequal. Moreover, through the instrument of the Act, Congress declared that work and the preparation for work are lifelong processes and that the opportunities to prepare for work should be made available to youth and adults alike. Congress essentially declared adult education to be an extension of the elementary and secondary public school systems, which in some states included the thirteenth and fourteenth years of schooling, and established its intention to provide financial support for selected school programs.

The third major reason for the historical significance of the Vocational Education Act of 1917 was that it provided a basis for defining vocational education. Up to that time, one might have expected the word *vocational* to refer to any program designated to educate for a calling, since the word comes from the Latin *vocare,* to call. To be more precise, *vocational education* might have denoted that part of education designed to prepare persons for differentiated work roles. In this sense, Harvard College, founded in 1636 to prepare persons for the ministry, medicine, and other professional callings, might have been considered the first "vocational education institution." Similarly, the land-grant system of colleges and universities, established by the Act of July 2, 1862 (commonly called the first Morrill Act) to prepare persons for callings in agriculture, engineering, and other practical and applied fields, might also have been thought of as vocational institutions. But by designating Public Law 64-347 as the Vocational Education Act of 1917, Congress unwittingly assigned the term *vocational education* to that part of education for work which is provided below the college level and which is financed in part with federal vocational funds. Thus not only did vocational education become limited by common usage to programs supported with federal vocational funds, but it apparently became associated with preparing persons for occupations that require relatively simple manual skills (Woerdehoff, Nelson, and Coster, 1960).

Because of this limited popular conception of vocational education, other terms were developed. The National Defense Education Act of 1958 introduced *technical education* to describe education for work chiefly at postsecondary levels for occupations that require greater competence in mathematics and science than is normally associated with vocational education. At about the same time, many educators were seeking a broad, comprehensive term to describe employment education at less than the college level and perhaps to lessen the dichotomy between education for professional work roles and education for other than professional work roles. *Occupational education* and *career education* evolved from this search, although career education partially emerged from career development theories (Holland, 1973; Osipow, 1968; Super and Overstreet, 1960). Career education came to denote a movement to bring together guidance, vocational education, and relevant general education to give increasing meaning to educational experiences. Marland (1971) reintroduced and popularized the idea of career education, which had been cited previously by the Educational Policies Commission (1956), and insisted that it not be bound by any one definition. One study of career education in six states reported that it was an outgrowth of dissatisfaction with existing educational programs (Porter and Coster, 1974). Career education appears to be more appropriately described as a concept than as a program—a concept directed toward philosophical changes in the educational system that would place a premium on the value of the immediate experience of individuals and their environment (for an earlier elaboration of the idea, see Dewey, 1916, pp. 228–242).

Concerned with the polyfurcation of education for work, Hamlin (1967) attempted to introduce *occupational education* into the educational vocabulary as a term that would encompass vocational, technical, professional, and prevocational education. As briefly described by Hamlin, this term has met with increasing acceptance, generally as a synonym for vocational education. The Congress first used it in the preamble to Part D, "Exemplary Programs and Projects," of the Vocational Education Amendments of 1968. Here, *occupational education* designates the downward extension of vocational education to include prevocational exploratory activities. Later, Congress created the Bureau of Occupational and Adult Education in the Office of Education of the Department of Health, Education, and Welfare, but one could argue strongly that the designation "Bureau of Vocational and Adult Education" would have been just as apt. There is no common pattern of usage of *occupational education,* and Marland (1974) reported that by 1974 more than 200 definitions of career education had been offered. For an interesting commentary on the use of the three terms—vocational, occupational, and career education—see Kahn and Wiener (1967, pp. 208–211).

The casual observer might reasonably expect that the career education movement would focus sharply on adult education. A career suggests a lifetime of occupational effort, and as Marland reasoned (1971), all persons have careers. With some notable exceptions, however, career education has been restricted to kindergarten through grade twelve or grade fourteen. Career education for adults has been limited, although not completely ignored.   .

The Expansion of Education

The establishment and growth of programs in the public schools to prepare persons for work is part of the larger pattern of expanding education in the United States. As we have seen, the history of preparation for work reflects the shifting of responsibility from the private sector, including the family, to the public sector. With the enactment of the first Morrill Act in 1862, the public's responsibility for preparing persons for professional work roles was firmly established. (This is not to say that private institutions of higher education have been relieved of this task, only that the public institutions have been able to provide preparation at a considerably lower cost to the individual student and for a wider range of professional roles than the private sector can.) Thus the stated principal objective of the Act (Section 3) was "to teach such branches of learning and the mechanical arts . . . in order to promote the liberal and practical education of the industrial classes in the several pursuits and professions in life." State-supported colleges and universities established with this objective as their guide, the land-grant colleges and universities, established pursuant to the first Morrill Act, represented an expansion, if not a change, in the mission of higher education.

They had a distinctly American character, in contrast to the state-supported institutions created before 1862, which were cast in the European mold. These new institutions were designed to educate the sons and daughters of farmers and mechanics who would be following in their parents' occupations, not pursuing the traditional learned callings. Although the first Morrill Act was specifically addressed to the need for professional workers in a rapidly developing technological society, its impact was broader and heralded a national concern for education for employment. One expression of that concern was the extraordinary response of the public higher education system. One century after President Abraham Lincoln signed the Act, President John F. Kennedy could proclam that "the land-grant system of higher education is the nation's largest single source of trained and educated manpower and now contributes more than one half of all regular and reserve officers entering the armed forces through the military program conducted at civilian institutions" (Brunner, 1962, p. 83). Although state legislatures occasionally have balked at state university and college budgets, the panoramic view is that the public accepts and supports educational programs designed to prepare persons for professional work roles.

The enactment of the Vocational Education Act of 1917 paralleled chronologically the movement to expand secondary education in the public schools. Every important set of educational aims published during this century listed education for vocational proficiency as a major goal (Commission on the Reorganization of Secondary Education, 1918; Committee on Curriculum Planning and Development of the National Association of Secondary School Principals, 1947; Educational Policies Commission, 1938). The strongest statement on salable skills was by the Committee on Curriculum Planning and Development of the National Association of Secondary School Principals (1947, p. 7) in the "Imperative Needs of Youth of Secondary School Age": "All youth need to develop salable skills and those understandings and attitudes that make the worker an intelligent and productive participant in economic life. To this end, most youth need supervised work experience as well as education in the skills and knowledge of their occupations." The Educational Policies Commission (1956) further stated its case for education for work in a publication entitled *Manpower and Education,* in which the Commission affirmed the need for public schools to take part in training manpower. And in a succinct statement on career education, the Commission asserted that education for careers should be a constant concern of all who plan educational programs.

Citizens' participation in vocational education in secondary and postsecondary institutions, which the National Advisory Council on Vocational Education (1968) found wanting, now can be reported as encouraging. From 1966 to 1975, the percentage of the total population between the ages of fifteen and nineteen who were enrolled in public secondary vocational programs—that is, programs partly supported by money appropriated pursuant to federal vocational education acts—increased from 25 percent to 45 percent. In that same period, the percentage of the population enrolled in postsecondary institutions offering vocational education (community colleges, technical institutes, area vocational schools, and junior colleges) increased from 3 percent to 20 percent. And the percentage of the population between the ages of twenty-five and sixty-four, classified as adults, who participated in federally assisted vocational programs increased from 3 percent to 4 percent

(National Advisory Council on Vocational Education, 1968; Lee and Fitzgerald, 1976). The total enrollment in vocational educational programs increased from 2 percent of the total population in 1961 to 3 percent in 1966 to 7 percent in 1975. Thus enrollments in postsecondary and adult vocational programs have increased rapidly during the past decade. The data show that in 1976 approximately four million persons were enrolled in adult vocational programs in public postsecondary schools and that another 374,000 were enrolled under the Comprehensive Employment and Training Act (CETA) of 1973 (Lee and Fitzgerald, 1976).

Education and Employment

Although the major statements of the aims of education that provided the goal-directed basis for the expansion of education were developed by educational groups and associations, educational philosophers have not dealt extensively with broadening the vocational aim—the notable exception is Dewey (1916). Instead, the impetus for expanding employment education in the public domain has come largely from vocational educators (chiefly through the federal Office of Education and the American Vocational Association) and from the Congress. Examples of the vocational educators' efforts are two reports of national significance that pointed out the need to extend vocational education: *Education for a Changing World* (Panel of Consultants on Vocational Education, 1963) and *Vocational Education: The Bridge Between Man and His Work* (National Advisory Council on Vocational Education, 1968). In the work of the Congress, which has really provided the major thrust, two themes have pervaded the findings and actions of the subcommittees—employment and the equalization of opportunity.

From the Vocational Education Act of 1917 to the Educational Amendments of 1976, the main purpose of vocational education has been "to fit [people] for useful employment." Indeed, the principal criterion for evaluating the effectiveness of programs supported under federal vocational education acts is the extent to which persons trained under those acts are employed, in addition

to how adequately they are trained. The emphasis on employment
was explicit in the Employment Act of 1946, Section 2:

> The Congress hereby declares that it is the con-
> tinuing policy and responsibility of the federal govern-
> ment to use all practicable means consistent with its
> needs and obligations and other essential considerations
> of national policy, with the assistance and cooperation
> of industry, agriculture, labor, and state and local gov-
> ernments, to coordinate and utilize all its plans, func-
> tions, and resources for the purpose of creating and
> maintaining, in a manner calculated to foster and pro-
> mote free, competitive enterprise and the general wel-
> fare, conditions under which there will be afforded
> useful employment opportunities, including self-employ-
> ment, for those able, willing, and seeking to work, and
> to promote maximum employment, production, and
> purchasing power.

Although education is not specifically mentioned in the Employment Act of 1946, and although it is hazardous to interpret
congressional intent, it does not seem unreasonable to state that the
Employment Act greatly influenced four major acts, passed in the
early 1960s and directed toward reducing unemployment, especially among the disadvantaged, by means of education. The four
acts are the Area Redevelopment Act of 1961, administered by the
Department of Commerce; the Manpower Development and Training Act of 1962, administered by the Department of Labor; the
Vocational Education Act of 1963, administered by the Department of Health, Education, and Welfare; and the Economic Opportunity Act of 1964, administered by a specially constituted
agency, the Office of Economic Opportunity. With the exception
of the Vocational Education Act of 1963, these federal acts were
intended to equalize economic opportunity and provide training
for unemployed and underemployed adults.

This legislation was augmented by two acts creating regional
commissions in geographical areas of economic need. The first and
largest of these commissions is the Appalachian Regional Commis-

sion, created pursuant to the Appalachian Regional Development Act of 1965. The Public Works and Economic Development Act of 1965 provided for the secretary of commerce to designate additional areas as targets for increased economic activity. The commissions established pursuant to this Act are the New England Regional Commission, the Coastal Plains Regional Commission, the Upper Great Lakes Regional Commission, the Ozarks Regional Commission, the Old West Regional Commission, the Four Corners Regional Commission, and the Pacific Northwest Regional Commission. The principal intent of these commissions is to equalize economic opportunity—that is, to stimulate the economy of the specific region especially by creating jobs. Vocational education programs have been established or expanded with money from these acts to train persons, chiefly adults, for employment in newly created jobs.

The Manpower Training and Development Act was superseded by the Comprehensive Employment and Training Act of 1973. The Vocational Education Act of 1963 was amended successively by the Vocational Education Amendments of 1968 and the Educational Amendments of 1972, 1974, and 1976.

Issues

Three major issues permeate the process of evolving a system or systems for preparing people for work in the United States: (1) Who is responsible for this preparation? (2) What is vocational education? and (3) How can we provide equal educational and economic opportunity?

Responsibility for Preparation. As I pointed out at the beginning of the chapter, the family and the private sector were historically responsible for preparing people for work. But for a variety of reasons, this responsibility shifted to the public sector—to publicly financed educational institutions and to government agencies. A reversal or a new shift may be occurring, however, because the Congress is not satisfied with the way the public education systems have been preparing the handicapped, the disadvantaged, those who dwell in the inner cities, members of minority groups, and women. Such persons have not had equal access to high-quality educational programs (more on this when I discuss the third issue), and the Congress, concerned about this inequality at least since the enactment of the Vocational Education Act of 1963, has criticized the efforts of the public schools and colleges. Indications that the Congress may shift the responsibility for employment preparation to agencies other than public education can be found in the Comprehensive Employment and Training Act of 1973 and in the expansion of the regional economic commissions cited earlier.

The Nature of Vocational Education. As we have seen, the term *vocational education* is usually restricted to educational programs supported in part by federal money. Even within this relatively narrow spectrum, however, educators do not agree about the nature and main characteristics of such programs. Although few would take exception to the aims of education that pertain to vocational proficiency, disagreement arises over what constitutes vocational proficiency. The definition depends partly on the status of the occupation for which the person is receiving vocational training. Generally speaking, the higher the prestige rating of the occupation, the more likely it is that becoming proficient will involve institutionally guided work experience specifically related to the occupation. Surgeons are not allowed to practice their skill unless there is evidence that they have done surgery under the direction and supervision of a competent instructor in a certified teaching hospital. But for occupations requiring less skill and enjoying less prestige, the prevailing belief is that adequate preparation consists of demonstrated competence in the fundamental processes of learning—the so-called three Rs and the development of basic learning skills (Mason, 1972, p. 42). Indeed, few persons can obtain employment who fail to demonstrate such competence, since these fundamental processes are the common element in preparation for work in contemporary American society. What it comes down to is whether educational institutions can ensure that the individual who seeks and needs a salable skill will be equipped with one, as well as ensure, by means of demanding practice under institutional supervision, that the person is proficient.

In a study sponsored by the Office of Education, Woerdehoff, Nelson, and Coster (1960) found evidence that disagreement on the nature of vocational education existed both among vocational educators and between vocational educators and others.

Respondents were asked to check which of four program descriptions most nearly matched their view of the nature of vocational education: (1) an educational program emphasizing the acquisition of a single mechanical skill and the related knowledge necessary to fit persons for useful employment; (2) a program stressing occupational adjustment, with special reference to selecting an occupation, developing abilities and understanding, and progressing in a vocation; (3) a program dealing with the relationship between vocational proficiency and societal welfare, with special reference to occupational information, preparation, and adjustment; or (4) a general educational program emphasizing knowledge and understanding sufficiently broad to serve as a basis for subsequent specialized training beyond high school. Choices 1, 2, and 3 were designed to represent the levels of complexity of vocational education. Choice 4 indicated a general education position. Yet about one tenth of the fifty-five agricultural educators, half of the eighty-six homemaking educators, and one quarter of the fifty-seven industrial educators who answered the questionnaire gave responses that reflected the general education position and did not differ significantly from those of the nonvocational educator groups, particularly the sociologists and educational philosophers. Thus, after almost fifty years of acceptance of preparation for work as an aim of education, in 1960 the question of what is vocational education apparently remained unsettled, even among vocational educators themselves.

Equalization of Opportunity. Equal educational opportunity is a perennial issue in the educational milieu. Two questions are involved: What constitutes equality? And how can it be achieved? This matter may be debated at length in educational circles, but the Congress has served notice that inequality in educational and economic opportunity is to be alleviated. The efficacy of social programs and strategies may be debated, but their intent is not subject to debate.

Perhaps equality should give way to quality. The questions should be focused on the quality of access, the quality of programs, and the quality of opportunities. A person who wishes to be an automobile mechanic should have access to high-quality training, and the standards of that training should be as high—within the context of the occupational requirements—as the standards for surgeons. The Commission of Occupational Education Institutions of the Southern Association of Colleges and Schools has demonstrated this point in its work on evaluation and accreditation (Childers, 1972).

Many areas of unequal access still exist, especially with regard to area, sex, racial and ethnic group, and age. Access to counseling and training must be equally available to all who want and need them if the goal of equal educational and economic opportunities, as mandated by the Congress, is ever to be achieved.

Toward a System of Education for Work

The traditional division of work (manual and mental, blue-collar and white-collar), the classification of occupations (professional, technical, semiskilled, and unskilled), and the stratification of the population (upper, middle, and lower class) all have militated against the development of a comprehensive system of work, and a comprehensive program of education for work. Added to this is the division of responsibility among and within the family, the private sector, and the public sector.

If one accepts the premise that a social system must include a manager in order for the system to function, then the education for work system in the several states does not qualify as a system unless the state legislature functions as the manager. At the federal level, responsibility for education for work is divided among several departments, and the management of the federal system is probably lodged in the Office of Management and Budget. The multiplicity of boards and agencies, coupled with the diversity of occupations and the divisions within each occupation, is not conducive to the development of a unified system under integrated management.

Nonetheless, there are indications that the nation is moving toward a quasi-system that may serve the interests of society and its members satisfactorily. This contention is based on certain observations: (1) The public school system has changed its policy of exclusion to one of inclusion. The range of occupations for which preparation is being offered and the range of people who are to be served are being expanded to include the universe in each case. (2) The strategy of diversification, in which the government distributes training funds to a variety of agencies, public and private, as in the Comprehensive Employment and Training Act, is likely to be continued to ensure that at least one agency will provide educational services to those who need them. (3) Those responsible for education-for-work programs are to be held accountable for achieving the goals set for the programs. And (4) power politics will ensure that no legitimate claim for educational services will be ignored.

Public education has evolved rapidly as educators, employers, politicians, and the public at large have sought to use this avenue increasingly as a means of preparing people for productive work of all kinds. Appreciable progress has been made, and the forces at work offer grounds for optimism about the continuing modification of arrangements at the federal, state, and local level to make the system effective and responsive to the changing needs of American society.

Chapter Twelve

Armed Forces and Veterans' Education

Thomas W. Carr
Richard M. Ripley

Formal adult education in the military began during the Revolutionary War. According to David Berry (1977, p. 23), "in 1778 General George Washington recognized the need for providing basic academic instruction to illiterate convalescent soldiers following the bitter winter at Valley Forge." In 1838 military-post schools were established to provide basic academic instruction for the illiterate. And following the Civil War, adult education for the military was expanded to include subjects intended to foster patriotism and cultural improvement. Adult education efforts by the armed forces were increased greatly during World War I, when Congress passed the Mobilization Act of 1916. This law provided for programs for military personnel that would enhance military efficiency and enable them to return to civilian life better prepared for civilian work and occupations (Berry, 1977). Hence, educational opportunities were expanded to include broad academic and vocational subjects, reflecting the nation's concern for the individual's contribution to society after completing military service. Unfortunately, interest in the education of military personnel declined after the World War I demobilization and remained low until the start of World War II, when the nation again acknowledged the importance of the role of education in the military, not only in the conduct of the war but also in demobilization.

The concept of general educational development in the military services began with the establishment of the U.S. Armed Forces Institute (USAFI) in 1942 at Madison, Wisconsin (Deighton, 1971). Begun as a wartime institution to provide correspondence courses in high school and college subjects, the USAFI was abolished by the Congress after three decades of service, when civilian institutions created programs to meet many of these needs. During its thirty-year existence, the USAFI, in cooperation with civilian colleges and universities and certain governmental agencies, developed correspondence courses as well as a high-school-equivalency program. Such innovations have exerted considerable influence on the adult education movement in this nation. Following World War II, the current patterns of education in the military were established. In 1946 the University of Maryland began providing baccalaureate-degree programs at military bases in the United States and overseas. These programs, along with those of many other schools, colleges, and universities, continue today as important contributions to military service. In recent years the number of colleges and universities providing off-campus graduate-degree programs at military bases has increased considerably. Also during the period after World War II, the armed forces organized an educational staff structure that extends from the Department of Defense in Washington, D.C., to military posts throughout the United States, overseas bases, and ships at sea. More than 2,000 combination education and testing centers operate where the armed forces serve (Rose, 1974). The staffs of these centers counsel military personnel in making educational choices and provide educational programs to meet their career needs.

Thus, several elements of adult education in the armed

forces took shape during and after World War II and, with only minor modifications, continue to this day. In addition to (1) cooperation with and reliance on civilian education institutions as major contributors to the education of military personnel, and (2) an educational staff to plan and operate educational programs and counseling services, which were outlined earlier, other important elements were (3) a tuition-assistance structure for encouraging and supporting adult education in the military, and (4) a belief in the ideas of standard testing, equivalency, and academic recognition for military training.

As one traces the proliferation of adult education in the armed forces, it becomes clear that the current patterns of education, which emphasize the general educational development of the individual, were informed both by the military services and by the civilian society. Over the years, education in the military has expanded from a focus on specific needs, such as literacy, to concern for development of military personnel as unique individuals, both as members of the armed forces in defense of the nation and as members of the larger society. Most certainly the scientific and technological advances made since World War II have affected the need for increasingly higher levels of education in civilian life and in the military services (Huntington, 1957; Janowitz, 1974).

Defense Department Programs

Education for an All-Volunteer Force. Education remains an important activity in today's technologically complex, volunteer military force. The policy of the military services (the army, navy, air force, and marines) is to present educational opportunities as an integral part of the life of military personnel through a system of coordinated career education and self-developmental education. This policy is based on the belief that education is a lifelong process that is essential if military personnel are to achieve their maximum potential in professional and leadership roles as members of the armed forces and as citizens. Educational programs are provided by schools within the armed forces and through civilian educational institutions.

The armed forces today are probably the world's largest

producers and consumers of adult education (Brodsky, 1970). The old saying "The military does only two things: fight and train" was never more true. Because this is a period of peace, the emphasis is on training. Each year the military graduates more than one million individuals from about 5,000 separate training courses produced within the Department of Defense. At the same time, about half a million service men and women are involved in education programs conducted by more than 1,000 civilian institutions. In short, education is big business in the Department of Defense—and the reasons are not hard to find.

When the draft is not in effect, the armed forces must rely on volunteers. In effect, the military services must compete with business, industry, the trades, and higher education for their share of the nation's eighteen-year-olds. And if the all-volunteer force is to remain successful (assuming women continue to join at the same or a slightly faster rate—about 40,000 per year), the military must attract almost one out of three male eighteen-year-olds who are qualified and available for military service. Therefore, because the chance to further their education provides a powerful incentive for many volunteers, the armed forces put heavy stress on education in recruiting, upgrading, and retaining outstanding young men and women. Today, the military provides a working environment in which the individual can choose from a wide range of career possibilities in which to receive training, enroll in educational programs for credit, learn occupational skills on the job, and move up the career ladder. For example, a person can learn about accounting, carpentry, church business administration, computer repair, dental assisting, food service, heavy equipment operation, law enforcement, mapping, masonry, personnel, plumbing, radio and TV maintenance, safety, surveying, and welding. Clearly, it is not pure altruism that motivates the Department of Defense to provide such opportunities. The Department wants to attract its share of the best eighteen-year-olds. And surveys show that youth who favor education (over such other inducements as money) get higher scores on intelligence tests, have higher occupational ambitions and self-esteem, and have a greater propensity to enlist and reenlist.

The Voluntary Education Program. Today, the Department of Defense assists and encourages military personnel to develop educationally and professionally through participation in the Voluntary Education Program (Rose, 1974). This is simply the military version of an adult education program in which the individual participates during off-duty time and for which he pays a portion, usually 25 percent, of the tuition. Support for educational activities exists throughout the armed forces: facilities and equipment frequently are made available for off-duty education, and many commanding officers urge participation to maintain both morale and combat readiness. These programs not only assist individuals to perform their military jobs more effectively but also help participants prepare for more responsible in-service jobs and promotion opportunities. Many military personnel are able to continue the academic or vocational training they began before entering the armed forces or to prepare for continuing their education after discharge. In any event, those who participate certainly enhance their value to the military and to the civilian manpower pool following active military service.

The unique circumstances of the military student must be kept in mind (Department of Defense, 1973). Physically mobile, the student body extends worldwide to training camps in the United States, remote locations in the Arctic, ships at sea, and American embassies in every capital of the free world. Military requirements determine when the student will be free to study, sleep, and eat.

Of the two million persons serving in the armed forces in 1977, approximately one fourth were taking part in the voluntary education program as part-time students. In fiscal year 1977, the Department of Defense's operating costs for educational activities totaled more than $80 million, while the Veterans Administration spent an additional $100 million for the education of active-duty military personnel. More than 1,000 civilian educational institutions support the programs of the four military services. And more than 2,700 full-time employees of the Department of Defense work at education centers and military headquarters to help carry them out. The opportunities range from remedial education through high school completion to graduate work. Because military life has become more technically oriented, more occupational opportunities are available than ever before.

The Army. Each military service operates and manages its own educational program under broad policy guidance from the office of the secretary of defense. The army's program, called General Educational Development (Department of the Army, 1975), involves more than 600 civilian colleges and universities. Almost 1,500 full-time employees, mostly civilian educators, staff the army's education centers worldwide. One interesting concept developed by the army is called Project Ahead, under which 1,300 colleges and universities have agreed to allow individuals to enroll before enlistment. Each institution advises and counsels these individuals while they are on active duty, with the expectation that they will return as full-time students following military service. Project Ahead was developed to help attract and upgrade army enlistees serving in the all-volunteer force. While on active duty, a Project Ahead soldier is counseled regularly on educational opportunities under the army's General Education Development program and is given assistance in getting enrolled.

The Air Force. The air force's voluntary education effort is called the Education Services Program. Its support staff numbers more than 900, and 300 civilian colleges and universities provide courses. Approximately 140,000 airmen and officers are part-time students in the program, which has a budget exceeding $21 million annually (Department of the Air Force, 1976). The air force is also proud of its Community College of the Air Force (CCAF), with central headquarters in San Antonio, Texas. The CCAF consists of an administrative headquarters and the seven major air force technical training schools, all of them accredited by regional accrediting associations. The CCAF has established a number of programs, each consisting of at least sixty-four semester hours and each leading to the associate degree in applied science. Airmen can complete these hours by attending one or more of the technical schools and working with regionally accredited civilian institutions that are associated with the Education Services Program. Generally, about 40 to 50 percent of the semester hours come from the air force's technical training, while the remainder, which consists of general education, must come from civilian institutions.

Currently, there are ninety-four associate degree programs built around air force training in 8 subjects, ranging from police science to computers. Normally, the average part-time student will take five or six years to complete the program. After finishing the degree, the airman is considered a master of his or her trade. Some colleges and universities will accept the degree-holder at the junior level, and many employers will hire the recipient without further training. Should the airman leave the service before completing the program, he will be issued a transcript showing progress.

The Navy. The navy works with more than 400 civilian institutions under a management system called the Navy Campus for Achievement (Department of the Navy, 1975). About 160,000 persons are participating in the navy voluntary education program, which includes the Program Afloat for College Education (Ducey, 1972). Under this program, college professors sail with the fleet and teach courses at sea. Several colleges working with the Navy Campus for Achievement have waived residency requirements for degree completion.

The Marine Corps. The smallest of the military services, the marine corps has almost 40,000 part-time students in its Voluntary Education Program (U.S. Marine Corps, 1977). Today, 272 civilian schools work with the Marine Corps.

Additional Educational Support. Several projects in the Department of Defense support all the armed forces' voluntary education programs. A unique one is the *Guide to the Evaluation of Educational Experiences in the Armed Services,* usually referred to as the *Guide* (J. W. Miller, 1975). Published under contract by the American Council on Education (ACE), the *Guide* includes a listing of formal courses including vocational-technical programs offered by each of the armed forces, with recommendations for credit at civilian institutions. Although the awarding of credit remains an institutional prerogative, the ACE's recommendations are designed to facilitate institutional decision making. The Office on Educational Credit of the ACE also provides an advisory service concerning credit recommendations. To ensure currency, a large number of the 5,000 formal military courses listed in the *Guide* are reevaluated each year.

Other opportunities available to all military personnel are provided by the Defense Activity for Non-Traditional Education Support (DANTES), located in Pensacola, Florida. Having replaced the U.S. Armed Forces Institute in 1974, DANTES offers academic credit by such examinations as the College-Level Examination Program anywhere in the world and the high school General Educational Development program at overseas locations only. Other activities of DANTES include the publication of a catalog of high-quality independent-study courses available from regionally accredited civilian institutions and the maintenance of a permanent file of transcripts of courses taken under the USAFI.

Finally, a network of more than 360 civilian institutions supports military education through adaptable residency requirements and a generous transfer policy. About half of these institutions are junior or community colleges. This system, called the Servicemen's Opportunity College, began in 1973 and is co-sponsored by twelve civilian associations such as the American Association of Community and Junior Colleges and the American Association of State Colleges and Universities (Department of Defense, 1973). The Servicemen's Opportunity College, funded jointly by the Department of Defense and the Carnegie Corporation, was established to help mobile military students in their efforts to reach an educational objective.

As noted earlier, the part-time military student can get monetary help to pursue additional education. Each military service, through a tuition-assistance program, may pay up to 75 percent of the tuition cost. Officers who receive such help must make an additional service commitment; enlisted personnel do not.

Veterans Administration Programs

Military students who came on duty before January 1, 1977, may use G.I. Bill benefits while in service if they prefer, although using them makes fewer benefits available on discharge. If G.I. Bill benefits are used while on active duty, the Veterans Administration pays all the costs of tuition, books, and fees. Recent changes in the

G.I. Bill increased benefits to veterans and military personnel and modified the entitlement for personnel coming on active duty after January 1, 1977. The Vietnam Era Veterans' Education Assistance Act provides for a contributory program for those joining the armed forces after January 1, 1977. The Act says that the individual must contribute between $50 and $75 per month for twelve consecutive months before becoming eligible for benefits. The Veterans Administration will then match the contribution two for one. The maximum contribution allowed is $2,700, matched by $5,500 from the Veterans Administration, for a total of $8,100. The total is divided into thirty-six equal payments to assist the veteran or service member in the pursuit of further education. Service personnel on active duty may use these benefits after they complete one term of enlistment.

A Model Educational System

The Department of Defense's voluntary education programs may represent, in microcosm, the future shape of adult education in the United States. The programs include professional educational counseling at the very beginning of an enlistment and at regular intervals during a career or period of service. Service training and off-duty education are integrated in a pattern of career development extending through retirement. Unique service programs, such as the Community College of the Air Force, the Navy Campus for Achievement, and Project Ahead, serve as important bridges to the civilian community. Accreditation of many service training schools is provided by regional accrediting associations, thus fostering civilian recognition of the high-quality training offered by the military services.

The Community College of the Air Force provides a transcript that lists, on a single computer-printed document, all the student's educational achievements in the armed forces and advanced-standing college credit from civilian institutions. The transfer of credits among institutions for the mobile military student is eased through the efforts of the Servicemen's Opportunity College. A possibility for the future is a Community College of the Armed Forces, patterned after the air force model, through which military personnel could receive college credit, or even an associate degree, for successful completion of military courses—augmented by prescribed college courses at civilian institutions.

Whatever the future holds, it is evident that voluntary adult education within the armed forces will remain dependent on civilian educational institutions for the bulk of its offerings. With the end of the draft and the advent of the all-volunteer force, education and training have become prime incentives for enlistment. A stronger partnership must be developed between the armed forces and civilian institutions of higher education, business, and industry as we seek creative ways to develop the future leaders of the nation—its young adults.

Chapter Thirteen

Labor Education

John R. MacKenzie

Labor education has been in existence as a separate educational subsystem since the International Ladies Garment Workers Union, AFL-CIO, established the first union education department approximately seventy-five years ago. The first postsecondary institution to concern itself with workers' educational needs and that of their unions, on a continuing basis, was the University of Wisconsin, whose program dates back to 1926. Labor education had a steady but uneven growth until ten years ago, when it entered a period of rapid expansion and change. This chapter focuses on those changes that have had the greatest impact on labor education in this decade and that promise to exert significant influence in the future.

The term *labor education,* or workers' education as it has been called in the past, usually is confined to the noncredit education of adult union members and to the educational needs of their organizations. Labor education is thus considered to be a part of adult education with a special clientele—trade union officers and members. Rogin (1970, p. 301) defined labor education as "the attempt to meet workers' educational needs as they arise from participation in unions. It is education directed toward action. Its programs are intended to enable workers to function more effectively as unionists, to help them understand society and fulfill their obligations as citizens and to promote individual development. It does not include training in job skills for the labor market, commonly known as vocational education."

This definition would have to be broadened today to include *labor studies,* the accepted term for a new academic field. Ten years ago there were no known degrees in labor studies, but by 1976 forty-two programs offering degrees (associate, bachelor's, or master's) were noted by Gray (1976) in her survey and analysis of the field. No doctorate had been awarded as of this writing, although at least two universities are considering a Ph.D program in labor studies, and Rutgers University offers the Ed.D. degree with a major in labor education. The development of labor studies as an academic field is surprising when one realizes that American universities and colleges are in a period of declining budgets and enrollments. Still, both the noncredit labor education programs and the labor studies degree programs give every indication of growth and continuity in the future.

Where do the students come from? The U.S. Department of Labor, in its 1975 *Directory of National and International Unions,* pointed out that 175 national and international (locals in Canada and the United States) unions and 37 professional and state associations are classified as trade unions in the United States. Together, these union organizations have between 60,000 and 70,000 local unions with a membership of approximately 21.5 million working men and women. The AFL-CIO represents 113 of these national and international unions, with approximately 14.2 million members. The national unions, affiliated or not, vary in size from the Horseshoer International, with its 291 members, to the giant International Brotherhood of Teamsters, with more than 2.5 million members. So the students for labor education come primarily from the ranks of these 21.5 million adult trade union members and, to a lesser degree, from unorganized labor. (Labor unions conduct educational programs to inform those who are not union members concerning the benefits of unionism. The unions do not operate general interest classes for all interested adults.)

Who provides the education programs? In the past, many organizations concerned themselves with workers' educational needs. These included the unions themselves, the Catholic Church, YMCAs, colleges and universities, school districts, and political groups. Today, regular labor education courses are conducted almost exclusively by two primary organizations—the trade unions and the land-grant universities and colleges. Together, they account for about 95 percent of all labor education activites. The remaining 5 percent of the programs are given on an ad hoc basis by unions and such other organizations as Catholic labor schools, the Brookings Institution, the Federal Mediation and Conciliation Service, and the Labor Management Services Administration of the Department of Labor, to mention a few organizations that show occasional interest in the educational needs of trade union officers and members. The courses provided by these organizations tend to be limited to the subject of labor relations.

What is the purpose of labor education programs? According to Gray (1966), these programs historically have had five aims: (1) to bring about an ideological understanding of society, especially of the class struggle, (2) to build union loyalty and participation, (3) to prepare union leaders, (4) to raise the educational level of the disadvantaged through remedial courses, and (5) to provide cultural enrichment for life's enjoyment. Of these, the third has predominated and continues to do so, partly because of a shortage of money to accomplish all five and partly because the rapid turnover among union officers made leadership training the primary need. Therefore, labor education classes conducted by universities, colleges, and unions are concerned primarily with professional development and the preparation of leaders. Such programs range from shop-steward training to the fast-developing programs for international union officers and staff members.

University and College Programs

The growth of university labor education programs in the past few years attests to the continuing interest in the field. In 1971, twenty-four universities had labor education programs; today, there are forty-two university and college programs in twenty-six states and the Commonwealth of Puerto Rico, and four new university programs have moved beyond the talking stage (University and College Labor Education Association, 1977). Along with the growth in the total number of institutional programs, older programs have expanded as the need to provide education to workers has made headway within the industrial states. Several programs have doubled or tripled their professional staffs since 1971.

Reasons for Expansion. This growth may be attributed to several factors. The first includes the increasing complexity of the labor relations process, the educational needs brought on by the bureaucratization of unions, and the increasing number and complexity of federal laws and regulations that govern both labor relations and the institution of labor itself. The Labor-Management Reporting and Disclosure Act, the Occupational Health and Safety Act, the Equal Employment Opportunity Act, the Employee Retirement Income Security Act, the Metric Conversion Act, and recent additions to the federal election laws all call for a much higher level of technical knowledge and understanding than was required fifteen years ago.

The second cause of growth is the recent organization of federal, state, county, and municipal employees into unions and associations. In attempting to meet the need to train these several million public employees to operate their new local unions, and in introducing them to the legal complexities of collective bargaining, university and union programs were overwhelmed. They have not yet fully recovered. The burden on the university programs, in particular, has been great because of the higher educational level of these public employees, compared to their union counterparts in the private sector. Included in this new wave were large numbers of teachers, college professors, social workers, engineers, nurses, economists, and members of other college-trained occupations, who turned to universities and colleges to fulfill their new educational requirements, as they had been conditioned to do in the past. The state universities and colleges either opened new programs or expanded existing ones to satisfy this new educational demand, a demand that helped to change noncredit labor education into credit education (labor studies) and moved it from the field into the classroom.

The third element in the growth of labor education was the rising educational level of the entire work force. In 1975 the average attainment of employed worker was 12.6 years of formal education; 71 percent of the civilian labor force had finished high school (Bureau of Labor Statistics, 1976). This brought the workers to the university gates, and although many institutions moved to meet workers' needs, most did not. Moreover, a sizeable number of workers were unwilling to accept the standard university offerings. Many of them, looking for courses that would help them develop and understand their unions or the problems they faced at the work place, found their organizations were ignored by most of the educational community. Whether the institution was an elementary or secondary school, a community college, or a university, the situation was the same. This situation is now changing, but slowly. Labor education or labor studies began to grow at a time when both enrollments and resources were declining in colleges. The new students were welcome, but their demands for labor education specialists or labor studies faculty members were not as welcome because of the cost pressures. This problem will have to be resolved by the infusion of new money from state legislatures, from the Congress, or from a reallocation of funds within the educational institutions.

A fourth reason for the expansion of labor education was the simple need for trade unions to replenish their leadership. The retiring unionists who had grown up with the modern trade union (born with the 1935 passage of the National Labor Relations or Wagner Act) were often replaced by persons new to this complex field who could not rely on experience as their primary teacher. So the new officers and staffs turned to universities and colleges, just as other professional or occupational groups had done in the past.

In addition, as the active members started to seek union offices, which they attain only through the internal electoral process, they often began their preparation through courses offered by union, university, or college labor education programs.

Trade unions, as institutions, often are more akin to political parties than they are to corporations or government. Union leaders are elected, and it is difficult, politically dangerous, and perhaps unlawful to groom a successor to the exclusion of others. If an elected leader attempts to bring along a second-line leader, this person may decide to run against the leader who helped him rise. The union leader who attempts to bring forward his own choice of a successor to replace him must do so within the federal law, or there will be a covey of Department of Labor officials standing ready to investigate the election and possessing the power to set the election aside if substantial political manipulation was shown by the incumbent. From the federal government's point of view, the electoral issue is always one of democratic procedure, not the organizational needs of the local or the national union. From the union's point of view, the issue is more complex. Who gets elected, and how, depends on who has the most power, not necessarily the best qualifications or the most experience. It may also depend on such vagaries as whether the person is skilled, male or female, young or old, black or white, with or without a pleasing personality, new to the union or with union experience, or part of the "in" or the "out" group. Trade union politics and the pressures of the representation process bring about a constant turnover of labor officials in the lowest to the highest positions. Although there are a few elected leaders whose terms of office have extended over many years, they are exceptional. The university labor educator must work with the elected leadership—and does so.

Structure. Labor education has traditionally been provided through the short course (one night a week for eight to twelve weeks), the weekend institute, or the one-day to week-long conference. Recently added, because of the changes noted above, have been credit courses and degree programs. The labor educator, like the circuit riding minister, usually carries the message or the program to the workers where they live and work within the state. In some situations, the state is covered from the state university; in others, the program is administered at the state university but has minicenters staffed by one or more persons working out of a branch campus, as in Pennsylvania, or operated in conjunction with other postsecondary institutions, as in Ohio.

The state university labor education programs often make use of many academic disciplines and resources within the university, whether the classes are held on or off campus. Part of the labor educator's function is to act as the go-between for the two organizations (the union and the college or university) and to provide an educational solution for the problems that face the trade union. This cooperation between the labor union and the college or university involves the joint planning of programs. The program developed is usually action-oriented and, because of its short duration, concentrates on possible solutions to current union problems.

Universities and colleges (the word *universities* will hereafter include colleges) have to provide some measure of autonomy to a labor education program, because its students are obtained through the union. The program must be flexible in setting fees, planning and developing courses, preparing the budget, selecting the faculty, and administering its courses in the field and within the university. The program director often needs policy guidance from the highest level within the university. Consequently, a rule of thumb is that with respect to administrative policy, no more than two reporting steps should exist between the program director and the president of the university. This accessibility is necessary for several reasons; first, because of the fast turnaround time that often is required in the development of labor education programs. (Two to six weeks is not unusual.) Moreover, the programs often involve elected or appointed state or national labor officials whose status often necessitates their having direct contact with top university officials. And the director's need to work simultaneously with several departments in different schools or colleges within the university may require the intercession of top university administrators to establish cooperation.

The program director is the person primarily responsible for interpreting the trade union to the university and the university to the trade union. Therefore, he should have a good understanding of trade unions, their structure, functions, needs, and politics, and should be acceptable to the trade union leadership within the state as well as to the university.

Unions have found that one of the best ways to develop a long-term relationship with the university is by setting up a statewide union-university advisory board. In fact, the national AFL-CIO recommends the establishment of such advisory committees in all university programs. For a state university program, this board, usually appointed by the university president and headed by one of the state AFL-CIO officers, is composed of major labor leaders from throughout the state, national-union labor educators, and one or more university administrators and faculty members who are interested in the program and who broadly represent various interested sectors of the university. The labor education director may serve as a member of the advisory committee or act as the executive secretary. The committee might convene two or three times a year to hear reports, make recommendations, assist with setting policy and priorities for the program, and lend support to the program within and without the university. Successful advisory boards have brought the two organizations much closer together by engendering a mutual understanding of the needs and responsibilities of each and by learning about the interplay between union policy and academic freedom.

Community College Programs

The most recent development in postsecondary labor education is the involvement of two-year colleges. This has resulted from two separate needs within the unions. The first is the desire primarily of the construction trade unions to have their apprentices receive educational credit for their extensive technical training. Second, trade union officers and members are looking for an associate degree, with a concentration in labor studies. They want to know more about their union, how it works, what it does, and how it relates to other institutions. The public college offers two advantages—its location in the community where the workers live and its low tuition.

The development of community college labor education has been spotty, however, for several reasons, not the least of which are the lack of professional labor educators at community colleges, the paucity of faculty members who can teach the necessary courses (from specialty fields within such disciplines as economics, sociology, history, psychology, and industrial relations), and the dearth of knowledge about how to relate to trade unions and their members. Solutions to these problems are being sought by the American Association of Community and Junior Colleges (AACJC), the national AFL-CIO, the University and College Labor Education Association (UCLEA), and such interested unions as the United Automobile Workers. These groups met in 1976 to work on the problem of developing labor education programs at community colleges. The AACJC itself has received a grant from the Department of Labor, and with the help of a long-time union and university labor educator, the Association has supplied some technical assistance in developing programs at its affiliate colleges. The UCLEA, through its Committee on Academic Standards and Degree Programs, is in the process of establishing academic and administrative guidelines that will assist new institutions, whether two-year or four-year, to develop both credit and noncredit programs. It should be noted that outside the technical and vocational fields, the unions themselves have not ventured into defining the specific long-term educational needs of their members.

The newness of the community college to labor education, the complexities arising from working with another organization, the trade union, and the competitive spirit within postsecondary education could cause difficulties for the two-year colleges. If they try to duplicate existing university programs, it will ultimately lead to political problems with the trade unions and to a waste of public money. But if the community colleges and the state university work together where labor education institutes or centers exist, then labor education and labor studies will progress, to the benefit of the worker students, their union, and the educational institutions too. One approach would be to have the community colleges develop credit courses for union members (when the demand is present) in their geographical area, in association with the state university labor education center. This would help assure cooperation, not competition; program quality; and future credit acceptance, should students wish to further their studies within the state university system. Once a working relationship is developed, a variety of cooperative arrangements become possible.

It should be remembered that trade unions are political organizations as well as economic and social ones; so community colleges will have to learn how to work with them in order to avoid political difficulty. What the university labor education programs have learned in fifty years of experience can and should be utilized to assure cooperation between community colleges and unions. There are no specific guidelines, as such, that can be used to guarantee cooperation between universities or community colleges and unions because the "mix" of unions and their concomitant needs in each state differ, just as the industries in which the union members work differ. The university and the community college programs within the state will reflect these differences to a greater or lesser degree. To provide for the orderly development of labor education, to husband scarce educational tax dollars, and to assure high-quality programming and smooth interactions between and among the educational institutions, the trade unions within each state should consider developing a statewide plan to meet their needs. In some states, it would not be realistic for more than one educational institution to offer programs. In others, only those institutions in areas containing many workers would be considered. In no case should postsecondary institutions jump into labor education without adequate preparation.

Union Programs

The trade unions in the United States conduct three types of education and training programs: apprenticeship training, vocational and manpower training, and labor education. An apprenticeship combines long-term (two- to four-year) on-the-job training with classroom instruction in method and theory. This form of learning is used in such highly skilled occupations as electrical engineering, tool and die making, plumbing, and operating engineering. The apprenticeship, one of the oldest forms of training, still maintains many of the same characteristics it had in Elizabethan England, where the Statute of Artificers was passed in 1577. The second type of program usually is aimed at developing new skills. Unions may conduct vocational and manpower programs alone or with employers, government agencies, public schools or community colleges, or some combination of these. Several unions have taken government manpower grants to train the disadvantaged to prepare them for entry into skilled occupations. Although I will not have more to say on these two types of program because they are outside the subject of this chapter, the reader should be aware that many unions conduct multimillion-dollar programs of apprentice and vocational training, usually with their employers, in a specific industry or occupation.

Continuing labor education programs, the type we are concerned with here, are conducted by the educational staffs of between 45 and 50 national and international unions and associations, or about 25 percent of the approximately 200 organizations recognized as unions by the Department of Labor. Among these are the American Federation of Government Employees (AFGE), the United Steelworkers of America, the United Automobile Workers, the International Association of Machinists, American Postal Workers, the Communication Workers of America, the International Ladies Garment Workers Union, the Amalgamated Clothing and Textile Workers Union, and the Amalgamated Meat Cutters and Butcher Workmen. As I mentioned earlier, almost all these programs are aimed at union leaders—local elected officers, appointed staff members, and active members, including business agents, organizers, union stewards or committeemen who have the responsibility for enforcing the collective bargaining agreement, and members of bargaining, legislative, or political committees. Rogin (1970) estimated that this group is equal to about 10 percent of the union membership and further noted that few, if any, unions have been able to educate this many of their members. Their educational programs aim primarily at providing officers and active members with the skills necessary to conduct their union affairs and to carry out the union's primary representation functions. Thus the topics include collective bargaining, grievance handling, arbitration, and methods for working within all the laws and regulations that govern labor relations. The participants might also study union administration, labor law, steward training, labor history, the structure and function of unions, communications, labor and social legislation, and politics. Most of these programs, conducted conference style, last from one to five days and are held on university campuses, at hotels, or in the unions' own training centers. Those sponsored by a union tend to be specifically geared to that union's needs or problems within a specific industry.

The local unions and the district or state councils of the national unions use university and college labor education centers within their states to meet specific needs not covered by their national unions and to involve more active members. Many of these members cannot afford to attend the regional conferences or workshops of their national union; the travel expenses, the loss of pay for time lost, and the costs of meals, accommodations, and the conference itself are too great. And reimbursing representatives who attend regional educational activities is costly to a local union. So the existence of conveniently located university labor centers provides educational opportunities that would otherwise be either unavailable or available only to a select few. The labor education centers carry the programs to the field where the unionists live and work and offer programs at "off-clock" times such as evenings and weekends to permit unionists to attend without loss of work or loss of time. In addition, many of the national and international unions that do not have their own education departments use universities to develop special programs for their own members or assist their locals in making contact with university centers.

Many state and local central labor bodies, or labor councils as they often are called, sponsor or cosponsor a number of educational programs for union members within their states or, in the case of the local labor council, within the territorial limits of that body prescribed by the national AFL-CIO. The primary purpose of the councils is to work on trade union legislation and on political and community concerns within their geographic areas. However, they carry on a variety of other functions, including assisting in meeting their members' educational needs. Many state councils, for instance, hold a week-long summer school for trade unionists throughout the state. These usually are cosponsored with the state university labor centers. Some state councils, such as Virginia's, sponsor weekend institutes in various parts of the state; still others band together to hold regional state schools, such as the states in the Rocky Mountain region or in the South where the Southern Labor School has operated for many years.

Many local central bodies conduct a series of educational programs on an interunion basis on a variety of subjects, usually union related, in conjunction with a state university labor education center. These may be short programs for particular needs or longer ones to meet broader requirements. One such program, the Union Leadership Academy (ULA), ties together three state university labor education centers—those of Rutgers, Penn State, and West Virginia. Each center conducts the program in conjunction with labor councils within its own state. Course materials are shared among the universities, and a single certificate is given for the completion of the eight short courses that make up the program. The one-thousandth graduate completed the program and was awarded his certificate in June 1977 at a special two-day graduation conference at West Virginia University. The ULA courses combine content from the social sciences and labor studies. The social science courses include "Labor and the Economic System," "Labor and the Political System," "Labor and the Social Systems," and "Labor History." These provide adult workers with insights into their institutions, communities, and work concerns.

The AFL-CIO Department of Education acts as a national resource, helping affiliated national unions and central bodies to develop labor education programs and providing them with educational materials. Several other departments within the AFL-CIO conduct labor education programs too from time to time or assist trade union organizations, primarily state and local central bodies, to do so. For instance, the Community Services Department aids its local counterparts in establishing programs to assist workers with their out-of-the-plant problems and is tied to the United Way and its affiliate agencies. In addition, the AFL-CIO has its own center for staff training, which began in the late 1960s. Located in Silver Springs, Maryland, the George Meany Center for Labor Studies has its own campus, classrooms, and residential facilities. The Center's primary activity is staff training, which extends from one to three weeks and covers the basic subjects of concern to union officers and staffs. The educational costs are borne by the AFL-CIO affiliates through their per capita tax to the AFL-CIO, and the students' unions usually pick up the room, food, and travel costs. The Center is well on its way to becoming a major adult labor education center; its facilities are made available to other AFL-CIO departments, such as Research or International Affairs, for special conferences and to affiliated unions for their staff conferences. The Center has developed an external bachelor's degree in labor studies through its affiliation with Antioch University in Yellow Springs, Ohio. In addition, several of its programs, such as the arbitration program, are carried to the Midwest and Far West, where they are held on university campuses that have labor education centers. The Center also has developed an extensive cultural enrichment program which includes Wednesday evening programs by a variety of performing artists and exhibits of paintings, etchings, and drawings by individual artists or from collections in a particular field.

A number of other unions, perhaps prompted by the success of the George Meany Center, have begun to develop their own residential education centers for their staff members. The United Steelworkers of America is developing its center in Pennsylvania, and the Retail Clerks International Association have theirs in southern Maryland. The United Automobile Workers center in northern Michigan serves more than union officers and members; it is a family education center offering recreation and child care along with a variety of educational programs.

Two coordinated efforts by labor councils deserve notice as well. District Council 37 of the American Federation of State, County, and Municipal Employees, which represents more than 100,000 New York City workers, has developed an educational opportunities program with New Rochelle College in New York. And District 65 of the Retail, Wholesale, and Department Store Employees Union is in the process of creating an educational program with Hofstra College in New York. Currently, both programs are outside the context of traditional labor education and may be developing a somewhat different trend in the relationship between unions and universities. Both make use of existing college programs, courses, and degrees to upgrade their members educationally while the unions carry on their own labor education program. The high concentration of union members in a small geographical area, the availability of money for education related to collective bargaining, and the needs of the members may have given impetus to a relationship that would not be practical elsewhere. This development will be watched by both unions and universities for application to their needs.

Recent Trends and Problems

Labor education, unlike many other fields of postsecondary education, is in a period of growth, both externally and internally. However, this expansion has coincided with a period of shrinking budgets and enrollments in higher education, a fact that tends to retard its potential and exacerbate the difficulties in establishing new labor education centers at state universities. Universities are reluctant to use their dwindling dollars to establish a new program, despite the need claimed by union leaders. The trade unions have attempted to remedy this by going to state legislatures and governors, or even boards of regents with some success, to gain acceptance and support for their projects. This process is not always a blessing to state universities, which have their own internal problems and priorities, but it has relieved them of the responsibility for having to choose between competing internal needs.

A second problem has to do with establishing new degrees and staffing new degree programs. In the community colleges, where many of the subjects that are part of labor studies are not taught, and where few attempts have been made to hire professional labor educators, unions often have insisted that union officers or staff members be permitted to teach many of the labor relations and labor studies courses on a part-time basis. This arrangement has proved successful in many cases, not so in others. One successful solution to the teacher-qualification problem is an arrangement between the community college and the state university whereby professional labor educators teach certain courses or help the community college screen the prospective instructors until such time as the community college is able to develop or hire its own labor studies teachers.

The problem of establishing a labor studies major or concentration is somewhat less complicated at the community college than at a university, owing to the college's flexibility and willingness to hire part-time instructors. This flexibility does not ensure that the program will be of high quality, however. In the long run the development of a top-notch program will require the hiring of additional labor educators to teach the necessary specialized classes or the hiring of a professional labor educator to coordinate and teach within the new labor studies concentration.

For the university, the problem of hiring faculty members, full time or part time, is much more complicated. Universities traditionally insist that their senior faculty members have a terminal degree, usually defined as a Ph.D. Yet when they try to apply the same rule to labor studies, a new field, they exclude many of the most able people, those directly involved with labor education. This impasse has led to difficulty at many institutions, but it seems to be on its way to partial solution in those universities that are allowing professional recognition and "executive" or "professional" experience in trade unions or in labor education to be substituted for the doctorate in the case of senior-level positions. The universities want the newer labor educators at junior levels to have a master's degree in labor studies, or a willingness to obtain one in an equivalent field, or a Ph.D. in a related discipline.

The establishment of a department of labor studies within universities has not always been easy. One reason is that those who teach it often prefer the somewhat autonomous institute or center in which labor studies has usually been housed, and thus they want any proposed department to be placed in that existing structure. Also, union leaders often believe that they can have more influence on the operation of an institute or center than they can have on a regular department. Another reason is that although labor studies does have its own core of knowledge—having to do with the problems of workers at the work place; their organization, the trade union; the union's internal and external functions; and the union's relations with other organizations in the United States and around the world—it is also interdisciplinary and usually requires courses from other disciplines, primarily in the social sciences. This overlap has caused one institution, the University of Massachusetts, to utilize interdisciplinary programs without departmental status. Others, such as Penn State, have enlarged the labor studies department to carry out a variety of functions, including adult education and specialized research. In still other institutions, the labor studies programs evolved in different schools and colleges at the same time, and so more than one department came into existence in one university. These departments were later tied together by a confederated structure, as at Rutgers University. A fourth approach, that of keeping an existing labor studies institute or center and placing the department within it (as mentioned earlier) is currently in use at the University of the District of Columbia.

The first approach, the interdisciplinary program, has serious problems. How are its operations to be reported, and who is to teach the labor studies courses? How is the program to be managed, and how are faculty and staff members to be judged, that is, by the standards of their own disciplines or on the basis of their labor studies program? And how will student advising be handled? Those students who have a real interest in working professionally in unions or in institutions that must deal with unions, or who wish to go to study unions, may well be confused and have difficulty relating to the program if the advisory arrangements are inadequate. Such problems are common to all interdisciplinary programs which seek to accommodate an external organization as well as to satisfy requirements of a university.

One recent development in collective bargaining that will have a great impact on labor education and the relationship between unions and postsecondary educational institutions is the negotiation of the educational fringe benefit. Unions have begun the process of bargaining about educational benefits for production and maintenance employees. Earlier these benefits were the preserve of management, technical, and professional employees. The Bureau of Labor Statistics of the Department of Labor, in an examination of 1550 negotiated settlements, found 60 contracts having tuition-aid packages that could bring together unions and postsecondary educational institutions. This benefit was negotiated by such unions as the auto workers, steelworkers, electrical workers, and machinists —unions which represent almost 4.5 million workers. The educational benefits in the auto industry alone can provide more than $900 per employee per year, within the limitations of the individual agreement and company plans. So far, however, not many workers have received these benefits. The Department of Education of the Auto Workers Union recently estimated that only 5 percent of its workers are taking advantage of the new educational benefit plans. So this union has developed an active program to assist its members with a variety of educational opportunities and activities. It seeks ways to help unions and universities to cooperate.

The second development that also may have a far-reaching impact on labor education is the call for labor education extension legislation by the presidents of two major international unions— Leonard Woodcock of the United Auto Workers and J. C. Turner of the International Union of Operating Engineers, AFL-CIO. Both referred to the Department of Agriculture's Cooperative Extension Service as one model that could be used to assist in developing educational opportunities for workers; and both have spoken out on behalf of labor education legislation. Most recently, Turner (1977, p. 13), one of the major speakers at the National Invitational Conference on Continuing Education, Manpower Policy, and Lifelong Learning, stated his views, in part, as follows: "A labor extension education program, through the state university system, could have as great a benefit for America's workers—the industrial classes—as the Agricultural Extension Service has had for farmers. I request your consideration of this during your deliberations."

The need for labor education legislation in the past, as now, seems to be predicated on certain assumptions. The first is that the educational needs of union officers and members have been accentuated by the increasing complexity of society. The recent passage of a variety of highly technical legislation has had a direct impact on them and their union and its economic, political, and social functions. But in passing major laws affecting the labor relations process and the unions, Congress paid no attention to ensuring that the worker-citizens and union leaders, the majority of whom are volunteers, gain a working knowledge of those laws.

The second assumption is based on the premise that, despite a long history of adult continuing education in the United States, such educational offerings have been geared to those who for the most part have had the advantage of a good education—the upper middle class—and not to worker-citizens. The workers have been reached only through labor education, which in its fifty years has demonstrated that it has served workers by reaching them through their union leaders. If labor education were expanded through legislation, more workers would be reached and a greater educational opportunity would be provided for more citizens.

The third assumption is that workers, like other groups of citizens, once they have been reached and have participated in relevant education programs, will go on in labor education and later continue their education on their own. Labor education has developed an "intake" system to reach a large portion of the American population that has not been reached by other forms of educational programs or by postsecondary institutions.

The fourth assumption is that state and federal governments have spent and are continuing to spend large amounts of tax money for a variety of programs that are used to educate managers in business, industry, and government, and this causes an imbalance that should be corrected. The situation can be corrected only by an even-handed approach, by providing educational funds to meet trade unions' educational needs.

The University and College Labor Education Association endorsed the principle of labor education legislation and requested its Committee on Legislation to draft laws for consideration. The result of this new thrust cannot be foretold at present, but one conclusion seems clear: American workers are continuing to assert their faith in the educational system through their demand for entry. If they are successful in their quest, their unions, their own development, their upward mobility, the educational system, and the nation will all be served.

A Period of Growth and Change

The role of labor education in the trade unions is both growing and changing. The unions are carrying out a traditional task by assisting members to understand their unions and their functions and to serve as better citizens. But in so doing, the unions are turning more and more to university labor education centers to help them develop programs to serve their members' educational needs. A second change is the unions' interest in labor studies, a term used to designate credit courses and degree programs. The growth in labor studies has been phenomenal, and the pressure is continuing for more educational opportunity in that field. The third change is the recent entry of community colleges into the field of labor studies and their work with trade unions on vocational and apprenticeship programs. It is too early to predict how this collaboration will go, but one can say that individual community colleges and unions continue to be interested. The fourth development is the new, if currently underutilized, educational fringe benefit, which has the potential to supply a variety of educational opportunities not only to union officers but also members and which should bring unions and postsecondary education closer together. The last type of change is the proposed financing of labor education by the federal government. Whether it will dust off the words *mechanic arts* in the original Smith-Lever Act, which developed the Agricultural Extension Service, and supply money for labor education extension is not known. However, there seems to be increased federal support ahead, which may provide greater educational opportunity for the approximately 25 percent of the work force that is unionized. If this increase occurs, then postsecondary education, whose pool of potential students is no longer overflowing, will be at least partially replenished. In addition, workers will have more chance to be upwardly mobile, and as the composition of the work force continues to change, the potential and opportunities of our manpower will grow too.

Growth and change bring challenges and opportunities. How many of the opportunities will be realized is not known, but the potential is present, and adult educators seem more alert to the possibilities than ever before.

Chapter Fourteen

Community Education for Community Development

J. Lin Compton
Howard Y. McClusky

Communities today face many problems: poorly developed and poorly operated schools, delinquency, few provisions for the mentally ill and the aged, inadequate housing and transportation facilities, crime, the economic dependence of the poor, indebtedness, blight, slums, and a lack of industrial development, to mention only a few. But of overriding concern is what might be labeled "the community problem," or the inability of the community to organize its forces to cope effectively with its specific ailments (Warren, 1973). Indeed, social analysts have expressed doubt about this nation's ability to produce enough problem-solving citizens to tackle, locally, the types of problems enumerated (Haney, 1972). Can problem-solving behavior be increased and sustained among citizens who have come to depend on the machinery of industry, technology, and government? This is a debatable issue, in view of the limits of our planet's natural resources, the dangers of a population explosion and consequent overcrowding, the socially disruptive effects of increased geographic mobility, and the inability of government, technology, and industry to deal with our difficulties (Meadows and others, 1972; Roberts, 1973; Schumacher, 1973).

The post–Great Society era has taught us many lessons. We have come to realize the limits of top-down approaches to community development, which generally have been unable to accommodate local variation or to obtain the needed local resources. Moreover, highly centralized strategies result in only minor mobilization of economic resources, little improvement in the planning and management skills of local people, and little incorporation of indigenous experience and knowledge in education and development efforts. We have also come to realize the magnitude of the top-heavy costs of big government. Thus the current situation calls for local problem solving: many things bothering us today would respond to local efforts at planned change. The participation of local citizens can be at least one means of coping with the problems of scale, of resource scarcity, and of adapting development efforts to local conditions. In addition, citizen participation is an important sociopsychological ingredient in both individual and community development. Involvement brings about a positive self-concept, a sense of control, and a sense of commitment and responsibility to others, which serve as a motivation for personal and community change. In fact, the importance of citizen participation in inducing a sense of identity and belonging—the foundation of development —cannot be overestimated.

Definitions

What, then, do we mean by *community education* and *community development*? Although these usually are treated as separate fields, they have a significant number of features in common. So perhaps we have now arrived at a time in dealing with community phenomena—with the problems and needs of a community's citizens and with the design and implementation of programs to serve them—when we can investigate those points at which community education and community development converge. And thus we arrive at *community education for development* (CED): a process whereby community members come together to identify their problems and needs, seek solutions among themselves, mobilize the necessary resources, and execute a plan of action or learning or both. This educative approach is one in which community is seen as both agent and objective, education is the process, and leaders are the facilitators in inducing change for the better. The inauguration of any such program involves the two processes of educating the community so that it understands its problems and of developing some organization for their solution.

Basic Concepts. The resources and social technology needed to achieve many of the objectives of CED already exist. They simply have not been applied in problem solving, and few efforts have been made to teach people how to apply them. Community education for development presents the how (practice and program) and the why (theory and principles) of teaching this social and behavioral technology to local groups for the sake of facilitating individual learning, group problem solving, and community building. The ultimate test of this approach, both as object and process, is how it affects those persons who make up the community being developed. Explicitly, then, the community itself is a developer of the people who live there. Concurrent with this notion should be the people's objective to help the community become a better teacher and, in doing so, help themselves become better educated. This approach is a direct method of teaching and helping learners make the connection between their learning and its direct application. It is a method of teaching adults the use of timing and the sequence of activities in bringing a project through successive stages to an acceptable closure.

CED is an effort through which the community is planned as a whole, with an integration of work, living, and play. In this context the community would be regarded as an external fact, a set of streets, buildings, parks, and services, as well as an internal experience of ideals and values held in common by the community. Thus it would be regarded as both place and spirit. Its physical environment may be considered in terms of housing, transportation, sanitation, aesthetic quality, spatial arrangements, and structures for social, recreational, and cultural outlets. Its internal environment, or psychological climate, should be a healthy one in which individuals, groups, and organizations (1) identify with the community and see themselves as an integral part of it; and (2) interrelate to achieve the good of the community as a whole and of different human systems within it.

Such a community would be characterized by mutual acceptance, participatory involvement, cooperation among systems, a high degree of mutual gratification from productive interdependence, a relatively high degree of power sharing (power defined as the ability to achieve one's ends, to influence the decision-making process, and to influence others), a communication system in which openness and authenticity are the norms, a high degree of utilization of available resources, and a tendency toward rationality as a guide to behavior. In any community the citizens' feelings and behavior may be placed on a continuum: from unfeeling to concerned to overheated and from inactive to active to out of control. The unfeeling and inactive end of the continuum represents the phenomenon of apathy; the overheated and out-of-control end represents the demonstrations and riots that have afflicted many American cities. In the ideal community described above, most citizens are concerned and active. Another set of continua may be labeled adjustmental: from defensive-neurotic to coping, from anxious-jittery to confident, from suspicious-closed to accepting-open, and from distorting or ignoring reality to facing reality. These kinds of attitude and behavior obviously relate to the psychological climate, which may help or hinder a community's attempt to facilitate its development. This climate is an expression of the members' accumulated experience: it may be accepted as is or be a target of a special effort at change. It may be a condition, a means, and a goal in CED. Either as a given or as something to be improved, climate is an important component of CED.

Also of basic importance in CED is the notion that people have not only the right but also the need to practice self-determination. The failures of institutionalized, bureaucratic models of programming, in which persons other than the users do the planning, have been clearly documented. We have come to realize the need for community change educators (Franklin, 1969; Compton, 1972), individuals who can assume a facilitative role in promoting self-actualizing, self-directed behavior in others, especially as this would take place within the social context of group and community building (Combs and Snygg, 1959; Freire, 1970; Maslow, 1968; Rogers, 1969).

Operational Basics. CED is the induction and educational management of certain interactions between a community and its members which lead to the improvement of both. Despite the apparent emphasis on interaction, however, much of CED deals with the learning of individual adults, largely because educators are increasingly aware that the formal schooling years have some limitations when it comes to preparing individuals adequately for a lifetime of learning. A sizable number of adults do not have the coping skills they need to survive at even a basic level of existence. And even those who are doing all right must, owing to rapid social and technological changes, constantly renew themselves with new knowledge and skills if they are to function well. Therefore, one element of CED consists of competency-based functional-literacy programs. Equally important are programs for spreading civic literacy, providing avenues for the development of an active, enlightened, and responsible citizenry. Community education for development, then, serves lifelong learning needs, provides special programs for the educationally disadvantaged, and promotes participatory democracy.

Community education for development can serve as an umbrella concept for three forms of learning: formal, nonformal, and informal (see Table 1). Formal education, of course, is schooling. Although many critics have cited its inadequacy as the sole means of meeting the vast array of society's needs as these continuously change, schooling does serve many useful ends, not the least of which is the socialization of children, or the provision of certain productive skills and attitudes they require to deal successfully with later life and work. Formal education can be related to CED in at least two ways: the concept of community is brought into the classroom for study and analysis (1) to develop children's awareness and knowledge of their own community and (2) to prepare them for active and responsible citizenship roles.

Nonformal education, like formal schooling, is structured

Table 1. Community Education for Development.

Needs and Interests		Modes of Education	
Political Subjects	Government Law/Legal Matters Crime Prevention Community Leadership International Affairs	Formal	Socialization Citizenship Training Career Preparation Intellectual Development Basic Skills Credentialing
Culture	Arts Forums Festivals Crafts Community Theatre History Human Relations Ethos (Philosophical, Spiritual)	Nonformal	Continuing Education Apprenticeships and On-the-Job Training Community Problem-Solving and Development Projects Regarding Needs and Interests of Special Groups
Economics	Home Management Industrial Development Business and Commerce Employment Occupational Training Career Education Consumer Economics	Informal	Family Life "Neighboring" Community Events Social Groups
Health	Sanitation Family Planning Nutrition Physical Fitness First Aid Preventive Medicine		

and has specific learning objectives, but it is conducted explicitly to satisfy the immediate and clearly identified learning needs of particular groups. Classes take place outside schools; usually they are short and flexible in terms of time and location; and they use a variety of human and material resources. No credits, diplomas or certificates, schedules, or set curricula are involved. Teachers may be either paid employees or volunteers. Community education for development emphasizes the use of nonformal channels to help people direct their own learning with the support of others who can mobilize resources and arrange proper learning environments.

Informal or incidental learning is what results from ordinary living at home, in the neighborhood, on the job. Unstructured and often subconscious, it is by far the most common type in the lifetime of any individual. CED affects but does not directly bring about informal learning. Obviously, the quality of what people learn informally depends on the quality of their physical and psychological environments. By encouraging people to improve their surroundings and in the process to improve themselves, CED not only provides direct opportunities to learn social values and effective social organization processes, but indirectly alters people's environmental conditioning and thereby their learning. So CED needs to be fostered by persons who appreciate the importance of incidental learning.

Forms and Functions

A study of the history of CED indicates several phases. First, beginning in the 1920s and continuing into the 1940s, was the development of community-based programs for the poor, ethnic minorities, or social deviants. In Michigan efforts were made to organize and provide leadership training for community councils in more than 300 communities during the 1930s and 1940s. The 1940s also witnessed various types of local self-help community development work, such as community self-study in the state of Washington and the cooperative approach in Nova Scotia. Also during this period various universities began training programs for change agents and planners. The second phase, which began in the early 1940s, focused on the community school as a force for change. A project in Flint, Michigan, for example, inspired by Frank Manley and backed by Charles Stewart Mott, attracted the attention of educators nationwide. In the third phase of CED's history, the community school movement continued, but now the school was seen as a focal point for input from all other agencies within the community. The current and fourth phase is marked by a renewed emphasis on defining CED more broadly; today, community schools collaborate with other agencies to provide education for the development needs of the public. In the next phase we may well see greater stress on citizens participating in decision making and problem solving through the workings of CED councils, and all agencies and institutions that have an educative potential will help to facilitate the whole enterprise.

Throughout these decades, most CED programs have focused on adults and adult learning, since adults, not children, make decisions about social change, and they need help in acquiring the perspective and insight needed to make wise decisions. Therefore, a well-endowed, nationwide adult education service is now essential in all societies. The reasons are both economic and social. Economic progress is achieved through the constant application of scientific, technical, and organizational skills to industrial and agricultural production at all levels. The implication here is that the optimum use of human ability can be made only by increasing the extent and efficacy of adult-learning. Moreover, adults must be helped to adapt to the effects of rapid change. They cannot be expected to perform a constructive personal role and to choose wise courses of action unless they know about the external forces that affect their own lives and the community at large. One noted author (Warren, 1972) clearly articulated the nature and extent of those forces and how they influence what takes place within the community. As a way to offset the bad effects, Warren advocated strengthening community building.

CED starts with a study of the community's problems, felt needs, and interests and then lays out plans in a cooperative fashion to meet them. This studying and planning is accomplished through encouraging enlightened citizen participation, fact finding, developing problem-solving support, coordinating community activities and services, and cooperative action. It is initiated by local citizens and facilitated by outside change agents; but those agents themselves can never implement CED, since by definition it cannot begin until local citizens make the necessary decisions for community improvement. Thus CED planners and educators must become students of the art of obtaining and strengthening citizens' involvement in local self-help education. One useful framework for analyzing this participation is provided by the "margin" theory, which suggests that the extent of a person's participation is largely a function of how much of a margin that individual has to apply to self-improvement pursuits. The margin is the ratio of load to power, the relationship between what people need to deal with their basic burdens and obligations to themselves and their immediate families (load) and the abilities and resources they have for handling that load (power). A challenge for the CED planner or educator is to find ways to help people either reduce their load or boost their power so as to increase what they have left over for self-improvement and community development (McClusky, 1970).

CED can lead the community into anticipating and keeping up with changes. It can help organizations do better what they are already trying to do for the community. CED can be flexible and can adjust to changing needs; if time and tasks change, so can CED patterns. Through the creation of an open atmosphere and deliberate solicitation of opinion, all citizens are encouraged to join in. CED can be particularly useful when several organizations with similar goals are competing for citizen participation and the community seems to have lost the sense of building its own future. Consideration of the myriad relationships among agencies, institutions, and groups within a community make it clear that CED basically focuses on three elements: first, individuals, for whom enrichment programs and activities are developed; second, those institutions that initiate and support CED; and third, those communities that stimulate people's interest in CED functions, which help people to assume the responsibilities of cooperative living.

From the standpoint of institutional programming, a number of key functions have to be carried out to effect a change in local conditions. Among these functions is the training of leaders, which has been performed well for many years by the community resource development arm of the Cooperative Extension Service (usually housed in each state's land-grant institution with operational units in every county). This service has a strong tradition of working with and training community leaders, of helping to establish community councils, and of providing assistance in the analysis of community problems and the assessment of needs. If CED is to be based on citizens' participation, then the expertise of community resource development specialists must trigger the overall effort. In highly urban settings, this triggering might be performed by community organization specialists of social service agencies or other groups who have had experience with social action.

The community services arm of community colleges also performs several functions that are basic to CED. It provides continuing education opportunities, locates courses in schools for the convenience of citizens, fosters high-quality instruction by providing workshops for paid and volunteer instructors on teaching methods, coordinates and houses research and evaluation, and provides staff training programs. Community schools manage and organize educational activities at convenient neighborhood sites. They are also potential headquarters for the coordination and planning of a "needs-resources-response" effort.

The meaning of CED, of people working together to plan the educational aspects of the community's future, is best expressed in CED councils. It is here that a cross-sectional representation of a community's concerned citizenry can best be organized. Such councils lend credibility to decisions concerning education and development; they work to assure that these decisions are pertinent to local situations, and they provide a means for the creative involvement of citizen leaders. Participation in these functions and the opportunities for a rotating membership make the CED council an excellent avenue of citizenship development. Probably most important of all is the council's role in preventing the tail from wagging the dog, of preventing institutions from dictating the scope and direction of a CED program. To function effectively, councils must involve both the providers of programs and representatives of the public.

From a personnel standpoint, then, the most direct contributors to the facilitation of CED programs are made by the community resource development specialists of Cooperative Extension Services, the community organization specialists of social services, the community services specialists of community colleges, the community school coordinators and community education directors of public school systems, and responsible citizens and lay leaders involved in CED councils. Other agencies, organizations, and associations that serve in some capacity include (1) libraries (serving as centers of program information, counseling, and referral); (2) YMCAs and YWCAs (providing additional facilities and staff members for recreational and educational activities); (3) various civic groups (sponsoring special programs related to culture, recreation, or the needs of special disadvantaged groups); (4) senior citizens' groups (serving as auxiliaries and special aides, bringing their knowledge and wisdom to bear on perplexing problems); (5) arts councils (supporting citizens' involvement in creative and aesthetic cultural activities, fostering the staging of special forums and festivals as cultural outlets); (6) various professional groups (doctors, lawyers, firemen, and policemen, among others, providing "protective," crisis-prevention instruction in such matters as preventive medicine, legal documents, safety, and crime prevention); and (7) parks and recreation departments (organizing special camps and environmental learning centers, especially for the benefit of urban youth, and administering community-wide sports programs for people of all ages and both sexes). Many of these potential learning resources, which can be found in most communities, have existed for decades, but their possibilities have never been realized. A central mission of the CED enterprise is thus to accent the existence of these groups and to involve them fully in programming for human development and community building.

Programming

Programming has two basic steps: first, specialists in community resource development or community organization or both, working with CED councils, analyze problems and assess the needs and interests of the community's citizens; and then armed with this information, school coordinators and community service directors, again working with the CED councils, plan, promote, and evaluate appropriate activities to meet those needs and interests. Analysis, assessment, planning, and promotion are continuing tasks. Community school coordinators and community services directors work continuously with the councils to mobilize resources and plan responses to the findings of the various analyses. A good example of CED councils at work is to be found in the Minneapolis area ("Community Education in Minnesota," 1973).

To make easier the interaction and coordinated planning of the many different agencies that work with the same clients and in cooperation with the same CED councils, an interagency team may be desirable. Since this teamwork requires considerable coordinated effort, a council of councils may be necessary too. In a county or a large city it may be desirable to bring together one or two citizen representatives of each local CED council and the community agents, planners, instructors, and administrators representing the different institutions in the area. This large group would deal with problems whose solutions call for resources beyond those represented in the individual council and which are of concern to a number of them. This combination of CED councils and an interagency task force constitutes an ideal mechanism for making decisions and resolving problems concerning large-scale education and development projects in counties and large cities.

Numerous models for educational and social change within communities have been created, validated, and used as guides to program development. Most of those models concern externally induced change (Compton, 1973; Reiff and Riessman, 1965). If the institutional elements, through an interagency task force representing external forces for change, can join ranks with citizen-based community education councils (internal forces for change) and collectively plan for the betterment of a given community, then the best of both worlds can be achieved. The advantages of institutional resources would thus be combined with local initiative. Obviously, under such an arrangement problems regarding power and influence, communication, organization, management, and priority setting often crop up. But the complexity of such an approach and the energies required to implement it would be small in comparison to its potential for community education and development.

The task of CED is neither to extend formal educational facilities nor to maintain the competence of the labor force. It must assist people to interpret what urbanization, social mobility, fluctuating employment demands, intergenerational conflicts, and other effects of rapid change mean for them and their own communities. It must help them to ascertain what positive contribution they can make to the general welfare and to the resolution of their personal problems. Wirtz (1975) advocated the establishment of "community education work councils" composed of representatives from all community employee groups, from those educational and training institutions that prepare people for employment, from the government, and from the general populace to map out the strategies for developing and promoting the human resource base within a community and for doing the broad planning to reconcile economic need and opportunity with educational response.

An optimum condition for CED program development would be the creation of the special position of "dean of community education for development," an individual who would work under the auspices of some local governmental unit, such as the county commissioners, city council, or other multiinstitutional planning body. The dean's function would be to smooth the coordination of the unit-wide CED programming. Having no axe to grind, this person would be in a position to improve communication among different agencies and institutions and individuals. Other functions would be to assist with the process of involving citizens in the decision making and problem solving related to CED, to orchestrate local efforts to obtain outside help, and to promote the public's awareness, understanding, and appreciation of the CED program.

Some key questions requiring the attention of community change educators in the future are these: What are the various modes of citizen participation in CED, and how can they be enhanced? What factors affect the formation and function of CED councils, what are their appropriate tasks, and how can a system of rotating membership in these councils be organized and maintained? What factors affect the formation and functioning of interagency cooperation? Does CED become a perceived threat to an agency's separate identity as the program expands? Should CED councils be viewed as serving agency personnel, should agency personnel be viewed as serving CED councils, or should councils and agency personnel be viewed as serving each other as equal partners working toward larger community goals? What specific effects does CED have on the community? These questions illustrate that experience with CED councils is still quite limited, and therefore those individuals who establish and work with such councils will be pioneers in providing guidelines for others.

Illustrative Programs

The programs we have selected for discussion here are ones we are familiar with. They are excellent examples of different levels and types of CED programming, although they do not necessarily exemplify the very best in each category. We offer them simply to show the diversity of CED, without assessing the soundness of their principles and concepts. We do, however, provide sufficient information so that follow-up contact can be made.

Community Library. Libraries, as learning and information centers, have a long-established tradition in CED. During the past decade, the Appalachian Adult Education Center at Morehead (Kentucky) State University worked extensively with public libraries in several states to expand and reinforce the library's role in adult basic education services, with special emphasis on providing services for disadvantaged individuals (Eyster, 1973). The program focused on assessing a community's needs for information and service, developing or collecting and making available special learning materials, using volunteers to expand library services, providing mobile and mail services for the community, serving as an information and referral center, recruiting disadvantaged learners, training teachers, developing audiovisual methods, facilitating cooperation between the library and other agencies, managing a speakers' bureau, stimulating coordination between public and school libraries, and developing special collections for disadvantaged adults. This program has won numerous national and international awards.

Community Resource Centers. An effort similar to the library extension program was launched by the National Self-Help Resource Center, Inc. (NSHRC), a nonprofit national broker of resources and technical assistance for community self-help initiatives (Davis, 1976). The NSHRC is also the developer and coordinator of the new "community resource centers" (CRSs), a national network designed to give people information on programs, policies, and services and to offer volunteer technical support for groups or individuals wishing to become more involved in community planning and decision making. The NSHRC acts as a catalyst for discussion among nongovernmental, nonprofit associations, organizations, and institutions so that problems may be resolved through the exchange of information and resources. The NSHRC staff has experience in communication and public relations, community organizing and planning, survey research, program management, and direct involvement with grass-roots community programs. In

1973 the center's organizers conducted the first nationwide study of the self-help movement for low-income people. Nearly 1,000 self-help projects were surveyed and 114 representative projects were studied. A product of that study was a book entitled *UPLIFT: What People Themselves Can Do* (National Self-Help Resource Center, 1976).

Integrated Model. The community education program in the Minneapolis area places special emphasis on local community education councils, interagency cooperation, and community schools and colleges. The program provides an excellent perspective on the broad definition of CED. State-level efforts in Minnesota also exemplify the important role of progressive and enlightened state leadership. The governor's office and the state legislature have worked together with a wide range of local agencies to prepare guidelines that encourage rather than stifle local initiative and diversity ("Community Education in Minnesota," 1973).

Community College Community Services. The development of strong community services programs by community colleges is portrayed best by the programs at Brookdale Community College in New Jersey and Oakland Community College in Michigan. Treating their total service area as their campus, these institutions tested and demonstrated the effectiveness of various methods of providing educational services that are low-cost, largely self-supporting, participatory, and judicious in the use of local talent. The models for human resource development that these programs provide for two-year colleges should become well known to policy makers and administrators across the nation in the years to come.

A County-wide Model. Exemplifying county-wide programming is the Durham County (North Carolina) Community Education Program, in which the local community college, a technical institute, the Cooperative Extension Service, and the schools cooperate to provide leadership in developing community advisory councils and in helping the councils plan educational activities. The program resulted from the efforts of a citizen's group in one community, was picked up and fostered by the county superintendent of schools, gained the favor of the county commissioners, obtained a seed grant from the U.S. Office of Education, and currently operates county-wide. This community education program also represents an attempt in one geographical area to develop, test, and refine a model for subsequent statewide support and diffusion. In addition, the program illustrates a development that seems to have taken place in a number of school programs: starting with centrally organized and coordinated programs, the Durham effort moved gradually toward wider participation by means of community education councils, a procedure referred to by others as moving from program to process (Minzey and Le Tarte, 1972).

A Multicounty Regional Model. The Alliance for Progress group operates in six northeastern counties in North Carolina. Initially supported by a Rockefeller grant, this group subsequently was able to obtain from the public school system a one-dollar-per-capita allotment for each school child enrolled, the amount of money needed to pay for the group's CED activities in the region. Strongly emphasized is the need to work with communities and with families to improve the quality of both as reinforcing agents for the learning and growth of children. This program also stresses the development of a public awareness, understanding, and appreciation of the cultural heritage of the multicounty area.

A Regional Culture Program. Another culturally based CED program that exemplifies the power of education in releasing human potential is the Highlander Folk School in New Market, Tennessee. For forty-seven years the school has been an adult education center working with Southerners to increase their capacities for self-determination, both as individuals and in groups. Emerging from the labor struggles of the 1930s, actively involved in the civil rights movement, and confronting situations similar to those faced by Alinsky (1969) in the United States and Freire (1970) in Brazil, the school most recently has been concerned with awakening Appalachian communities. Through Highlander's programs, many Appalachian people have been encouraged to find beauty and take pride in their own way of life, to speak their own language without humiliation, and to comprehend their own power to accomplish self-defined goals through social movements built from the bottom up.

Organizing Senior Citizens. Programming for older adults has become one of the urgent tasks of adult education. The Action Coalition to Create Opportunities for Retirement with Dignity, Inc.

(ACCORD), an advocacy organization in Onondago County, New York, has had a major educational impact on the community by increasing public awareness of senior citizens and by changing the public image of the elderly. The Coalition began with a broad-based community conference sponsored by the United Way and called "Up with Older People," which led to a consensus that the greatest catalyst for better services for the aging would be an organization for older adults themselves. Following the conference, and with the help of a federal and state grant to support a small staff, ACCORD gradually emerged as senior citizens were brought together in small groups to discuss and plan the resolution of various problems confronting them. Emphasis was placed on open and free membership, enlisting the elderly themselves as volunteer workers, and developing numerous branch chapters drawn from various institutional sources (labor unions, retired executives, public housing tenants, and churches). These emphases resulted in the establishment of a delegate assembly, a board of directors, and various task forces and communities. All these developments led to tackling the special problems of elderly minority group members, building public awareness of the elderly, and gathering specific information on the status of various difficulties faced by the elderly. The organizational structure of ACCORD fosters the most strength possible within a community, but it is probably the process by which AC-CORD functions that has had the greatest educational effect on older adults themselves and on the general community.

A Literacy Project. A further demonstration of the power of CED is provided by a small project in Cumberland County, North Carolina. Designed to be run by volunteers, this literacy program was initiated by one of the authors and conducted by the field supervisor of the adult basic education program of the local technical institute. The program focused on testing whether it was a good idea to give the responsibility for literacy programming to the leaders of three communities in the area. The leaders' awareness of literacy problems, in general and within their own communities, was promoted through dialogue and the use of educational materials and films. Following their acceptance of the notion that their communities should and could undertake efforts to tackle their illiteracy, committees were formed, students were recruited, volunteer instructors were trained, money was raised, materials were developed, and facilities were prepared for classes. The accomplishments in terms of enrollment and learning were considerable. But more important perhaps were some subsequent developments: the communities reorganized their forces to deal with the educational needs and problems of the older adult and with community health problems. Thus the confidence gained from their initial efforts at eradicating illiteracy resulted in community action on a broader scale. This project exemplifies the spirit of CED programming.

The foregoing illustrations portray a number of basic CED principles and concepts, from which we developed the following guidelines:

1. State government has a legitimate role in CED as long as it gives support which encourages and facilitates rather than controls and directs local initiative (Minnesota).

2. Different levels and types of initiative in CED programming can be integrated through the establishment of CED councils (Minnesota).

3. Cooperation can be facilitated at many levels, from the small local group to the county and region (Alliance for Progress, North Carolina).

4. Each region has a cultural history and an integrity of its own. Themes of cultural preservation and revitalization can be used to trigger CED programming (Alliance for Progress, North Carolina; Highlander Folk School, Tennessee).

5. Cooperation among agencies, based on the recognition that their resources complement each other, can bolster CED if it allows citizens to participate in making decisions about program development (Durham County, North Carolina, CED program).

6. CED often begins as an effort by a special-interest group to meet its needs and then matures into a wider concern for the welfare of the larger community (ACCORD, New York; Literacy Project, North Carolina).

7. An organization having too few staff members and other resources to deliver its services to those people who are most difficult to reach can multiply its value to the community many times by involving volunteers (Appalachian Adult Education Center, Kentucky).

8. Information resource centers can serve as catalysts by providing access to information vital to the solution of community problems (NSHRC, Washington, D.C.).

9. The effective delivery of educational services by a formal institution is enhanced through the CED approach of regarding the community as the campus of the institution (Brookdale Community College, New Jersey; Oakland Community College, Michigan).

10. Extraordinary efforts are sometimes required of community change educators facing conditions of oppression that are not responsive to conventional approaches (Highlander Folk School, Tennessee).

11. Community change educators must be adept at fostering group-centered leadership and action permitting the civic maturation of both individuals and whole communities (Cumberland County, North Carolina).

These are only some of the many guidelines that could be deduced from analyzing CED programs and projects. Perhaps none is more important than the realization that effective CED programs call for integrated effort along horizontal and vertical lines (Warren, 1972), across organizational boundaries within communities, and between local community forces and related extra-community forces.

Resources

The post World War II era witnessed an explosion of knowledge and activity in the CED field. That CED emerged as a professional field of practice is indicated by the wide range of professional journals that treat this topic as well as by the creation of numerous centers and associations. The American Association of Community and Junior Colleges has recently established a Center for Community Education, one of whose primary purposes is to encourage the development and strengthening of community service programs in community colleges. A Community Development Society of America, formed in the late 1960s, now serves the professional needs of community development practitioners. Professional associations such as the National University Extension

Association, the Adult Education Association of the U.S.A., the National Association for Public Continuing and Adult Education, and the Rural Sociological Society established special-interest sections on community development. The National Community Education Association (NCEA), formerly the National Community School Education Association, caters to the needs of community educators regardless of their institutional affiliation. The National Center for Community Education in Flint, Michigan, provides short-term training for community educators. Other professional associations active in the CED field are the American Association of Health, Physical Education, and Recreation, the National Council on Aging, the American Association of School Administrators, the National Recreation and Parks Association, and the American Association of Colleges of Teacher Education. These organizations have been active in research and development related to CED programming and information dissemination.

Universities and state departments of education were brought into the enterprise with the establishment of more than fifty university-based regional resource centers and cooperating centers, many with initial seed money from the Charles Stewart Mott Foundation in Flint, Michigan. Currently, more than fifty universities and thirty-one state education departments have formally organized CED programs. The University of Michigan operates an Office of Community Education Research that conducts and documents studies and disseminates reports on various research matters. It provides a research monograph series, a newsletter, assistance in research design and data-collection procedures, and information retrieval.

Other primary sources of literature and information are the new federal Office for Community Education housed in the Office of Education and the Pendell Publishing Company in Midland, Michigan. Pendell, a primary contributor to the early literature on community schools, has more recently published a series of how-to pamphlets dealing with funding, community surveys, establishing priorities, using volunteers, interagency cooperation, public relations, problem-solving skills, evaluation, case histories, and emerging models. The Mott Foundation also made available to various universities and state agencies a variety of audiovisual materials useful in promoting the message of community schools. The U.S. Office of Education community education program is responsible for defining, implementing, and monitoring federal grants which provide support to local educational agencies, state educational agencies, and institutions of higher education. Unfortunately, the provisions of the federal legislation reflect a continuing bias toward defining community education in terms of public schools and not in terms of the community and all its institutions having educative potential.

This review of developments yields a picture of rapid growth in the field of practice, accompanied by an increasing diversity of participating institutions, programming patterns, and supportive arrangements. There is still much room, however, for qualitative improvement in the art of CED programming.

Prospects and Issues

CED carries the notion that change and growth should bring about improvement. Persons trying to stimulate growth should consider what has gone before, the available resources and their current allocation, and the interrelatedness of various forces at work in a given area at a given time. Congruent with these basic notions is the principle that facilitators should take into account what happens as it happens, to reorganize and redirect all community forces to achieve a desired end.

Ironically, one of the greatest hindrances to the development of a CED movement in the United States has been the excessive seed money for special pilot projects. All too often the patterns and processes initiated in these projects could not be duplicated elsewhere simply because the programs intended to replicate the pilots lacked the resources to sustain the type of effort expended at the pilot site. Private foundations and the federal government have perpetuated strategies that benefit only the immediate recipients of large grants. Even worse is the stagnating effect that the awareness of such money has on local initiative. Rather than do the work needed to mobilize community resources, many local groups choose to spend exorbitant amounts of time and energy in developing grant proposals. The regressive effect that the rejection of such proposals has on the continuity of local initiative has never been adequately measured.

The argument is often advanced that strategies should be tried out at test sites before their large-scale diffusion. As a general principle aimed at avoiding the wasteful expenditure of scarce resources, this approach is unarguable. However, history is clear: pilot projects have consistently failed to act as catalysts of comparable change and development at nontest sites. Although some good may come from pilot projects—the staff may better understand the nature of certain problems and the conditions that sustain them—seldom do they learn much that can be applied to other areas. Perhaps the cause of this nontransferability is the failure of the special project staff to document adequately the process of development in the target area. Most projects tend to conduct only pre- and post-project evaluations. As a result, the staff has considerable difficulty explaining the dynamics of program development to interested planners.

Considerable debate has ensued about whether CED programming should emphasize program or process, should be school-based or community-based, should be oriented toward education or social problems; a related issue is whether CED should take place within a hierarchical organization or as a part of a community-wide social system. Unfortunately, much of this debate revolves around a set of false dichotomies. Although community education and community development do represent opposite positions to those who consider learning and social action as separate, ideally CED represents complementary and mutually reinforcing efforts at improving both citizens and their community. And although educational activities quite frequently take on the appearance of programs, this does not deny the value inherent in a process approach to learning. Whereas certain types of learning activities may take place in schools, others are apt to occur at several locations. For many types of learning, a classroom is the least appropriate atmosphere. CED activities may be primarily educational or directed at social problems, depending on the objectives of those involved. Some CED activities may be well placed in the hierarchical framework of one institution, whereas others may call for the coordinated work of many different groups and institutions, all part of a larger social system. Most important is keeping the community and its residents at the center of the enterprise. Otherwise, an institution may tend to launch programs that satisfy its immediate requirements but fail to reflect the felt needs of the community.

A central principle in our formulation of CED is that of the community as the school. The community provides the physical environment and the social context within which nonformal and informal learning take place. If these two forms of learning are to be deemed at least as important as formal schooling, and if the interplay of influence among these three forms of learning is acknowledged, then surely the community and the total set of resources and facilities that it contains must be the base for CED activities. Attempts to focus attention solely on the school must yield to a new emphasis on the community as a whole and on the workings of CED councils. Schools will always be in great demand as sites for learning activities, but if public school educators, for example, unilaterally try to control CED, it is highly unlikely that they will be able to obtain the kind of participation, representation, and coordination necessary to bring about a self-sustaining movement.

Another key issue in CED concerns the involvement of laypeople, as we have pointed out earlier. Should programs grow from their participation in decision making and problem-solving, or should select or elite groups design programs and then try to solicit citizens' acceptance of the results? Can we train a change agent who can help get things started and then willingly step into the background as others grow in confidence and ability and become willing to assume leadership? Should the rates and levels of participation serve as indicators of a people's involvement in the self-actualizing growth of themselves and their community, or should *citizen participation* be viewed as synonymous with *volunteerism*?

Our judgment is that CED has a future as a philosophy, a program area, and as a movement. A continuing effort to define and articulate the field is needed, however, if all participants are to understand each other, achieve a sense of common purpose, and establish a necessary "modus cooperandi."

Chapter Fifteen

Adult Education for Home and Family Life

Myrtle Lutterloh Swicegood

The family is expected to perform such essential societal functions as nurturance, protection, and renewal for family members—and all this by people who have received little prior or on-the-job training and who face unprecedented social and technological upheaval. The miracle is that the family has persisted. Whether it can continue to do so is a question, however, for it is undoubtedly deeply troubled. What, then, is the future of the family? And what is the future of the American way of life, which has depended so heavily on this basic social unit? Help in answering these questions is being sought by the family and society.

In response to a coalition of family organizations and other concerned leaders, President Carter called a White House Conference "to examine the strengths of American families, the difficulties they face, and the way in which family life is affected by public

250

policies. The Conference examined the important effects that the world of work, the mass media, the court system, private institutions, and other major facets of our society have on American families" (National Council on Family Relations, 1978, pp. 1–2)." Thus families are becoming a focal point for scholars, lay leaders, and policy makers. And this attention has generated increased demands for family life education, although the resources required to conduct the programs have not been forthcoming. Adult educators, foreseeing this trend, began to clarify their position (Vincent, 1973). A preliminary position statement on the American family, entitled *American Families: Trends, Pressures, and Recommendations, a Preliminary Report to Governor Jimmy Carter* (Califano, 1976), intensified study of this subject and encouraged some expansion of thinking. As a consequence, adult educators have come to view the American family as "an arena for education intervention" (Cromwell and Bartz, 1977, p. 162) that should have a high priority. Families have been the foundation of every culture and society throughout history. Adult educators are committed to helping them continue to be so. Such action seems appropriate because meeting human needs and coping with and planning for change are known abilities of adult educators.

The sections that follow treat four subjects of concern in adult education for home and family life (HFL): (1) significant trends in the changing conditions of families, (2) the development of skills for home and family life, (3) adult education by home economists, and (4) the current limitations and future opportunities of HFL educators.

Trends

To assess the sources of family-related problems and needs, we should look at some changes affecting the family. For one thing, the definition of a family has been altered as living styles have become more diverse during the past several decades in the United States. Even when defined conservatively, the word *family* now generally means the nuclear family—husband, wife, and children— rather than the extended family (the nuclear family and other relatives), which prevailed earlier. More radical definitions of *family*

include such varied living arrangements as communes, single parents
with children, singles in their own households, unmarried couples living together, and two or more individuals of like sex living together.
For instance, in *Home Economics, New Directions II* (American
Home Economics Association, 1974–75, p. 1), a family is defined
as "a unit of intimate, transacting and interdependent persons who
share some values and goals, responsibility for decisions and resources, and have commitments to one another over time." The
changes that these definitions reflect have come about first of all
because of industrialization and subsequent urbanization and second
because of altered values and ideas about individual satisfaction and
fulfillment. The definition quoted earlier challenges those who believe that the nuclear family offers particular values that need to be
retained and reinforced. And the diversity represented by the definition also challenges adult educators, who must work hard to
meet the requirements of a varied clientele.

　　Expectations. Accompanying the new definitions are several
trends having to do with people's expectations of marriage. Does it
have any value at all? At what age should people marry? And how
long should marriage be expected to last? Should the primary purpose of marriage be to help the partners find more meaning in life,
both individually and together? Or to achieve material goals? Or to
carry on the race? *If* one aim is to produce children, when should
they arrive? People's answers to these and other questions are not
traditional, and often they produce considerable stress. As is well
known, for instance, couples who marry today may neither plan nor
promise to live together "until death do us part." The 1976 *Annual
Report* of the Bureau of the Census on the marital status and living
arrangements of Americans showed that there were then 84 di-
vorced persons for every 1,000 persons who were then married, a
79 percent increase since 1970. The freedom to divorce with little
or no social stigma does permit greater individual choice, which
seems to be an important objective today, but it has not brought a
concomitant freedom from the pain and stress of marriage breakup.
This pain does not seem to dissuade people from trying again, however. The statistics also show that those who divorce are likely to
remarry, engaging in what some HFL educators have termed
"serial monogamy" (Mace and Mace, 1974, p. 34).

　　Many young people no longer choose marriage. Those who

do are likely to be older than their predecessors—in 1976, 43 percent of women in their early twenties were single as compared to 28 percent in 1960—and to postpone having children until the woman is older and until the couple's educational, economic, and career desires have been satisfied. Even in the twenty-five to twenty-nine age group, 22 percent of the married women in 1976 were childless. These factors help to account for the decreasing fertility rate, which fell to a record low of 1.76 children per woman in 1976 as compared to 2.4 children in 1970 (Bureau of the Census, 1976b). The economic, social, and physical stresses of child rearing in addition to the increasing career options for women appear to be among the reasons for childlessness.

Those who choose to marry also expect more meaning from the relationship, more personal fulfillment, than did their predecessors. One might say, with Bernard (1972), that marriage is therefore better, or at least that it would be better if these expectations were met because the partners worked at achieving them. But so often, of course, rising expectations lead only to greater dissatisfaction, to a refusal to tolerate forms of marital behavior that were accepted in the past. In a study of upper-middle-class families (Cuber and Harroff, 1965), 80 percent of the couples were classified as simply existing in their marriage relationship, which was not a significant source of satisfaction. Children frequently were cited as sources of dissatisfaction and marital stress.

As the foregoing paragraph suggests, many of the changes in people's attitudes toward marriage, and therefore in the structure of families, reflect the increased focus on self. Self-fulfillment is not always deemed compatible with a commitment to others, a feeling of societal obligation. And when an individual is unwillingly obligated to a relationship, cohesion, stability, and growth are lacking in that relationship, which then produces developmental problems for both adults and children, if the latter are involved (Satir, 1972).

Orientation Toward Work. Another obvious trend is the increasing employment of married women. In 1975 nearly half of all husband-wife families had two workers or more (Hayghe, 1976). And this trend is likely to persist as training and job opportunities are opened to women and as more women seek personal fulfillment outside the home or are forced into the labor market by divorce.

This movement undoubtedly offers important benefits: a higher standard of living for the family with two incomes, greater self-esteem and economic power for many working women, more egalitarian marriages in which men and women share tasks at work and at home. But there are drawbacks, too. As more and more energy and time are directed toward the work world by both parents, and increasingly by the teen-age children as well, the home as the center of family life is eroded. This is exacerbated by the mobility of American families in search of employment opportunities and advancement. According to Califano (1976, p. 4), the average American family now moves fourteen times in a lifetime. Many of these mobile families have not achieved needed friendships and community identification. So family members try to meet their individual needs by turning to one another, just at a time when family communication and opportunities for learning and growing together have diminished. When several members work outside the home, they are rarely together as a complete family because of conflicting work and personal schedules. All this produces marital and physical strains that use up energy needed for nourishing relationships. Families are becoming more aware of the ravages of this way of life, however, and parent workers are more often rejecting job transfers or promotions in order to maintain some stability.

Care for the Young and the Elderly. Many of the changes outlined above, particularly the disappearance of the extended family and a lack of the increase in working mothers, have led to unsatisfactory care for children and senior citizens. Day care provisions and other community services are inadequate. In 1975 licensed group-care facilities were available for less than one-sixth of the nation's nearly six million children under age six whose mothers worked away from home (Day Care and Child Development Council, 1976). Increasing levels of child abuse are a related concern. The U.S. Children's Bureau in 1974 conservatively estimated that there were 50,000 to 75,000 cases of child abuse per year (Irwin, 1974). An additional 150,000 children were in detention centers and training schools for delinquents. Many of those children had committed no chargeable offense but were in need of supervision (Advisory Committee on Child Development, 1976).

With more people living to an advanced age than ever before, the number of elderly who are not able to care for themselves continues to increase. Inflation, fixed incomes, and increased longevity have caused the resources of the elderly to become even more inadequate. Frequently, adults now find themselves supporting two generations—their children and their parents. The resulting physical and economic stresses of work and family responsibilities are so great that many family units are stretched beyond their ability to cope. In some communities senior citizen centers and meals have been made available for the elderly, but owing to a lack of transportation and to their physical disabilities, many have not availed themselves of these opportunities. Other senior citizens struggle alone, clinging to their puritan work ethic and their determination to remain independent. We can expect a growing demand for supplementary family services and decreased resistance to the government's taking a role in family life.

The foregoing is only a sampling of the changes that have come to American families. In the past, change occurred relatively slowly and adjustment could be gradual. But accelerating change appears to be characteristic of the present and the foreseeable future. So how to plan ahead to prevent personal and family disintegration has become a major challenge for adult educators, especially since prevention has proven to be less costly than correction. What to do with the years that have been added to the human lifespan is another growing concern. Education for satisfying use of leisure time will be a major demand. Home and family life education can both prepare people for new vocations and provide pure enrichment.

We do not know what families of the future will be like, but we do know they will be different from those of today, as will their environment. The American family is work oriented; much of family life revolves around the various members' vocations. Thus the blending of several life roles into a meaningful whole will be an increasinging challenge.

Developing Skills for Home and Family Life

Home and family life education deals with humans' basic needs for food, shelter, and clothing; with the resultant need to manage family resources wisely; and with the development of harmonious relationships.

The Basics. Obviously, human beings must eat, and therefore they need to learn about food. Adult educators can supply knowledge and skills related to producing, buying, preparing, and conserving food, as well as information about good nutrition, food safety, and additives. Unfortunately, people also need to learn how to deal with the often misleading information that bombards them and how to change the poor eating habits many have acquired. An adequate food supply and knowledge of good nutritional practices do not necessarily result in behavior that assures proper diet. Most people eat food because they like it, not because they think it meets their nutritional requirements. Another subject treated by HFL education is the different nutritional problems and needs of each stage of human development. These various aspects of food education are of particular concern to adult educators because adults control the food supply of children, and thus whatever skills they acquire will benefit many more people than just the learner.

The second basic, shelter, not only protects humans from the elements but satisfies their needs to have their own space, to build nests, and to have tangible evidence of belonging. A house to live in is usually the single largest investment for most families and one of lasting consequence. Choosing that house—if they are fortunate enough to be able to afford one at all—is often a more confusing process than it was to past generations because of the myriad and expensive forms of currently available housing. Furnishing the house, too, is a costly and often difficult task. Many of the psychological and physiological effects of space arrangement, color, texture, and other elements of interior design are identifiable to the specialist but a mystery to the novice. And learning through experience in the case has proven to be painful and expensive: A poor choice of house plan and furnishings may have to be endured for a lifetime, because the large initial investment may preclude change. Clearly, then, home and family life education can help a great deal by developing people's ability to make informed decisions and thereby avoid costly mistakes.

Clothing enables humans to meet physical, social, and psychological needs; it protects, reveals social status, and expresses their identity and creativity. The wide range of ready-made clothing available, coupled with escalating costs and cónfusion about the proper care of clothing, makes education for the consumer increasingly important. Education for the producer or creator is also becoming more important as the desire for creativity, economy, and satisfying use of leisure time leads to an increased interest in home sewing and clothing-construction skills.

Since meeting the basic needs for food, shelter, and clothing consumes a large portion of the income and time available to the individual and the family, and since most adults acknowledge their feelings of inadequacy with respect to these requirements and their desire for assistance, adult educators have a large and productive field to work.

Home Management. This subject may be considered an extension or part of meeting basic needs. People need to manage their money carefully, to recognize and deal with the fact of finite environmental resources, to develop a division of labor in the home that suits the new dual-career families, and so on. Home and family life counselors indicate that money management often is the dominant issue in marital troubles. Formerly, decision making was not so difficult; now, with the "over-choice" in the marketplace that is characteristic of a technological and industrial society, the simple purchase of a box of detergent may require selecting among twenty brands of different size, price, weight, and alleged value. This factor, combined with the prospect of continuing inflation and an increasing life span, indicates the necessity of long-range planning and education for the management of resources. Living in the century ahead, with ever-greater resource limitations, will require still more wisdom and self-reliance. There will be heavy demands on the so-called normal person, not to mention the handicapped, the illiterate, the poor, and those with particular health problems, who will have special managerial needs. Home and family life education can help provide the lifelong learning and adaptability necessary in a changing world.

Human Relations Skills. The third major domain of HFL education is the development of open, trusting, and productive relationships among family members as well as among persons of different backgrounds, ethnic identities, values, and beliefs. For too long we have believed that when the need arises, people will automatically develop the ability to be good mates, effective parents, and cooperative community members. As has been observed, increasing disenchantment with marriage and childbearing may be less an indictment of the family than a symptom of the problems stemming from humans' inability to establish and maintain harmonious relationships at home and at work. Interpersonal skills essential to home and community relations in a mobile society can be taught and learned and thus are appropriate to HFL adult education curricula.

Adult Education by Home Economists

Home economists have been a major force in education for home and family living. Over the years these professionals have applied the basic philosophy of helping people identify their own problems and aspirations and then have provided practical, research-based information to help solve difficulties and achieve personal goals. The home economics profession first charted this direction at the 1902 Lake Placid Conference. There, the now-classic definition of the emerging field was established: "Home economics in its most comprehensive sense is the study of laws, conditions, principles, and ideals which are concerned on the one hand with man's immediate physical environment and on the other hand with his nature as a social being, and is the study especially of the relation between these two factors" (Lake Placid Conference on Home Economics, 1902, p. 71). Such a broad definition allowed for the synthesis and integration of various disciplines in one defined body of knowledge. In recent years comprehensive ecological and systems approaches have also been incorporated.

The American Home Economics Association, formed in 1908, has helped to develop and carry out educational programs designed to integrate and apply knowledge in meeting families' needs. Numerous services and educational projects have evolved from these programs. One of them, the Cooperative Extension Service created by the 1914 Smith-Lever Act, provided for cooperation between the U.S. Department of Agriculture and the land-grant institution in each state in conducting agricultural and home economics extension work. Such work was to "consist of the giving of instruction and practical demonstrations in agriculture and home economics to persons not attending or resident in said colleges in the several communities, and imparting to such persons information on said subjects through field demonstrations, publications, and otherwise" (Vines and Anderson, 1976, p. 7). The Smith-Hughes Act of 1917 supported the establishment of vocational agriculture classes and home economics in the public schools. There was also an adult education component. Community canneries and classes were inaugurated for men and women according to the needs and interests of that time (Roberts, 1965).

In her book *When We're Green We Grow*, McKimmon (1945, p. 46), a pioneer in cooperative extension education, described homemakers in 1916 as follows: "They were hungry for the new experience of learning to do things through seeing them done; for the opportunity of coming together in interesting work; for the chance to produce an income which would furnish them with things they had so long desired; and for an outlet through which they could express themselves and get recognition from others for what they had done. All of these things satisfied fundamental urges, and I believe they furnish a solid foundation upon which a successful work for any group of human beings may be built." This description gives historical insight into how the Cooperative Extension Service became the largest U.S. organization for the education of adults. Through this agency millions of families have achieved better homemaking practices in informal teaching situations which are structured to meet individual requirements and goals.

Through the years home economists have retained a practical approach to dealing with humans' basic needs, the families within which they are nurtured, and the community in which they live and are a part. The translation of theory and research for dissemination and application has been a major objective of the home economist in adult education. This person, usually a woman, also has had the unique opportunity of working directly with the consumer (the learner) to identify additional interests and needs for research and knowledge, thus enabling academia to remain contemporary. Olsen (1976, p. 569) suggested that the unification of theory, research, and application is essential: "Research cannot be properly conducted without the guidance of theory, nor can theory be adequately developed or substantiated without empirical verification. If in addition theory-oriented research investigated real-life problems, the coordinated approach would facilitate a complementary cycle of development in each area." The home economist has facilitated this cyclic development, which in turn has enabled her to remain abreast of needed knowledge and to develop a reputation as a credible source of research-based, reliable information.

The recognized leadership of the home economist in adult education has enabled her to work effectively with other agencies. One example of such effort is the "Lap Reader Project," to provide an enriched environment for preschool children. The North Carolina Extension Homemakers Association (a volunteer group), the North Carolina public libraries, the North Carolina Department of Public Instruction, and the School of Home Economics at the University of North Carolina at Greensboro, with the North Carolina Agricultural Extension Service as project coordinator, have joined forces in this Project. Partial monetary support is provided by the Small Grant Division of the American Association of Home Economics and Land-Grand Administrators.

The logo for the Lap Reader Project symbolizes the spirit of this cooperative endeavor. The central figures are an adult and a small child seated in a rocking chair and sharing a book. The words beneath the figures invite the viewer to "Open the World, Become a Lap Reader." The beliefs that reading is basic to learning and that learning to read when the prerequisites have been attained is a natural step in a child's development made reading the focus of the project. Any adult can become a Lap Reader, for it is not only reading and communicating with a child but the good feelings associated with this experience that produce positive results. This project uses the cooperative extension volunteer, whose knowledge has been provided through special training, through experience as an adult learner, and often through experience as a parent. In addition to reading, educational experiences with toys that teach, imaginative role play, visits in the community, labeling objects, learning shapes and sounds, and learning communication skills are some of this project's components. Both the child and the parents benefit, as the Lap Reader volunteer becomes a source of parent education and often serves as a role model for parents.

It is through volunteers like these that learning has been extended to the masses and that the work of the professional home economist has been multiplied. The Cooperative Extension Service is one agency that has relied heavily on the use of volunteers. In 1973 the National Extension Homemakers Association conducted a survey to determine who extension homemakers are, how they extend their leadership to others, and what contributions they make to meeting local, national, and international needs. The survey showed that Extension Homemakers Club members had given an average of seventy-nine hours of voluntary service per member during a twelve-month period. If those services had been paid for at a wage of two dollars an hour, their total value for a year would have exceeded $90 million (Vines and Anderson, 1976, p. 94). The adult educator—the cooperative extension home economist—was the facilitator. Home economists are being used as home and family educators in social services departments, health departments, daycare centers, and nursing homes.

Limitations and Opportunities

If adult education for home and family life is so good, why are there any problems? To begin with, in spite of more than fifty years of effort to inform the public, many adults are unaware of such education. Many others are reluctant to ask for help even though they know it is available. Still others have not embraced the concept of lifelong learning; hence, they are not seeking learning opportunities. Finally, there are those adults who feel that their lives are so hopeless that no solution to their problems can be found through education. These are certainly significant difficulties, and probably we ought not to expect education to handle all of them. Fortunately, however, formal HFL educators have help from libraries, museums, social service agencies, industries, churches, and even the media. Churches and religious groups are leaders in new endeavors to teach the skills of marriage and family enrichment and interpersonal relationships. In addition the yellow pages in the telephone directory of even a small town are likely to list counselors who can provide individual or family assistance. Many of the highly rated television programs deal with relationship problems too, as do radio talk shows and newspaper columnists. A possible future source of informal education is the electronic home learning center, which may assist in solving specific individual problems.

Another set of problems confronting adult educators has to do with the changing structure of the family and its functions. The family most likely to succeed in the future will probably be the one that creates a growth-centered, not a child-centered, home environment (Otto, 1972). This change in focus will tend to strengthen the whole unit as well as satisfy individual members' needs. The family can be a learning community. But if adult educators are to help to achieve this projected change, they will have to make a special commitment to that goal. To facilitate organized commitment, in 1973 the Adult Education Association of the U.S.A. established a working committee to analyze the educational requirements of the American family. The committee's work was highlighted in "The American Family: Its Impact on Quality of Life," a paper by Cromwell and Bartz (1977), who suggested that four changes are needed in the attitudes and practices of adult educators and adult learners.

First, people need to drop the idea that it is not normal for families to need assistance in bringing about a truly satisfying family life. Vincent (1973) suggested that Americans are victimized by the myth of naturalism. Many adults feel that one should instinctively know how to be a good spouse or parent and how to manage efficiently, that this all comes naturally when various roles are assumed. This myth often leads people to believe that they eventually will learn what is needed and that to seek help is an admission of personal inadequacy. Additional insight is needed regarding how and what adults want to learn, why they do not avail themselves of proffered learning opportunities, and what assistance or encouragement is required to stimulate self-directed learning through each step of maturation.

The second change suggested by Cromwell and Bartz is a focus on the family as the basic unit for education rather than on the individuals who happen to be family members. This altered emphasis supports Otto's previously stated belief that the successful family of the future will be a growth-centered group. A total-family approach would enable family life educators to respond to the role

changes of family members and would call attention to the necessity of serving more than housewives. Males have been welcome
learners in the past but have not been conspicuous participants
in home and family life education, which they usually view as
education for females in female roles. The third needed change
relates to the first one: adult educators must stress more than they
have the notion that effective family relationships do not just happen, that they result from deliberate efforts by all members of the
family unit.

And finally, Cromwell and Bartz and many of their con-
temporaries feel that adult educators should facilitate the development of a support system for families by promoting the delivery,
coordination, and integration of family-development resources at
the local, state, and national level. Since every sector of life is
affected by public policy, a knowledge of existing policy and careful
planning for future policy are essential. The current fragmented
approach to dealing with human needs has been severely criticized.
The positive effects of this criticism have been an increased awareness of the multiplicity and complexity of human needs, an expanded articulation of needs, and in many instances aroused determination to find a better way. Several HFL authorities have suggested that a cabinet post in the federal government be created to
speak for the family. In the current atmosphere of government and
agency accountability, it appears logical to expect that more support systems for the family will be created. The political arena may
eventually become the meeting ground for educators, policy makers,
and other human rights advocates who share a concern for the
American family.

Policy makers and educators are hearing new, demanding
voices. The blue-collar wife is seeking more education for herself
and her children, for she is coming to believe that education will
provide access to a more truly satisfying life. Women in general are
seeking learning that will lead to new work opportunities, a trend
that is likely to continue and to increase. Thinking persons are planning ahead to adjust to the role changes and opportunities resulting
from what has been termed the women's movement, but which
might be more aptly identified as the humanizing movement. There
is increased recognition that no one sex or group of people exists in

isolation; hence, all tend either to benefit from progress or to suffer from stagnation.

In home and family living programs, adult educators are trying to adjust to what comes, whatever its direction. They continue to be concerned about the effects of social and technological changes on the home, family, and community. Whether those changes concern solar energy or family planning, malnutrition or food safety, cultural arts or land-use planning, adopting will be a continuing process. Adult educators who are capable of generating knowledge and of translating and applying new knowledge are one key to satisfying the current and future educational interests of adult learners. As more kinds of learning become available, adults will become more selective in their educational pursuits, choosing only those they consider to be of value to them. Constant professional improvement and foresight will be essential for the successful adult educator of the future.

To summarize: Through their attitudes and valuing of human worth and potential, adult educators help adult learners become aware not only of their limitations but especially of their ability to select those options that will develop their fullest potential. As home and family life educators, we can facilitate the acquisition of those physical, interpersonal, and managerial skills that, in the third century of our nation, will be essential to social stability and a more satisfying life. Individual adult learners and their families are the final decision makers; our role as adult educators is simply to pave the way.

Chapter Sixteen

Nontraditional Study: Translating the Ideas into Action

John A. Valentine

College credit for "experiential" learning, educational brokering as a new form of adult counseling, and the University of Mid-America as a counterpart in the United States of the Open University in the United Kingdom—these are among the developments of the mid 1970s stimulated by the eruption of ideas and activities in the late 1960s and early 1970s that is called by some "the nontraditional study movement." Though concerned in the main with describing these and other current or very recent developments, this chapter also considers how such developments drew inspiration and support from the early ground swell of the movement, and particularly from the activities and recommendations of the Commission on Non-Traditional Study.

265

The Movement

The nontraditional study movement was not confined to educational arrangements for those beyond the usual college age. Much attention was given to more flexible and productive structures for full-time students who went directly to college from secondary schools. The movement increasingly tended, however, to focus on older adults who desired to undertake or resume their education some years after high school and who could only manage part-time study. It is not unusual, in fact, to hear adults referred to as "nontraditional" learners, particularly within the context of higher education, which must raise the eyebrows if not the hackles of those who have devoted their professional lives to adult education. Although the period when the nontraditional study movement was at its peak is still in the recent past, it is difficult now to comprehend fully the eagerness and confidence with which various attempts were made or planned then to make postsecondary education more accessible, more convenient, and more effective. The educational scene was not as darkened as it is today by clouds of doubt and uncertainty. It was a time of bright hopes and exciting developments.

The Open University was suddenly a reality overseas, and American educators trouped in droves to England, seeking to find ideas in that bold and ambitious venture in bringing a university education within the reach of thousands of "left-out" persons which could be put to work here. New York State launched its Regents External Degree Program, answering in affirmative action the question of Carnegie Corporation President Alan Pifer (1970–71): "Is it time for an External Degree?" The University Without Walls project, Empire State College, and Minnesota Metropolitan State College implemented individualized degree programs based on the use of mentors, learning contracts, and resources for learning available in the world outside as well as inside college walls. Miami-Dade College formed consortia of colleges to attract the critical mass of students and money necessary to produce high-quality educational television programs that capture the sights and sounds of the world at large, and not just those emitted by a professor speaking in an office, classroom, or television studio.

Examining and reflecting on these and other developments were a number of study groups, including the U.S. Department of Health, Education and Welfare's Newman Task Force on Higher Education, the Carnegie Commission on Higher Education, the Study on Continuing Education and the Future, and the Commission on Non-Traditional Study. To the latter commission, chaired by Samuel B. Gould, sponsored by the College Entrance Examination Board and Educational Testing Service, and financed by the Carnegie Corporation, goes the credit, or blame, for bringing the term *nontraditional study* into wide usage. This Commission, through its final report, *Diversity by Design* (Commission on Non-Traditional Study, 1973, p. xv), also is responsible for the suggestion that nontraditional study is "more an attitude than a system," an attitude which, in Gould's oft-quoted words, "puts the student first and the institution second, concentrates more on the former's need than the latter's convenience, encourages diversity of individual opportunity rather than uniform prescription, and deemphasizes time, space, and even course requirements in favor of competence and, where applicable, performance"; an attitude, further, "that has concern for the learner of any age and circumstances, for the degree aspirant as well as the person who finds sufficient reward in enriching life through constant, periodic or occasional study"; and finally, an attitude "that is not new: it is simply more prevalent than it used to be. It can stimulate exciting and high-quality progress; it can also, unless great care is taken to protect the freedom it offers, be the unwitting means to a lessening of academic rigor and even to charlatanism."

Although the outlook of the Commission on Non-Traditional Study differed in some respects from that of the other study groups, the members of all the groups tended to share certain common perceptions, including a sense of the direction in which education must head to fulfill its promise for society as a whole and for its individual members. They saw accelerating change as a fact of life of increasing significance. They saw the concept of equal educational opportunity as requiring a broader definition that would embrace those in their middle and later years, as well as the young. They recognized the potential of many resources for learning outside the formal educational system. They saw the logic of a technological society using technology to serve educational ends. Lastly, they saw the need to build many more bridges for people to use in making their way from education to the working world, or back into education, or from one educational institution to another.

Emerging from these perceptions was a vision of a learning society, a society so rich in inducements, facilities, and supportive arrangements for learning that every person with an itch and ability to learn something new would have opportunities to do so. In its most idealistic form, this vision assumed that the desire to learn is a fundamental part of human nature, on which society places such value that the means for its expression would enjoy both high political favor and substantial economic support. But even if cut back to correspond with more conservative views of humans and society, the vision was filled with a strikingly new diversity and abundance of learning opportunities.

The various recommendations of the Commission on Non-Traditional Study all dealt with creating such diversity and abundance. Directed toward many different institutions, both governmental and private, the proposals aimed to provide new arrangements for people frustrated by existing educational institutions. Some recommendations were directly concerned with better ways of helping students learn; others with more satisfactory methods of counseling, assessing, and crediting students. Still others addressed problems of financing, institutional accreditation, and interinstitutional cooperation. Whether what was recommended in each case was in some sense "nontraditional" was regarded to be of less moment than that it would lead to more people finding paths of learning open to them.

It is beyond the purpose and scope of this chapter to examine all fifty-seven recommendations of the Commission and the extent to which events since 1973 have fulfilled them. This would be a monumental task. The more modest and manageable task at hand is to describe a few developments related to the education of adults that I happen both to be acquainted with and to regard as significant, and by way of background to relate each development to a specific Commission recommendation. In relating developments to certain recommendations of the Commission, I have to leave open the elusive question of how much the Commission in fact influenced those developments. The Commission and its recommendations have been cited in many proposals submitted to governmental agencies and private foundations, but possibly each of the activities to be described would have been proposed, funded, and undertaken, even if the Commission had not been created.

New Modes of Assessing Learning

One recommendation of the Commission on Non-Traditional Study (1973, p. 125) was that "new devices should be perfected to measure the outcomes of many types of non-traditional study and to assess the educational effect of work experience and community service." A project undertaken in 1974 that has made remarkable progress in both creating and implementing such devices is the "Cooperative Assessment of Experiential Learning," or CAEL. The purpose of this project is to develop methods of assessing learning acquired outside classrooms that are accurate in a measurement sense, feasible in practical terms, and acceptable within the academic community. Drawn into the project from the beginning were representatives of institutions already evaluating experiential learning in various ways, as well as representatives of the Educational Testing Service and the Carnegie Corporation, which provided the initial funding. Under the direction of a steering committee, chaired by Morris T. Keeton, CAEL produced working papers, a resource book, institutional reports, and a newsletter. A series of theoretical papers commissioned by CAEL became the basis of a book entitled *Experiential Learning: Rationale, Characteristics, and Assessment* (Keeton and Associates, 1976). Representatives of more than 200 institutions have participated in the CAEL assembly, which has met several times in various parts of the country to hear reports, exchange views, and consider questions of policy. Workshops for faculty members also are sponsored by CAEL.

The interest of many educators active in CAEL has centered as much in the educational potential of experiential learning as in the problem of assessing and crediting such learning. The further development of internships, work and study arrangements, travel, and other sources of experiential learning is becoming the major CAEL objective. The overriding concern up to now, however, has been evaluation. Since experiential learning by its nature is individualized and frequently takes place independently of faculty direction, as in the case of prior learning for which academic credit is sought, the assumption underlying conventional testing procedures, that all those tested have run the same race, is not valid. The challenge of making individual assessments competently enough to be accurate and fair, and efficiently enough to be practical and affordable, is enormous.

In CAEL's efforts to meet this challenge, the "portfolio" played a prominent role. A portfolio is an organized set of materials that describe, exhibit, and document what the individual has done. It provides a basis for judgments about the nature and amount of learning that an individual has achieved. The CAEL identified six stages involved in creating and using portfolios and the educational questions posed by each of those stages (Keeton and Associates, 1976, p. 227):

1. Identify the learning, whether acquired through life experience or incorporated in a sponsored program. (What types of experiential learning justify college-level credit; to what extent must learning be specified?)
2. Connect such learning to the educational goals or academic degree of the student. (Does crediting experiential learning change the meaning of the B.S. degree?)
3. Document the fact that the student has participated in the learning experience. (Should credit be based on experience or learning?)
4. Measure the extent and character of the learning acquired. (When learning experiences differ widely, how can assessment be consistent and equitable without being standardized?)
5. Evaluate whether the learning meets an acceptable standard and determine its credit equivalence. (When learning standards differ widely, how can educational standards be publicly understood and maintained?)
6. Transcribe the credit or recognition of learning. (How should

the qualitative value of learning achievements be communicated
to the student and to third parties?)

The Commission on Educational Credit of the American
Council on Education lends support to the efforts of the CAEL to
develop and promote the use of portfolios and other devices for
measuring and crediting the outcomes of experiential learning. This
commission, the successor to the Commission on the Accreditation
of Service Experiences, regards experiential learning as one of four
equally legitimate sources of college credit, the other three being
grades awarded by faculty members for satisfactory performance
in regular college courses; satisfactory performance in courses
offered by noncollegiate sponsors (including business, industry, and
labor unions, as well as the armed forces); and satisfactory performance on standardized examinations, such as those in the
College-Level Examination Program.

Educational Brokering

The Commission on Non-Traditional Study was concerned
with the fact that many persons who desire to learn either do not
know where to turn for information and advice or find the counselors they do contact knowledgeable only about the offerings of a
particular institution and capable of giving little personal attention,
advice, or support. The Commission (1973, pp. 34–35) therefore
recommended that "student guidance and counseling services, in
specially created centers when necessary and appropriate, should
provide expert advice relevant to both individual needs and available resources." In the past several years a number of agencies
engaged in this type of recommended service began using the term
educational brokering to describe the particular form of counseling
they offered. With encouragement and financial support from the
Fund for the Improvement of Postsecondary Education, representatives of nine such agencies in Alabama, Connecticut, Massachusetts,
New Jersey, New York, Vermont, and Washington met to pool
their views and experiences and the lessons they had learned. The
dialogue thus generated became the basis for a monograph, *Educa-*

tional Brokering, New Services for Adult Learners. This monograph described educational brokering agencies as functioning "as
middlemen between adult learners and educational institutions and
resources. At the one hand of the broker are several million Americans whose education has been interrupted by the responsibilities
of early parenthood, economic pressures, social and cultural deprivation, frustrations and low achievement in the classrooms of their
youth, or by other impediments. At the broker's other hand is a
vast and complex array of educational programs: private and
public colleges and universities, community colleges, proprietary
schools, correspondence schools, public schools' adult programs,
employer-sponsored training programs, labor union and church-
sponsored institutions and programs, and local, state, and federal
agencies involved in education" (Heffernan, Macy, and Vickers,
1975, pp. viii–ix).

Two characteristics distinguish educational brokering agencies from the majority of counseling centers. Brokers, neutral with
respect to the institutions chosen by their clients, aim to inform
clients about the offerings of all such institutions. They are not
neutral, however, on the matter of the learners' interests versus
the institutions' interests. They serve as learners' advocates and as
such may intercede in negotiations between the learners and an
institution and even try to change institutional policies that pose
obstacles without clear justification.

Educational brokering agencies vary in their organizational
structure and setting. The Regional Learning Service of Central
New York is an example of a free-standing agency; the Community College of Vermont is a unit of the state college system;
the Regional Continuing Education for Women Program in Philadelphia is a coordinated activity of counselors in five colleges; the
Okanagan County Educational Service in Omak, Washington, is
a unit of Wenatchee Valley College but carries out its brokering
role independently, as does the School for New Learning of De
Paul University, Chicago. A National Center for Educational
Brokering was established in 1976 to promote the proliferation of
brokering programs, improve the quality of their services, and
facilitate their financial vitality. Originally housed in the Regional
Learning Service of Central New York and subsequently in the

National Manpower Institute in Washington, D.C., with support provided by the Fund for the Improvement of Postsecondary Education and the Carnegie Corporation, the Center sponsors conferences and workshops, a consulting service, and the publication of a monthly bulletin. Another type of broker is the public library, identified by the Commission on Non-Traditional Study as a promising source of information and advice for adult learners. Building on the experience gained, materials developed, and publicity generated by the College Board's Office of Library Independent Study and Guidance Project, a Consortium of Public Library Innovation, formed in 1976, is working to increase the scope and caliber of library activities of an educational brokering type.

The University of Mid-America

When the Commission on Non-Traditional Study was active, there was growing interest in the educational potential of computers, cable television, audio and video cassettes, and satellite broadcasting, and a counterbalancing awareness that the actual use of instructional technology in American schools and colleges continued to be both limited in extent and primitive in nature, despite such a shining exception as "Sesame Street." In recommending that "strong and systematic efforts should be made to reexamine the possibilities offered by educational technology" (Commission on Non-Traditional Study, 1973, p. 96), the Commission was mindful of the formidable difficulties of achieving appropriate organizational arrangements, faculty understanding and acceptance, and necessary economies of scale. "As colleges and universities have used television," noted the Commission in its final report, "the production of 'software' has been analogous to raising homegrown vegetables in a cottage garden" (1973, p. 108).

The University of Mid-America (UMA), founded in 1974, is a notable example of an institution that worked hard to solve those difficulties. With the Open University of the United Kingdom as both a model and a stimulus, UMA represents a cooperative effort of Midwestern universities to produce and deliver high-quality multimedia instruction to people where they live. Although television is emphasized, newspapers, toll-free telephone lines, and the postal service also are brought into play, and the use of radio and cable television is anticipated. The special strengths of printed materials and of audio casettes are capitalized on, and learning centers provide opportunities for the human interaction for which so many learners hunger. The charter participants in UMA are Iowa State University, the University of Kansas, Kansas State University, the University of Missouri, and the University of Nebraska. The University of Iowa, the University of Minnesota, the University of South Dakota, and South Dakota State University have more recently joined the fold, and other institutions have expressed interest. The presidents of the participating institutions serve as the governing body, and faculty and staff members from each institution compose the UMA academic council, headed by the UMA vice-president for academic affairs.

The UMA evolved as an extension of the State University of Nebraska formed in 1971, which carried out a number of studies and developmental projects—most of them supported by the U.S. Office to Education—to find out who the "takers" of mediated instruction might be, what kinds of instruction they were interested in, how teaching materials could most effectively be produced and delivered, and, not least, what organizational and financial strategies would enable the whole operation to function successfully. Essentially a consortium of independent universities, UMA grants no credits or degrees: those remain the prerogative of each participating institution. The principal function of UMA is planning and developing curricula; working out how all this will be "delivered" is the responsibility of each participating state. Multimedia courses which have been developed by UMA cover a broad range of topics as is indicated by the following selected list of such courses: "Anyone for Tennyson?"; "Principles of Accounting"; "Pests, Pesticides, and Safety"; "Introduction to Symphonic Music"; "Going Metric"; "Japan: The Living Tradition"; "A Survey of the World Food Problems"; "Great Plains Experience"; and "A Critical Review of the American Revolution." Just as the UMA makes its sources available to colleges and universities outside its membership, the UMA institutions lease courses produced by others. For example, two Dallas County Community College District tele-courses, "It's Everybody's Business" and "Writing for a Reason," have been used successfully by several UMA member institutions. More than 3,500 students have enrolled formally in UMA courses, and thousands more have watched TV programs or read course-related newspaper articles. There are no admission requirements. Most people enroll for credit, although many report they simply want to learn, for their own pleasure or to become better developed as persons and citizens.

Although foundations also have contributed, the National Institute of Education has provided the principal financial support of the UMA in the amount of more than four million dollars. Plans call for the UMA to become sufficiently self-supporting within the next few years that grants will be needed only for research and for developing new courses. The returns from the large investment in the UMA need to be measured not only in terms of the creation of a viable regional university that exploits the possibilities of educational technology but also in terms of the wealth of experience and knowledge gained that may help with the development of new opportunities for people to learn conveniently and efficiently what they want to learn.

Surveys of Would-Be Learners

In the ongoing planning and evaluations of the UMA surveys of potential clients and of enrolled students were conducted as a matter of course, and such surveys are becoming more common, particularly at the state level. *In The Third Century: Postsecondary Planning for the Non-Traditional Learner* (Hamilton, 1976), a report of such a survey in Iowa, cited surveys completed or under way in California, Colorado, Florida, Illinois, Massachusetts, Minnesota, Nebraska, New Jersey, New York, Texas, Vermont, and Wisconsin.

This trend was anticipated as necessary by the Commission on Non-Traditional Study (1973, p. 36), which recommended that "the survey of clientele for non-traditional study begun under the auspices of the Commission should be continued and expanded." When it first addressed the question of making education more accessible to more people, the Commission could find few facts about the actual numbers and kinds of persons whose desires to learn were frustrated and also about the nature of both their desires and their frustrations. The consequent questionnaire survey on the learning interests and experiences of U.S. adults, initiated by the Commission, yielded data that stimulated widespread interest. The questionnaire used in the survey was adapted for use in surveys of learner interests in more than twenty states or localities, including California, Iowa, and metropolitan St. Louis. The increasing interest in conducting such surveys has been accompanied by an increasing awareness of their limitations, as well as their potential for purposes of planning and marketing. The report of a recent conference at which experience with such surveys was discussed carries the provocative title *Meeting (New?) Needs With (New?) Resources* (Hamilton and Valley, 1976).

The final act of the Commission on Non-Traditional Study in 1973 was to hold an invitational conference at which its final report was presented to and discussed by representatives of a wide variety of associations, institutions, and agencies. The last of the Commission's fifty-seven recommendations was that a follow-up conference be convened in 1975 "to determine what significant progress non-traditional study has made" (Commission on Non-Traditional Study, 1973, p. 141). Three national conferences, on "Open Learning and Non-Traditional Study," subsequently took place—in 1974, 1975, and 1976. Those conferences were occasions for people at work on undertakings of the sort recommended by the Commission to report on their progress and to exchange words of advice, encouragement, and criticism. Communications technology received growing attention at the conferences. (The University of Mid-America joined with the Joint Council on Educational Telecommunications to sponsor the 1975 conference, and with the Corporation for Public Broadcasting and the National Association of State Universities and Colleges in sponsoring the 1976 conference.) Practical problems of implementation, including problems of marketing and cost-benefit analysis, also received increasing attention. Advances and successes continue to be reported, but difficulties and frustrations also are evident. A summary of the 1976 conference was significantly titled "Confidence and Diffidence in Open Learning" (Gross, 1976). Problems of gaining support, recruiting students, maintaining standards, controlling costs, and building useful alliances, acute these days for most if not all educational institutions, often are even more pressing for institutions that are striking out in new directions.

But the army of those engaged in creating the new abundance and diversity of opportunities for learning that the Commission on Non-Traditional Study saw as the essential point of the nontraditional study movement grows ever larger. This chapter actually dealt with only a small fraction of the total participants. Other chapters of this book identify additional participants, and there are many more who deserve recognition.

Evidence of Forward Movement

Does the sum of the outcomes of the efforts of all those builders suggest that a learning society has been achieved? Few would claim that it does. Far too many obstacles and frustrations exist in the lives of too many men and women who have a desire to learn. For tangible evidence of forward movement, however, one can certainly look with satisfaction at the CAEL Project, the agencies engaged in educational brokering, the University of Mid-America, the surveys undertaken to understand better the learning interests of particular groups of adults, and the annual Conference on Open Learning and Non-Traditional Study. To appreciate fully the significance of these developments, one has only to realize that they have moved in the space of less than eight years from ideas in the minds of a few to facilities and practices enriching the lives of many.

Chapter Seventeen

◆◆◆◆◆◆◆◆◆◆◆◆◆◆◆◆◆◆◆◆◆◆◆
◆◆◆◆◆◆◆◆◆◆◆◆◆◆◆◆◆◆◆◆◆◆

Mass and Instructional Media

◆◆◆◆◆◆◆◆◆◆◆◆◆◆◆◆◆◆◆◆◆◆◆
◆◆◆◆◆◆◆◆◆◆◆◆◆◆◆◆◆◆◆◆◆◆

Thelma M. Cornish
William L. Carpenter

The impact of mass media and instructional media on adult education results from their power to transmit great quantities of information quickly to a large number of adults in nontraditional ways. Television, radio, print, computer-assisted instruction, telephonic systems, and combinations of these reach increasing numbers of persons of all ages. It is manifestly apparent, as McLuhan (1964, p. ix) observed, that "in terms of the electronic age, a totally new environment has been created."

Although mass media and instructional media are not the same, the difference is principally one of scale, and both can be used to teach adult learners. So it makes sense to treat them together in this chapter. The *mass media,* obviously, are those modes of communication that reach a lot of people, the masses: commercial newspapers, radio, television, movies, books, and magazines. When these modes and the techniques they use are adapted for classroom use, they become *instructional media*. In an excellent book on the subject, *Big Media, Little Media,* Schramm (1977) restricts instructional media to "the electronic and photographic media that came into use in the nineteenth and twentieth centuries: photographs, slides, films, recordings, radio, television, computers" (pp. 12–13). He points out that, like print, "these are not specially designed for instruction; they are simply information-carrying technologies that can be used for instruction." Thus the oldest medium, print, is often not included in what most people mean by *instructional media* or *educational media* or *mediated instruction*— various terms that have been in vogue at one time or another during the past decade. The parent term, *audiovisual aids,* which was popular when slide, film, and filmstrip projectors were the newest developments, shows both that print was excluded from the beginning and that these other modes were first considered supplements to the teacher and the book. Be that as it may, however, we will examine all these media as they apply to adult education, looking at how they are used not only as devices in the classroom but also as a means of publicizing programs, as a primary means of teaching students in settings outside the classroom, and as a tool for instructing instructors.

But before we do so, let us briefly highlight the history of these media in order to regain some perspective on the incredible swiftness with which these developments have become part of our lives, taken for granted already. It has been only a relatively few centuries since the Chinese and Egyptians each independently invented paper. Then Gutenberg's movable type in 1450 ushered in modern printing. The advent of photography made it practical to illustrate textbooks. The invention of the rotary press in 1846 and the web-fed press in 1865 mechanized printing. Greatly assisting the distribution of all this printed material in the United States was the development of the Postal Service around 1900, including the Rural Free Delivery, which brought newspapers and magazines within everyone's reach. And then the establishment of the Cooperative Extension Service in 1914 made possible the broad distribution of more explicitly instructional material for adults. The federal legislation creating the Service specified that up to 5 percent of the budget could be applied to printing and distributing publications; and before the year was out, an agricultural editor was on the staff in most states, sending out press releases to newspapers and printing bulletins with instructions for farmers.

Commercial radio broadcasting began in 1920, television in 1941. Color television became available about the same time the first communication satellite went up in 1962. Radio, highly important as an information medium, has not been developed as an in-school medium in the United States, but when television came along, educators were quick to see its potential. Educational channels were allocated and programming was begun in the early 1950s. Accompanying these major breakthroughs in the past twenty years has been an explosion of other electronic devices designed or adapted for the classroom: audiotapes, and cassettes, videotapes and videocassettes, overhead projection materials, and 8 mm filmloops, among others. With such a variety from which to choose, today's educators may be more confused than comforted when they want to select communication media to use in their educational programs. But for the sake of their students' learning and their own professional competence, it will behoove them to understand these new media and learn to apply them.

Illustrative Uses

To further acquaint adult educators with the range of ways in which the communications media are and can be used, we present the following examples, arranged roughly in five categories according to their purposes: (1) to promote programs and recruit students, (2) to deliver more or less formal education outside the school, (3) to provide nonformal education, (4) to enrich classroom teaching, and (5) to train adult educators.

Promotion and Recruitment. Personal contact is still the most effective means of recruiting for or promoting any type of program. But in view of the masses that must be reached, personal contact is not usually feasible, and therefore educators must turn to other forms of advertising. Some educational programs are presented to the public via paid advertising. But for educational endeavors, much free time and space is available in the commercial media. For example, three radio spots developed in 1976 by the National 4-H Service Committee to promote this national youth program were presented as a public service by an estimated 4,000 radio stations. In Maryland, a toll-free telephone service was operated by the State Department of Education to supplement a coordinated program of spot announcements on a state-sponsored General Educational Development Instructional Television (GED/ITV) program. In a six-month period, 7,000 people called in to find out more about the GED program. A toll-free telephone number also was used to receive inquiries generated by spot announcements on the four state television channels used by the Maryland Center for Public Broadcasting. One of the programs being promoted by this means was "Speak for Yourself," a thirty-two lesson television course in conversational English.

A program on energy conservation conducted by county extension agents in New York State was advertised by radio spots (18,000 airings) and special newspaper feature articles in a campaign which invited the public to contact their county extension office for free copies of twenty "Consumer Fact Sheets." During the first half of 1977, more than two million copies were distributed. The College of Agriculture at the University of Illinois used radio and TV spots, along with a two-screen slide-tape show and a brochure, to present its case for new facilities on the campus. The package presented the story of Illinois agricultural research to both "critical support audiences" and the public.

A promotional and recruitment spot for broadcast can vary from the filmed-on-location TV spot costing $2,000 to the single one-dollar slide accompanied by a script read by the station announcer. The same production techniques used to sell commercial products can be used in such spots—announcer-read statements, interviews, testimonials, hidden cameras, and musical jingles. A newspaper announcement may cost no more than a single sheet of paper and typing time.

Formal Education Outside the Classroom. In this category fall those programs offered, generally by educational institutions, to people in their homes or in other settings away from conventional classrooms. Such media programs are developed either because they are the most efficient means of teaching a large number of people or because certain isolated groups of adults can only be reached by these means. Thus mass media techniques are used to serve many adults who have transportation problems; who hesitate to admit to their families and communities that they do not possess a high school education and who therefore feel they cannot or will not participate in organized classes; who lack confidence and fear failure and the reactions of others; and who may be unable to leave home or job for any reason. The programs therefore range from quite formal replicas of classroom courses, with lectures, texts, papers, and so on, to structured but less traditional courses which emphasize self-instruction and require a minimum of guidance by a teacher.

The oldest and most basic medium of "distance teaching" is print, in existence at least since the correspondence schools began. A modern example of the use of this medium, as well as an example of how educational and public agencies are cooperating to present programs, was the General Educational Development Newspaper project in Philadelphia. This was conducted successfully by the local board of education in conjunction with two daily newspapers, ten public libraries, and the Pennsylvania Department of Education. With the help of counseling and assessment at centers established in public libraries, adults were able to study lessons published five days a week. In the first six weeks of operation, more than 1,300 adults participated. The newspaper—the most accessible print medium around the world—has also been put to use in several African, Asian, and South American countries to help adults with limited reading abilities (UNESCO, 1977). In these programs, the newspaper is often employed both as a supplement to classroom teaching and as a means of self-instruction. In some African countries such as Ghana, for example, newspapers are produced by the newly literate to serve their minimally literate countrymen.

The addition of the broadcast media to the tools of distance teaching has of course enriched the possibilities greatly. Not only do they stimulate the auditory sense and, in the case of television, present pictures instead of words to the eye, they also offer "live" teaching, and their regular scheduling tends to bring about disciplined study (Schramm, 1977). One long-standing example of the use of television is the complete two-year curriculum presented since 1956 by Chicago City College. Students who complete this course earn an A.A. degree, with which they can usually transfer to a four-year institution. Televised lectures are supplemented with texts and assigned papers, and in some cases with class meetings on campus. Two-thirds of the students registered for credit in this program are in their twenties and thirties, but almost half of the noncredit viewers are in their forties and fifties. Another college-level television course is the innovative degree program for working adults instituted by Wayne State University. Since 1973, adults have been able to earn a general studies degree in four years. The unique delivery system combines television programs, weekly workshops, and intensive weekend conferences over three years. During the fourth year of advanced studies each student writes a major essay. Most participants combine full-time employment with full-time study.

Television is being applied in other exciting ways, too, as its technology continues to advance. Within the next five years, for instance, farm families in isolated areas of eastern North Carolina may be able to take courses that have been stored in a unit attached to their television sets. This will be made possible through the recently funded North Carolina Rural Renaissance Project sponsored by the North Carolina Community College System. The project will make use of a new development that allows programs to be transmitted rapidly over the airwaves to a receiver connected with a television set, where they are stored for later playback. Television sets that can receive the signal could be located in churches, community centers, prisons, and homes. The project is aimed at making life in isolated towns and farm country more attractive. There is no limit to the subject matter that can be covered in such a program.

The other broadcast medium, radio, is also used to transmit adult education classes, though much less frequently than television. Since 1969, for example, Purdue University has offered regular courses on the radio that closely resemble those in the classroom. Reading lists and sample examinations are sold to the students.

More than fifteen courses in some years have been offered by this method (Schramm, 1977).

A less well-known auditory medium of adult instruction is the telephone, whose use is exemplified by the Direct Instruction for Adult Learning (DIAL) system, originated in Roanoke, Virginia. The system incorporates tapes and materials which are designed to meet an individual's needs by instructors who work at program centers. The adult students work at their own pace and hear tapes as many times as desired. The system now exists in nine Virginia counties.

Not to be omitted from the list of communication media used in adult education is the computer. A computer-based instructional program, developed in Urbana, Illinois, operates in cooperation with the University of Illinois. The program includes planned lesson routines and an instructional aide at each of three sites, which are a considerable distance from Urbana. The system develops a series of instructional units to increase vocabulary and improve reading comprehension for adults reading at the fourth- to seventh-grade level (Garth, 1977).

Nonformal Education. This category overlaps somewhat the preceding one; so the assignment of a particular illustration to one section or the other was rather arbitrary in some cases. But the general principles of selection were that the media program described was usually developed by other than an educational institution—often by a government agency—and offered no academic credit. As defined by Ahmed and Combs (quoted in Schramm, 1977, p. 226), nonformal education is "the motley assortment of organized and semiorganized educational activities operating outside the regular structure and routines of the formal [educational] system, aimed at serving a great variety of learning needs of different subgroups in the population, both young and old. Some nonformal programs cater to the same learning needs as the schools and in effect are substitutes for formal schooling."

The mass media have excelled as carriers of nonformal education. And the Cooperative Extension Services have excelled at using the mass media. In presenting their educational material to the public, they have amassed an impressive array of statistics in this respect: a 1977 survey of 15 state Cooperative Extension

Services indicated that the average number of news releases from the various state offices was 752 per year. In Illinois alone, in a recent six-month period, county and area agents prepared 6,494 news articles, wrote 4,365 regular news columns, submitted 3,596 feature photographs to newspapers, prepared 10,034 radio programs, and participated in 513 television shows (Illinois Cooperative Extension Service, 1975). And the Kansas Cooperative Extension Service reported that in 1976 its 465 professional members made an estimated 20 million indirect contacts with clients through the mass media—newspapers, magazines, newsletters, radio, and television.

Television, in particular, as we noted in the previous section, has been used imaginatively. In a program of Vermont Cooperative Extension Service, twenty-seven videocassettes were made of specialists discussing various topics about which the Service wished to inform people. The ability of county agents to turn the specialists on and off when and where they needed them was a prime advantage of this technique. The fifteen-minute color cassettes were played over cable television at local fairs and shopping malls, where people could phone in questions and get answers from an agent at the time the tapes were being shown. Comparative tests in 1976 demonstrated that the use of specialists on videocassettes equaled the results gained by having specialists appear in person. However, the ability of the county agent to field questions and administer the videocassette showings was cited as a key ingredient in the program's success.

Another case of videotape used effectively is "Farm Marketplace," a ten-program series designed and produced by Kentucky Educational Television with the Kentucky Cooperative Extension Service and the Kentucky Farm Bureau in 1977. The goals of the program were to acquaint farmers with the nature and complexity of the marketing system and to show them how they could make their own informed decisions about selling their products. More than 5,000 farmers ordered the workbook prepared to go along with the telecast. A third example is provided by the Oregon Cooperative Extension Service, which used four thirty-minute videotapes, broadcast over educational stations and five commercial stations, to prepare private and commercial pesticide applicators for certification. A viewer's guide and two reference manuals were supplied to each person who registered for the training. The result: a test was administered by the Oregon Department of Agriculture a few days after the last of the four broadcasts, and 94 percent of the nearly 5,000 persons who took part in the video short course received authorization to apply selected pesticides.

A more formal application of television can be found in the high school preparation series produced by Kentucky Educational Television. The telelessons are broadcast in Kentucky and are also available on videocassette tapes in other parts of the country. Some adults study independently at home; others are supported through a variety of organized programs. Evaluation studies of the series showed these telelessons to be as effective as any other method or instructional mode.

An interesting example of the use of several media comes from New York, where in 1974 the Extension Service made available a twenty-four-hour information system on topics of consumer interest to radio stations through an automated telephone-tape hookup. Nearly 150 stations in six states and Ontario, as well as the wire services and radio networks, have access to the call-in service. Do radio stations like the service? Calls from radio stations in 1976 totaled 3,756.

Even comic books have been found to be a useful means of delivering nonformal education to adults. More than a million copies of a comic book on nutrition produced by the U.S. Department of Agriculture were ordered. And a recent North Carolina survey showed that leaflets, circular letters, and cartoon booklets were all acceptable to low-income homemakers and were effective in conveying nutrition information (Trent, Kinlaw, and Pintozzi, 1977).

We ought to mention too in this category a few of the myriad educational films available from government and other organizations. From the productive National Film Board of Canada comes "Following the Plough," a twenty-seven-minute film showing the change in farming practices and farms in Canada. A unique adjunct to the film was a modern troubadour, who hired on at farms acrosss Canada in 1977 and wrote songs about farm life and his travels. In the United States, the National Wheat Institute offers a seventeen-minute film tracing the history of wheat in human nutrition and emphasizing the nutrients necessary for good health. Colleges and universities are among the film producers as well. The University of Wisconsin, for instance, produced twenty-one feature films from 1968 to October 1976 on such diverse topics as land use, hog marketing, community development, Christmas trees, wildflowers, and solid waste disposal. Of course any of these films could be used as the center of a one-shot nonformal adult education program or as a supplement to a formal course.

Supplementing and Enriching Classroom Teaching. Speaking of films brings us to the next category. Bretz (cited in Schramm, 1977, p. 176) described the supplementary use of the media as "that directly related to the curriculum, but carrying a minor part of the responsibility, in comparison to the teacher. Media used for enrichment are less directly related [than supplements] to the syllabus, but rather are intended to contribute new insights, new experiences, variety, or enjoyment." Whatever way they are used, however, most of the instructional media available to the educator today are designed to present a visual image along with a verbal presentation. Visualizing a message focuses attention, avoids misconceptions, saves time, shows concepts, presents new experiences, provides multiple use and flexibility, and makes learning easier (Stephen, 1969). However, Schramm (1977, p. 273) cautions that educators need to consider the quality of their media use. After analyzing some 1,000 studies and finding that there is more variance in quality within than between media, he concluded that "how a medium is used may therefore be more important than the choice of media, if the scale of use or the need of pictorial or auditory material does not dictate the need of one certain family of media rather than another."

As a hypothetical case, suppose that the literature class instructor wants the students in a given class to analyze a piece of writing. All that is really needed is a printed copy of the story, but it might add interest to have a copy of the original handwritten manuscript. Or suppose in a speech class the teacher wants students to analyze a person's speeches. Some judgments could be made by simply reading a printed copy of one of the speeches, but to analyze his speaking, the students must at least have the speaker's voice on audiotape. Further, if he were on film or videotape, his arm motions and facial expressions, for example, could be critiqued. In analysis of either the writing or the speaking, the students might do an even better job if they knew something about the person's life. For this purpose a filmed dramatization, if available, would be useful. And yet, perhaps none of these media supplements is really necessary for effective teaching; perhaps the printed form is quite sufficient. This is but a sample of the analysis a teacher must make in selecting media to use. Creativity and good judgment are the keys to success here.

Training Adult Educators. The mass media, especially television, are being used increasingly to train both prospective and practicing teachers. Because of the diversity and phenomenal growth of adult education over the past decade, there were too few instructors with experience in working with adults to satisfy the demand. As a result, many elementary and secondary teachers were hired who then needed to adapt their earlier training to the characteristics and psychology of adult learners. These teachers, who are frequently employed on a part-time basis, have little time for professional upgrading and little incentive for engaging in further training if it were made available. A program to alleviate the problems of crash training and to capitalize on the power of television as a teaching mode was developed by the Maryland State Department of Education. The series, entitled "Basic Education: Teaching the Adult, A Teacher Education Series" (Division of Instructional Television, 1973a), consists of thirty telelessons, with an accompanying teacher's manual. This survey course uses a how-to format combining lectures, demonstrations, and discussions. The telelessons are designed for use in conjunction with seminars and other means of exchange.

As the Maryland Department of Education prepared to produce the series, staff members involved in the project began to ask the crucial question "What can television do that the classroom cannot do?" They found seven answers, five of which were that television can illustrate teaching models, ensure that the content of a course is presented uniformly to different groups of students and yet be flexible enough to meet varying needs and situations, maintain interest by presenting the subject matter in a variety of ways, explain and illustrate key concepts in a short time, and allow segments of a series to be singled out for special use. The remaining advantages were that many staff members representing varied disciplines could help to develop and then use the series and that episodes could be packaged in cassette form to allow institutions and local education agencies to repeat the lessons any number of times.

In planning the project, the creators sought the broad participation of the State Education Department and personnel in community colleges and public schools engaged in teaching adult basic education. Five colleges and universities were involved in its development. When the state-funded project was completed, a special federal grant was received from the Division of Adult Education of the U.S. Office of Education to make the product available to colleges and universities in the ten Office of Education regions. During 1974–75, the year of implementation, the series was viewed by 430 students in twenty-five institutions. By means of cassette tape, the telelessons were presented on closed-circuit systems as a college course or as part of in-service activities.

The project was evaluated by Curriculum and Evaluation Consultants (1976). They found that teachers have backgrounds and attitudes that would enable them to benefit from this type of experience. Ninety-eight percent of the teachers responding to the evaluation felt that television is a good medium for learning, at least part of the time. The evaluation survey also established that (1) the tapes and manuals can be used to teach both graduate and undergraduate students in a variety of ways; (2) students with no prior adult basic education training achieved more than students who had had such training; (3) there was no difference in achievement among students with different levels of teaching experience; (4) the telelessons were best used to supplement and reinforce an instructional program; (5) state departments of education reported that the series was used effectively in general orientation sessions, in skill-development activities, and in stimulating interest. The use of this Adult Basic Education Instructional Television series has since spread rapidly throughout the country, the U.S. territories, and several provinces of Canada. The evaluation of the Maryland series did not include a control group; therefore, comparative data are not available. However, Campeau (1974) reviewed some of the research comparing television with live instruction in the education of adults. These studies generally found no significant differences between them.

Equally important is the use of electronic media to teach adult educators how to employ communications technology. The inflexibility of many adult education programs discourages the use of electronic media. Rigid scheduling, the application of traditional elementary and secondary education techniques, and the ineffective use of available facilities and staff all serve as barriers. Seeking to change the attitudes of professionals and improve their skills, the Maryland State Department of Education developed another series of telelessons, this one on the use of instructional-television (Division of Instructional Television, 1973b). A work manual is part of the credit course combining television lessons, on-campus seminars, and assignments from the manual. Teachers like the course because it develops their confidence in employing this new teaching device in the classroom.

Some Problems

Thus far we have painted a rather rosy picture of media users doing all manner of interesting things. But we must point out some drawbacks and cautions too. A primary one, of course, is the cost, which can be prohibitive. To have a commercial company produce a three-minute film, for instance, will cost between $30,000 and $50,000, outside the budget of many agencies of adult education. The equipment to make and present material is usually expensive as well. There are ways to control cost, however. Films can be rented or purchased. Hardware can sometimes be pooled. And instructors can make their own graphics, although—and here we come to a second drawback—even the use of simple materials requires a certain amount of ability. Not just anyone can write a newspaper article or perform well before a microphone or television camera. Some artistic talent is necessary to develop first-class visuals. However, many agencies provide art and editorial services to their members. Newspaper reporters can be encouraged to write special-interest stories, and a station announcer can read the radio spot.

Also, through the process of adult education, one can be taught skills in these particular areas.

Third, the mass media and their managers are not always reliable or easy to work with. The equipment may break or be in use elsewhere when you need it. The newspaper may not print the article you submit. Attention must be given to developing harmonious relationships with representatives of the mass media if adult educators are to make optimum use of the media.

Another difficulty is that feedback is limited, and evaluation is frequently hard to do. One can provide exact scores and count students in a classroom. But for a radio or television broadcast it is often not possible to make even a good estimate of how many people were tuned in. Some administrators want to see more concrete results of such efforts than can be obtained routinely with the mass media. And then there is the risk involved. How do adult educators know they will succeed when they change their teaching style and try something new? What if the projector breaks down? As in any situation where something new is tried, failure lurks around the corner. But because adult educators are always encouraging others to change their practices, they have an obligation to improve their own practices as well.

Finally, instructional media must be used judiciously and in combination with human contact. Eyster (1976b) and other researchers have established that the most critical element in the successful application of electronic media is person-to-person contact, however nominal. This is necessary for students' involvement, retention, perseverance, and achievement. Many students get bored and cannot concentrate, for instance, when served a steady diet of self-instruction materials. In other words, these technological devices, especially television, are not the panacea that educators might once have thought. But there is no question they have brought vital new means to the end of adult education.

Future Growth

Two models of education face today's educator: "One results from our past history and assumes that people can prepare for

life most effectively by attending school and college for a length-
ened period of time. This model assumes people used to be 'educated' in order to be employable; learning, however, is assumed to
be largely finished when an individual leaves school or college. The
alternative model, being developed now, proposes a continuing
learning process conducted largely within the real-life situation of
the community, rather than within the schoolroom and the 'ivied
halls of academe' " (Theobold, 1976, p. 25). The movement toward the second way of looking at education coincides with
society's transition from the industrial era to the age of communications. What does all this mean to adult educators? It means they
must move with alacrity and insist on implementing what they have
begun: the lifelong learning movement. And they must confront
their own shortcomings. The use of mass and instructional media
should contribute significantly to their efforts.

As we enter this new period, we shall find increasing emphasis on education suited to the individual adult learner. As
Theobold (1976) explained, information systems will be designed
to provide people with the specific data, human contacts, ideas,
and models they need to deal with their specific concerns at particular moments of their lives. Rigid, teacher-dominated classroom
learning and imposed curricula, with their sprinkling of semi-
individualization, will die out as the means of learning expand. The
institutionalization and formalization so common today will diminish, as will the emphasis on academic credit. A distinction will be
made between schooling and learning. Adult learning centers and
public libraries will function as service centers for guidance and
assistance, for information and referral, materials, assessment,
and career planning. Opportunities will be provided for peer learning. The entire community will be viewed as a learning laboratory.

In this creative learning environment, mass and instructional media will be used increasingly to provide options for adult
learners. Even commercial television will provide more educational
offerings along the lines of such past contributions as the 1977
National Broadcasting Company series on parenting skills, the
Columbia Broadcasting System's family reading program, the
American Broadcasting Company's GED program in the metropolitan Washington area, and the Westinghouse Broadcast series on

consumer education. This last resulted from a study of adult performance levels, which revealed that the average American lacks basic consumer skills. A commercial television station in Baltimore, Maryland, which has aired the "Listen to Read" series for the past fifteen years, is no longer one of the few that broadcast adult education programs; it is now one of the many.

The possibilities of cable television are just beginning to be explored and developed. It is already an excellent means of disseminating practical information, and it offers community people opportunities to enter into the telecommunications field. In Sweden, for example, the first noncommercial cable television project (CABLE Communications and Resource Center, 1977) employed programs produced by local residents who had learned production techniques at a weekend course. This medium deserves local community support and control. Communication satellites, which can deliver signals to areas which have not been served or have had inadequate service, will also achieve new and wider applications, combining several media (Kreitlow, 1976).

In the world of print, the increasing popularity of magazines appealing to the mass audience of the college-educated who are interested in pursuing additional learning is apparent. *The Smithsonian,* a magazine published by the Smithsonian Institution Press, Washington, D.C., is an excellent example. After only seven years, *The Smithsonian* has emerged as one of the most successful monthlies in the United States, with a June 1977 circulation of more than 1.5 million. Thus, in this electronic era, there is still a role for print media.

Clearly, mass and instructional media can and will play a vital role in adult education. These can assist adult educators in removing barriers to diversity, in encouraging people to take responsibility for learning, and in promoting lifelong learning. Adult educators would be remiss if they ignored these tools as they strive to serve the ever-growing body of potential and actual students.

References

ABT ASSOCIATES. *An Evaluation of MDTA Training in Correctional Institutions.* 3 vols. Washington, D.C.: Manpower Administration, U.S. Department of Labor, March 1971.

ACADEMY FOR EDUCATIONAL DEVELOPMENT. *Never Too Old to Learn.* New York: Academy for Educational Development, 1974.

Act of July 2, 1862 (First Morrill Act). 12 Stat. 503 (1862), 7 USC 301, 1970.

ADKINS, W. R. "Life Skills: Structured Counseling for the Disadvantaged." *Personnel and Guidance Journal,* 1970, *39,* 108–116.

ADVISORY COMMITTEE ON CHILD DEVELOPMENT. *Toward a National Policy for Children and Families.* Washington, D.C.: National Research Council, National Academy of Sciences, 1976.

ALINSKY, S. D. *Reveille for Radicals.* New York: Vintage Books, 1969.

"American Higher Education: Toward an Uncertain Future." *Daedalus,* 1974, *103*(4); 1975, *104*(1).

AMERICAN HOME ECONOMICS ASSOCIATION. *Home Economics, New Directions II.* Washington, D.C.: American Home Economics Association, 1974–75.

APPALACHIAN ADULT EDUCATION CENTER. *Long-Range Follow-Up*

Study: West Virginia Module. Morehead, Ky.: Morehead State University, 1972.

Appalachian Regional Development Act, 79 Stat. 5, 1965.

Area Redevelopment Act, 75 Stat. 47, 1961.

ARENBERG, D. "Cognition and Aging: Verbal Learning, Memory, Problem Solving, and Aging." In C. Eisdorfer and B. P. Lawton (Eds.), *The Psychology of Adult Development and Aging.* Washington, D.C.: American Psychological Association, 1973.

"ASTD Has Good News—Five Years from Now." *Adult and Continuing Education Today* (Today Publications), February 2, 1976, pp. 19–20.

BAKER, K., IRWIN, J., LEONARD, D., HABERFELD, S., and SEASHORE, M. *Summary Report: Project Newgate and Other Prison College Programs.* Office of Economic Opportunity Contract B-2C 5322. Washington, D.C.: Bureau of Prisons, April, 1973.

BALTES, P. B., and SCHAIE, K. W. *"The Myth of the Twilight Years." Psychology Today,* 1974, *7,* 35–40.

BARLOW, C. E. *The Unconquerable Senator Page.* Washington, D.C.: American Vocational Association, 1976.

BARLOW, M. L. *History of Industrial Education in the United States.* Peoria, Ill.: Charles A. Bennett, 1967.

BARLYN, L., and SCHEIN, E. H. "Life/Career Considerations as Indicators of Quality Employment." In A. D. Biderman and T. F. Dury (Eds.), *Measuring Work Quality for Social Reporting.* Beverly Hills, Calif.: Sage, 1976.

BARRON, W. *Teacher Awareness and Counseling in Adult Basic Education.* Austin: Extension Teaching and Field Service Bureau, University of Texas, 1969.

BATES, F. L. *The Structure of Occupations: A Role Theory Approach.* Raleigh: Center for Occupational Education, North Carolina State University, 1968.

BAY, OVID (Ed). "The Editor's Letter." Washington, D.C.: Extension Service, U.S. Department of Agriculture, June 15, 1976–July 15, 1977.

BENEDICT, R. *Patterns of Culture.* New York: New American Library, 1934.

BENNE, K. "The Processes of Re-Education: An Assessment of Kurt Lewin's Views." In K. D. Benne, L. P. Bradford, J. R.

Gibb, and R. O. Lippitt (Eds.), *The Planning of Change*. (3rd ed.) New York: Holt, Rinehart and Winston, 1976.

BERNARD, J. "The Status of Women in Modern Patterns of Culture." In C. F. Epstein and W. J. Goode (Eds.) *The Other Half*. Englewood Cliffs, N.J.: Prentice-Hall, 1971.

BERNARD, J. *The Future of Marriage*. New York: World, 1972.

BERRY, D. C. *Higher Education in the United States Army*. New York: Carlton Press, 1977.

BERRY, J., and LORING, R. K. "Continuing Education for Women." In R. M. Smith, G. F. Aker, and J. R. Kidd (Eds.), *Handbook of Adult Education*. New York: Macmillan, 1970.

BILINGUAL EDUCATION SERVICE CENTER. "Need Statement." In *Proposal for Providing Supportive Services for Adult ESL Education Programs*. Arlington Heights, Ill.: Bilingual Education Service Center, 1976.

BILOVSKY, D., and MATSON, J. *Community Colleges and the Developmentally Disabled*. Washington, D.C.: American Association of Community and Junior Colleges, 1977.

BION, W. R. *Experiences in Groups*. New York: Basic Books, 1959.

BISHOP, C. E. (Chairman). *The People Left Behind*. A Report by the President's National Advisory Commission on Rural Poverty. Washington, D.C.: U.S. Government Printing Office, 1967.

BISHOP, J. H. *The General Equilibrium Impact of Alternative Antipoverty Strategies: Income Maintenance, Training, and Job Creation*. Madison, Wis.: University of Madison Institute of Research on Poverty, 1977.

BOTWINICK, J. *Cognitive Processes in Maturity and Old Age*. New York: Springer, 1967.

BRADFORD, L. P. *National Training Laboratories—Its History: 1947–1970*. Privately published, Bethel, Maine, 1974.

BRODSKY, N. "The Armed Forces." In R. M. Smith, G. F. Aker, and J. R. Kidd (Eds.), *Handbook of Adult Education*. New York: Macmillan, 1970.

BROWN, E. G., JR. "State of the State." Governor's Address to the California State Legislature, Sacramento, 1976.

BROWN, J. W., LEWIS, R. B., and HARCLEROAD, F. F. *AV Instruction Technology, Media, and Methods*. (5th ed.) New York: McGraw-Hill, 1977.

BRUBECK, T. "Twenty Ways to Open a Door." *American Rehabilitation*, 1976, *1*, 23.

BRUNNER, H. S. "Federal Laws and Rulings." In *Land-Grant Colleges and Universities: 1892–1962*. Washington, D.C.: U.S. Department of Health, Education and Welfare, 1962.

BUREAU OF BASIC CONTINUING EDUCATION. *Adult Basic Education, New York State: A Two-Year Study of Title III, P.L. 89–750, 1965–1967*. Albany: New York State Education Department, 1967.

BUREAU OF THE CENSUS. *Annual Report*. Washington, D.C.: U.S. Department of Commerce, June 1, 1976a.

BUREAU OF THE CENSUS. *The U.S. Fact Book: The American Almanac: The Statistical Abstract of the U.S.* (96th ed.) New York: Grosset and Dunlap, 1976b.

BUREAU OF EDUCATION FOR THE HANDICAPPED. *Proceedings of the Conference on Research Needs Related to Career Education for the Handicapped*. Washington, D.C.: Office of Education, U.S. Department of Health, Education and Welfare, 1975.

BUREAU OF LABOR STATISTICS. *Educational Attainment of Workers*. Special Labor Force Report No. 193. Washington, D.C.: U.S. Department of Labor, 1976.

BUREAU OF PRISONS. *Education for Tomorrow*. Washington, D.C.: U.S. Department of Justice, 1976.

BURKE, J. G. "American Engineer Rates High on Skill, Low on Social Responsibility." *UCLA Weekly*, May 10, 1976, pp. 1–4.

BYERS, K. T. (Ed.). *Employee Training and Development in the Public Service*. Chicago: Public Personnel Association, 1970.

CABLE COMMUNICATIONS AND RESOURCE CENTER. "The Expanding Cable Picture." *CABLE Lines*, 1977, *5*, (1) and (2).

CALIFANO, J. A., JR. *American Families: Trends, Pressures, and Recommendations, A Preliminary Report to Governor Jimmy Carter*. Washington, D.C.: Press Office, U.S. Department of Health, Education and Welfare, August 1976.

CALIFANO, J. A., JR. "Statement by Joseph A. Califano, Jr." *HEW News*, April 28, 1977, p. 2.

CAMPBELL, T. M. *The Movable School Goes to the Negro Farmer*. Tuskegee, Ala.: Tuskegee Institute Press, 1936.

CAMPEAU, P. L. "Selected Review of the Results of Research on the Use of Audiovisual Media to Teach Adults." *A-V Communication Review*, 1974, *22*, 5.

CAPLAN, E. H., AND LANDEKICH, S. *Human Resource Accounting: Past, Present, and Future.* New York: National Association of Accountants, 1974.

CAPLOW, T. *The Sociology of Work.* New York: McGraw-Hill, 1954.

CARKHUFF, R. R. *Helping and Human Relations.* Vol. 1. New York: Holt, Rinehart and Winston, 1969.

CARLSON, N. A. "The Future of Prisons." *Trial*, 1976, *12*(3).

CARNEGIE COMMISSION ON HIGHER EDUCATION. *A Chance to Learn.* New York: McGraw-Hill, 1970a.

CARNEGIE COMMISSION ON HIGHER EDUCATION. *The Open Door College.* New York: McGraw-Hill, 1970b.

CARNEGIE COMMISSION ON HIGHER EDUCATION. *Less Time, More Options.* New York: McGraw-Hill, 1971a.

CARNEGIE COMMISSION ON HIGHER EDUCATION. *New Students and New Places.* New York: McGraw-Hill, 1971b.

CARNEGIE COMMISSION ON HIGHER EDUCATION. *Priorities for Action: Final Report.* New York: McGraw-Hill, 1973a.

CARNEGIE COMMISSION ON HIGHER EDUCATION. *Toward a Learning Society: Alternative Channels to Life, Work, and Service.* New York: McGraw-Hill, 1973b.

CARNEGIE CORPORATION OF NEW YORK. *Carnegie Quarterly*, 1975, *23*(4).

CASSELL, R. *Strengthening Extension Education Programs for All Segments of Society Through Effective Program Development.* Washington, D.C.: Federal Extension Service, 1970.

CENTER FOR CONTINUING EDUCATION OF WOMEN. *New Research on Women and Sex Roles.* Ann Arbor: University of Michigan, 1976.

CHEYNEY, A. B. *Teaching Reading Skills Through the Newspaper.* Newark, Del.: International Reading Association, 1973.

CHICAGO PLANNING COUNCIL ON AGING. *The Chicago Plan for the Elderly and the Handicapped.* Chicago: Mayor's Office for Senior Citizens and the Handicapped, 1976.

CHILDERS, B. E. "Vocational Program Evaluation." In A. H. Krebs (Ed.), *The Second Yearbook of the American Vocational As-*

sociation. Washington, D.C.: American Vocational Association, 1972.

CITY UNIVERSITY OF NEW YORK. *The Status of Women at the City University of New York—A Report to the Chancellor.* New York: City University, December 1972.

Civil Rights Act. Public Law 88-352, 88th Cong., HR 7152, July 2, 1964.

CLARENBACH, K. F. "Can Continuing Education Adapt?" *Journal of the American Association of University Women,* 1970, *63* (2), 62–64.

COBB, H. V. (Ed.). "Mental Retardation: Century of Decision." In *President's Committee on Mental Retardation.* Washington, D.C.: U.S. Government Printing Office, 1976.

COLEMAN, J. S. *Equality of Educational Opportunity.* Washington, D.C.: National Center of Educational Statistics, 1966.

COLES, G. S. "U.S. Literacy Statistics: How to Succeed With Hardly Trying." *Literacy Work,* 1976, *5,* 47–68.

COMBS, A. W., and SNYGG, D. *Individual Behavior: A Perceptual Approach to Behavior.* New York: Harper & Row, 1959.

COMMISSION ON NON-TRADITIONAL STUDY. *Diversity by Design.* San Francisco: Jossey-Bass, 1973.

COMMISSION ON THE REORGANIZATION OF SECONDARY EDUCATION. *Cardinal Principles of Secondary Education.* Bull. 35, U.S. Bureau of Education. Washington, D.C.: U.S. Government Printing Office, 1918.

COMMITTEE FOR REVISION OF 1954 MANUAL. *Manual of Correctional Standards.* New York: American Correctional Association, 1970.

COMMITTEE ON CURRICULUM PLANNING AND DEVELOPMENT OF THE NATIONAL ASSOCIATION OF SECONDARY SCHOOL PRINCIPALS. "The Imperative Needs of Youth of Secondary School Age." *Bulletin of the National Association of Secondary School Principals,* 1947, *31,* 45.

COMMONER, B. *The Poverty of Power: Energy and the Economic Crisis.* New York: Knopf, 1976.

COMMUNITY COLLEGE OF BALTIMORE. "Success of the Sneak Preview of Orientation Week." Unpublished report. Baltimore, Md.: Community College of Baltimore, 1976.

"Community Education in Minnesota." *Community Education Journal* (Pendell Publishing), May 1973 (whole issue).

Comprehensive Employment and Training Act, 87 Stat. 839, 1973.

COMPTON, J. L. "Factors Related to the Role of the Primary School Teacher as a Mediator Facilitator in the Communication Process Between the Rural Village Community and the Larger Social System in Northeast Thailand." Unpublished doctoral dissertation, University of Michigan, 1972.

COMPTON, J. L. *Community Teamwork: What It Is, How It Starts, What Makes It Succeed.* Silang, Cavite, Philippines: International Institute of Rural Reconstruction, 1973.

Continuing Education for Women: A Five-Year Report of the Minneapolis Plan. Minneapolis: University of Minnesota, 1967.

Cooperative Agricultural Extension Work Act, 87 Stat. 839, 1973.

CORBALLY, J. E., JR. "Change, the Professions, and Continuing Education." In D. E. Moore, Jr. (Ed.), *Mandatory Continuing Education: Prospects and Dilemmas for Professionals.* Urbana-Champaign: Office of Continuing Education and Public Service, University of Illinois, 1976.

CORTWRIGHT, R., and BRICE, E. W. "Adult Basic Education." In R. M. Smith, G. F. Aker, and J. R. Kidd (Eds.), *Handbook of Adult Education.* New York: Macmillan, 1970.

COSTER, J. K. "Some Characteristics of High School Pupils from Three Income Groups." *Journal of Educational Psychology,* 1959, *50,* 55–62.

COSTER, J. K. (Ed.) *A Guide to Preparing Courses of Study in Vocational Agriculture for High School Students in Indianapolis.* Lafayette, Ind.: Purdue University Press, 1964.

COUNCIL FOR EXCEPTIONAL CHILDREN. "Full Educational Opportunities for Handicapped Individuals." In *The White House Conference on Handicapped Individuals.* Vol. 1: *Awareness Papers.* Washington, D.C.: U.S. Government Printing Office, 1977.

CRAIG, R. L. *Handbook of Training and Development.* New York: McGraw-Hill, 1977.

CROMWELL, R. E., and BARTZ, H. W. "The American Family: Its Impact on Quality of Life." *Adult Leadership,* 1977, *25,* 162.

CROSS, K. P. "Learner-Centered Curricula." In D. W. Vermilye

(Ed.), *Learner-Centered Reform*. San Francisco: Jossey-Bass, 1975.

CROSS, K. P. *Accent on Learning*. San Francisco: Jossey-Bass, 1976.

CROSS, K. P., VALLEY, J. R., and ASSOCIATES. *Planning Non-Traditional Programs*. San Francisco: Jossey-Bass, 1974.

CUBER, J. F., and HARROFF, P. B. *The Significant Americans*. New York: Appleton-Century-Crofts, 1965.

CURRICULUM AND EVALUATION CONSULTANTS. *An Evaluation of the Instructional Television Program "Basic Education: Teaching the Adult."* Prepared for the Division of Instruction, Maryland State Department of Education. Merchantville, N.J.: Curriculum and Evaluation Consultants, 1976.

DAVIS, S. A. *Community Resource Centers: The Notebook*. Washington, D.C.: National Self-Help Resource Center, 1976.

DAY CARE AND CHILD DEVELOPMENT COUNCIL OF AMERICA. *Child Care '76*. Washington, D.C.: Day Care and Child Development Council of America, 1976.

DE CROW, R. *New Learning for Older Americans: An Overview of National Effort*. Washington, D.C.: Adult Education Association of the USA, n.d.

DE CROW, R. "Learning for Older Americans: Why Adult Educators Must Work at the Behest of Others." Memorandum to the Council of Affiliated Organizations. Washington, D.C.: Adult Education Association of the USA, Oct. 1974.

DEGLER, C. N. "Revolution Without Ideology: The Changing Place of Women in America." In R. J. Lifton (Ed.), *The Woman in America*. Boston: Houghton Mifflin, 1964.

DEIGHTON, L. C. (Editor-in-Chief). *The Encyclopedia of Education*. Vol. 3. New York: Macmillan and Free Press, 1971.

DEPARTMENT OF THE AIR FORCE. *Operation and Administration of the Air Force Education Service Program*. AFM 213-1. June 1976.

DEPARTMENT OF THE ARMY. *General Education Development*. AR621-4. Nov. 1975.

DEPARTMENT OF DEFENSE. "Defense Education." *Commanders Digest*, 1973, *14* (5).

DEPARTMENT OF THE NAVY. *Educational Services Manual.* CNET 1560. 3. May 1975.

DERVIN, B., ZWEIZIG, D., BANISTER, M., and others. *The Development of Strategies for Dealing with the Information Needs of Urban Residents: Phase I, Citizen Study.* U.S. Office of Education Project No. L0035JA. Seattle: School of Communications, University of Washington, 1976.

DERVIN, B., ZWEIZIG, D., BANISTER, M., and others. *The Development of Strategies for Dealing With the Information Needs of Urban Residents: Phase II, Information Practitioner Study.* U.S. Office of Education Project No. 475AH50014. Seattle: School of Communications, University of Washington, 1977.

DE TOCQUEVILLE, A. *Democracy in America.* New York: Oxford University Press, 1947.

DEWEY, J. *Democracy and Education.* New York: Macmillan, 1916.

DIVISION OF INSTRUCTIONAL TELEVISION. *Basic Education: Teaching Adults, A Teacher Education Series.* Owings Mills: Maryland State Department of Education, 1973a.

DIVISION OF INSTRUCTIONAL TELEVISION. *Instructional Television Utilization, A Teacher Education Series.* Owings Mills: Maryland State Department of Education, 1973b.

DONNELLY, R. S. *Continuing Professional Education: An Appraisal.* Amherst: Division of Continuing Education, University of Massachusetts, 1976.

DUBLIN, M. K. "Foreword." In *Continuing Education Programs and Services for Women.* (rev. ed.) Washington, D.C.: U.S. Department of Labor, 1968.

DUCEY, A. L. "Higher Education for the Military." *Change,* 1972, *4*(3), 27–30.

Economic Opportunity Act, 78 Stat. 508, 1964.

EDUCATION COMMISSION OF THE STATES. *Correctional Education: A Forgotten Human Service.* Report No. 76. Washington, D.C.: Education Commission of the States, 1976a.

EDUCATION COMMISSION OF THE STATES. *An Overview of Findings and Recommendations of Major Research Studies and National Commissions Concerning Education of Offenders.* Report No.

81. Washington, D.C.: Education Commission of the States, March 1976b.

EDUCATIONAL POLICIES COMMISSION. *The Purposes of Education in American Democracy.* Washington, D.C.: National Education Association of the United States, 1938.

EDUCATIONAL POLICIES COMMISSION. *Federal Activities in Education.* Washington, D.C.: National Education Association of the United States, 1939.

EDUCATIONAL POLICIES COMMISSION. *Manpower and Education.* Washington, D.C.: National Education Association of the United States, 1956.

EHRENBERG, R. G., and HEWLELT, J. G. "The Impact of the Win 2 Program on Welfare Costs and Recipient Rates." *Journal of Human Resources,* 1976, 2 (2), 219–232.

EISDORFER, C., and LAWTON, B. P. (Eds.). *The Psychology of Adult Development and Aging.* Washington, D.C.: American Psychological Association, 1973.

EMPLOYMENT AND TRAINING ADMINISTRATION. *Comprehensive Employment and Training Act Review and Oversight. Part I: Background and First-Year Report. Part II: Public Policy Issues.* Washington, D.C.: U.S. Department of Labor, Dec. 5, 1975.

Employment Act, 60 Stat. 23, 1946.

EPSTEIN, C. F. "Positive Effects of the Double Negative: Sex, Race, and Professional Elites." Paper presented at annual meeting of the American Sociological Association, Denver, Colo., August 31, 1971.

Equal Employment Opportunity Act, Public Law 261, 92nd Cong. March 24, 1972.

ERIKSON, E. H. *Childhood and Society.* (2nd ed.) New York: Norton, 1963.

ETZIONI, A. "Old People with Public Policy." *Social Policy,* 1976, 7 (3), 21–29.

EVENSON, W. M. "The Experimental Approach." In H. B. Long, R. C. Anderson, and J. A. Blubaugh (Eds.), *Approaches to Community Development.* Iowa City, Iowa: National University Extension Association, 1973.

EYSTER, G. W. *The Interrelating of Library and Basic Education Services for Disadvantaged Adults: A Demonstration of Four Alternative Working Models.* Annual Report, Vols. 1 and 2. Morehead, Ky.: Appalachian Adult Education Center, 1973.

EYSTER, G. W. "Barriers in the Community." In *Synergy '76.* Eugene, Ore.: Parks and Recreation Society, Community Education Association, and Association of Health, Physical Education, and Recreation, 1976a.

EYSTER, G. W. "ETV Utilization in Adult Education." *Adult Leadership,* 1976b, *2,* 109–111.

FEENEY, H. M. "Interest Values and Social Class as Related to Adult Women Who Are Continuing Their Education." Unpublished doctoral dissertation, New York University, 1972.

FISHER, A. C. "Cost-Effectiveness Analysis for the War on Poverty." In T. A. Goldman (Ed.), *Cost-Effectiveness Analysis.* New York: Praeger, 1967.

FISHER, F. D. "Educating for Underemployment." *Change,* 1976, *8* (1), 16.

FOUGHT, C. A. "The Historical Development of Continuing Education for Women in the United States: Economic, Social, and Psychological Implications." Unpublished doctoral dissertation, Ohio State University, 1966.

FRANCIOSA, G. *The Implementation of a Cognitive Style Mapping and Diagnostic/Prescriptive ABE Program.* Niagara Falls, N.Y.: School District of Niagara Falls, 1974.

FRANK, H. E. *Human Resource Development:The European Approach.* Houston: Gulf Publishing, 1974.

FRANKLIN, R. *Toward the Style of the Community Change Educator.* Washington, D.C.: National Training Laboratories Institute for Applied Behavioral Science, 1969.

FREEMAN, R. B. "Investments in Human Capital and Knowledge." In E. Shapiro and W. L. White (Eds.), *Capital for Productivity and Jobs.* Englewood Cliffs, N.J.: Prentice-Hall, 1977.

FREIRE, P. *Pedagogy of the Oppressed.* New York: Herder and Herder, 1970.

GANS, H. J. "Social Protest of the 1960s Takes the Form of the Equality Revolution." In N. R. Yetman and C. H. Steele (Eds.), *Majority and Minority.* Boston: Allyn & Bacon, 1971.

GARRETT, J. F. "Handicapped Americans—Overview." *American Rehabilitation,* 1976, *1,* 5.

GARTH, J. *Adult Reading Comprehension Skills: A Computer-Based Instructional Program.* Urbana, Ill.: Urbana School District #16, 1977.

GEAKE, R. R. "Professional Services and Quality: Continuing Education as a Guarantee." Paper presented at the Conference on Mandatory Continuing Education for the Professions, Southern Methodist University, Dallas, 1976.

GENTILE, E. "Handicapper." Paper presented at 1st annual Conference of the Mid-American Association of Educational Opportunity Program Personnel, Green Bay, Wis., November 10, 1975.

GIGES, B., and ROSENFELD, E. "Personal Growth, Encounter, and Self-Awareness." In M. Rosenbaum and S. Snodowsky (Eds.), *The Intensive Group Experience.* New York: Free Press, 1977.

GINZBERG, E., and ASSOCIATES. *Life Styles of Educated Women.* New York: Columbia University Press, 1966.

GLASSER, D. J. *The Effectiveness of a Prison and Parole System.* Indianapolis, Ind.: Bobbs-Merrill, 1974.

GLASSER, D. J. "Achieving Better Questions: A Half-Century's Progression in Correctional Research." *Federal Probation,* September 1975, *39,* 9–14.

GOOD, C. V. (Ed.). *Dictionary of Education.* (3rd ed.) New York: Merriman, 1974.

GRABOWSKI, S., and MASON, W. D. (Eds.). *Learning for Aging.* Washington, D.C.: Adult Education Association of the USA and ERIC Clearinghouse on Adult Education, n.d.

GRAY, L. *The American Way of Labor Education.* Reprint Series 184. New York: New York State School of Industrial and Labor Relations, Cornell University, 1966.

GRAY, L. "Labor Studies Credit and Degree Programs: A Growth Sector of Higher Education." *"Labor Studies Journal,* 1976, *1* (1), 34.

GREEK, W. J. "The Impact of Mandatory Continuing Education Requirements on Professional Associations." In D. E. Moore, Jr. (Ed.), *Mandatory Continuing Education: Prospects and Dilemmas for Professionals.* Urbana-Champaign: Office of Continuing Education and Public Service, University of Illinois, 1976.

GROSS, R. "Confidence and Diffidence in Open Learning." In *Forum '76: Proceedings of the Third Annual Conference on Open Learning and Non-Traditional Study.* Lincoln, Nebr.: University of Mid-America, 1976.

HAMILTON, I. B. *The Third Century: Postsecondary Planning for the Non-Traditional Learner.* A report prepared for the Higher Education Facilities Commission of the State of Iowa under the auspices of the Office of New Degree Programs of the College Entrance Examination Board and Educational Testing Service. Princeton, N.J.: Educational Testing Service, 1976.

HAMILTON, I. B., and VALLEY, J. R. (Eds.). *Matching (New?) Needs with (New?) Resources.* Princeton, N.J.: Educational Testing Service, 1976.

HAMLIN, H. M. *Citizen Evaluation of Public Occupational Education.* Raleigh: Center for Occupational Education, North Carolina State University, 1967.

HANEY, J. E. "Can America Produce Enough Problem-Solving Citizens?" *Research News* (Office of Research Administration, University of Michigan) July 1972.

HARBESON, G. E. "The New Feminism." *Journal of the American Association of University Women,* 1970, *63* (2), 53–56.

HARRILL, L. R. *Memories of 4-H.* Raleigh: North Carolina State University Print Shop, 1967.

HARRIS, L., and ASSOCIATES. *The Myth and Reality of Aging in America.* Washington, D.C.: National Council on Aging, 1975.

Hatch Act of May 2, 1887, as amended August 11, 1955 (Public Law 352).

HAUSER, P. "Breaking the Poverty Cycle." In S. Tax (Ed.), *The People vs. the System.* Chicago: Acme Press, 1968.

HAVELOCK, R. G. *A Guide to Innovation in Education.* Ann Arbor: Institute for Social Research, University of Michigan, 1970.

HAVIGHURST, R. J. "Changing Status and Roles During the Adult Life Cycle: Significance for Adult Education." In H. W. Burns (Ed.), *Sociological Backgrounds of Adult Education.* Notes and Essays on Education for Adults, No. 41. Chicago: Center for the Study of Liberal Education for Adults, 1963.

HAVIGHURST, R. J. *Developmental Tasks and Education.* (2nd ed.) New York: McKay, 1970.

HAVIGHURST, R. J. *Aging in America: Implications for Education.* Washington, D.C.: National Council on Aging, 1976a.

HAVIGHURST, R. J. "Education Through the Adult Life Span." *Educational Gerontology,* 1976b, *1,* 41–51.

HAYES, A. P. "Community Colleges Serve Some of the People." *Community College Review,* 1973, *1,* 38–42.

HAYGHE, H. *Families and the Rise of Working Wives: An Overview.* Special Labor Force Report 189. Washington, D.C.: U.S. Department of Labor, 1976.

HEFFERNAN, J. M., MACY, F. U., and VICKERS, D. F. *Educational Brokering: New Services for Adult Learners.* Syracuse, N.Y.: National Center for Educational Brokerage, 1975.

HENDRICKSON, A. *A Manual for Planning Educational Programs for Older Adults.* Tallahassee: Department of Adult Education, Florida State University, 1973.

HERZBERG, F. *Work and the Nature of Man.* New York: World, 1966.

HILL, R. W. "The Constitutionality of Continuing Education Requirements." Paper presented at Conference on Continuing Education Requirements, National Association of State Boards of Accountancy, New York, 1975.

HILLS, J. "On Accountability in Education." In R. M. Pavalko (Ed.), *Sociology of Education.* Itasca, Ill.: Peacock, 1976.

HOLLAND, J. L. *Making Vocational Choices.* Englewood Cliffs, N.J.: Prentice-Hall, 1973.

HOLLINGSHEAD, A. B. *Elmtown's Youth.* New York: Wiley, 1949.

HOULE, C. O. *Continuing Your Education.* San Francisco: Jossey-Bass, 1964.

HOULE, C. O. *The Design of Education.* San Francisco: Jossey-Bass, 1972.

HOULE, C. O. "Continuing Education for the Elderly." Unpublished paper, Committee on Human Development, University of Chicago, 1975.

HOULE, C. O. "Evidence for the Effectiveness of Continuing Professional Education and the Impact of Mandatory Continuing Education." In D. E. Moore, Jr. (Ed.), *Mandatory Continuing*

Education: Prospects and Dilemmas for Professionals. Urbana-Champaign: Office of Continuing Education and Public Service, University of Illinois, 1976.

HUNTINGTON, S. P. *The Soldier and the State.* Cambridge, Mass.: Belknap Press, 1957.

HUXLEY, A. "Education on the Non-Verbal Level." *Daedalus,* 1962, *91* (1), 279–293.

ILLICH, I., and VERNE, E. "Imprisoned in the Global Classroom." *London-Times Educational Supplement,* March 21, 1975, pp. 21–23.

ILLINOIS COOPERATIVE EXTENSION SERVICE. *Mass Media Survey.* Urbana: University of Illinois, 1975.

INGHAM, R. *Design and Application of Educative Systems.* Tallahassee: Department of Adult Education, Florida State University, 1973a.

INGHAM, R. *The Learning Resources Counseling Center for Tallahassee.* Tallahassee: Department of Adult Education, Florida State University, 1973b.

IRWIN, T. *To Combat Child Abuse and Neglect.* New York: Public Affairs Committee, Inc., 1974.

JANOWITZ, M. *Sociology and the Military Establishment.* Beverly Hills, Calif.: Sage, 1974.

JARVIK, L. F., EISDORFER, C., and BLUM, J. E. (Eds.). *Intellectual Functioning in Adults: Psychological and Biological Influences.* New York: Springer, 1973.

JENSEN, G. "Education for Self-Fulfillment." In R. N. Smith, G. F. Akers, and J. R. Kidd (Eds.), *Handbook of Adult Education.* New York: Macmillan, 1970.

JOHNS, R. J., GOFFMAN, I. J., ALEXANDER, K., and STOLLAR, K. H. (Eds.). *Economic Factors Affecting the Financing of Education.* Gainesville, Fla.: National Educational Finance Project, 1970.

JOHNSTONE, J. W. C., and RIVERA, R. J. *Volunteers for Learning.* Chicago: Aldine, 1965.

KAHN, H., and WIENER, A. J. *The Year 2000: A Framework for Speculation on the Next Thirty-Three Years.* New York: Macmillan, 1967.

KEETON, M. T., and ASSOCIATES. *Experiential Learning: Rationale, Characteristics and Assessment.* San Francisco: Jossey-Bass, 1976.

KIRKWOOD COMMUNITY COLLEGE, CEDAR RAPIDS, IOWA. "Community Services ACCtion Center." *ACCtion,* 1976, *1,* 5.

KNOWLES, M. S. *The Modern Practice of Adult Education.* New York: Association Press, 1970.

KNOWLES, M. S. *The Adult Learner: A Neglected Species.* Houston: Gulf Publishing, 1973.

KNOWLES, M. S. *Self-Directed Learning.* New York: Association Press, 1975a.

KNOWLES, M. S. "Toward a Model of Lifelong Education." In H. Dave (Ed.), *Reflections on Lifelong Education and the School.* Hamburg, Germany: UNESCO Institute for Education, 1975b.

KOPECKY, L. "There Is Always a 'Depression.' " *Mainstream,* May 1977, p. 4.

KORIM, A. S. *Older Americans and Community Colleges: A Guide for Program Implementation.* Washington, D.C.: American Association of Community and Junior Colleges, 1974a.

KORIM, A. A. *Older Americans and Community Colleges: An Overview.* Washington, D.C.: American Association of Community and Junior Colleges, 1974b.

KRAUSE, F. J. "Century of Decision in Mental Retardation." *American Rehabilitation,* 1976, *1,* 16–19.

KREITLOW, B. W. "Innovation in Organizing Learning for Adults— The New Technology." In R. W. Smith (Ed.), *Adult Learning: Issues and Innovations.* Information Series No. 8. DeKalb: Clearinghouse in Career Education, Northern Illinois University, 1976.

KREPS, J. *Sex in the Marketplace: American Women at Work.* Baltimore: Johns Hopkins Press, 1971.

LAKE PLACID CONFERENCE ON HOME ECONOMICS. *Proceedings of the Fourth Annual Conference, September 16–20.* Washington, D.C.: American Home Economics Association, 1902.

LE BLANC, M. A. "Patient Population and Other Estimates of Prosthetics and Orthotics in the U.S." *Orthotics and Prosthetics,* 1973, *27,* 38–44.

LE DONNE, M. *Survey of Library and Information Problems in Correctional Institutions.* Washington, D.C.: Office of Education. U.S. Department of Health, Education and Welfare, January 1974.

LEE, A. M., and FITZGERALD, D. *Learning a Living Across the Nation.* Vol. 5. Flagstaff: Northern Arizona University, 1976.

LEIBERG, L. *The Mutual Agreement Program.* Resource Document #3, ACA Parole-Correction Project. College Park, Md.: American Correctional Association, 1973.

LEIBOW, E. *Talley's Corner.* Boston, Mass.: Little, Brown, 1967.

LESTER, C. N. "Selected Personal and Environmental Factors— Influencing Conformity or Nonconformity to Organizational Norms in the Virginia Cooperative Extension Service." Unpublished doctoral dissertation, Florida State University, Tallahassee, 1969.

LEVY, L., and ROWITY, L. *The Ecology of Mental Disorders.* New York: Human Services Press, 1973.

LEWIS, C. E. "To Whom Does/Should the Patient's Chart Belong?" *UCLA Daily Bruin,* October 25, 1976, p. 11.

LIND, A. "The Future of Citizen Involvement." *The Futurist,* 1975, *6,* 316–328.

LINDEMAN, E. C. *The Meaning of Adult Education.* New York: New Republic, 1926.

LIPTON, D., MARTINSON, R., and WILKS, J. *The Effectiveness of Correctional Treatment.* New York: Praeger, 1975.

LOGSDON, J. D. "Role of the Community College in Community Education." *Phi Delta Kappan,* 1972, *54,* 197–199.

LONDONER, C. A. "Survival Needs of the Aged: Implications for Program Planning." *Aging and Human Development,* 1971, *2,* 113–117.

MC CLUSKY, H. Y. "Education for Aging: The Scope of the Field and Perspectives for the Future." In S. Grabowski and W. D. Mason (Eds.), *Learning for Aging.* Washington, D.C.; Adult Education Association of the USA, n.d.

MC CLUSKY, H. Y. "A Dynamic Approach to Participation in Community Development." *Journal of the Community Development Society,* 1970, *1,* 25–32.

MC COLLUM, S. G. "New Designs for Correctional Education and Training Programs." *Federal Probation,* 1973, *37,* 6–11.

MC COLLUM, S. G. "College for Prisoners." In D. W. Vermilye (Ed.), *Learner-Centered Reform.* San Francisco: Jossey-Bass, 1975.

MC COLLUM, S. G. "What Works." *Federal Probation,* 1977, *41,* 32–35.

MC DONALD, A. *Four-Year Study of Mexican-American Children Whose Parents Were and Were Not Enrolled in Adult Basic Education.* 2 vols. Brownsville, Tex.: Board of Education, 1975.

MACE, D., and MACE, V. *We Can Have Better Marriages If We Really Want Them.* Nashville, Tenn.: Abingdon Press, 1974.

MC FANN, H. H. "Training Strategies and Individual Differences." In W. S. Griffith and A. P. Hayes (Eds.), *Adult Basic Education: The State of the Art.* Chicago: Department of Adult Education, University of Chicago, 1970.

MC GREGOR, D. *Human Side of Enterprise.* New York: McGraw-Hill, 1960.

MC HOLLAND, J. D. *Human Potential Semniars: Participants' Workbook,* Evanston, Ill.: Human Potential Seminars, 1975.

MC KIMMON, J. S. *When We're Green We Grow.* Chapel Hill: University of North Carolina Press, 1945.

MC LUHAN, M. *Understanding Media: The Extensions of Man.* New York: American Library, 1964.

MAEROFF, G. I. "The Growing Women's Studies Movement Gets Organized." *New York Times,* January 18, 1977, p. 23.

MALONE, V. "A Plan of Action to Implement a Job Stability Program for an Extension Advisor in an Urban Area." Unpublished doctoral dissertation, Florida State University, 1973.

MANGANO, J. "Head-Start Parents' Adult Basic Education Project, New York City." In W. S. Griffith and A. P. Hayes (Eds.), *Adult Basic Education: The State of the Art.* Chicago: Department of Education, University of Chicago, 1970.

MANGUM, G. L. *Contributions and Costs of Manpower Development and Training.* Policy Papers on Human Resources and Industrial Relations, No. 5. Ann Arbor, Mich.: Institute of Labor and Industrial Relations, 1967.

Manpower Training and Development Act, 76 Stat. 23, 1962.

MARCUS, E. E. "Effects of Age, Sex, and Socioeconomic Status on Adult Education Participants' Perception of the Utility of Their Participation." Unpublished doctoral dissertation, University of Chicago, 1976.

MARLAND, S. P., JR. "Career Education Now." Paper presented at

1971 convention of the National Association of Secondary School Principals, Houston, 1971.

MARLAND, S. P., JR. "The Problem." In M. W. Shook and S. J. King (Eds.), *National Invitational Conference on Occupational Education for Chief State School Officers*. Raleigh: Center for Occupational Education, North Carolina State University, 1974.

MARSHALL, T., and others. "An Evaluation of 'Newgate' and Other Programs." *Summary Report: Project Newgate and Others*. Prison College Program, Office of Economic Opportunities Contract B-2C 5322. Washington, D.C.: Bureau of Prisons, April 1973.

MASLOW, A. H. *Toward a Psychology of Being*. New York: D. Van Nostrand, 1962.

MASLOW, A. H. *Toward a Psychology of Being*. (2nd ed.) New York: Van Nostrand Reinhold, 1968.

MASLOW, A. H. *The Farther Reaches of Human Nature*. New York: Viking Press, 1971.

MASON, R. F. *Contemporary Educational Theory*. New York: McKay, 1972.

MEAD, M. (Ed.). *Cultural Patterns and Technical Change*. New York: New American Library, 1955.

MEAD, M. "Introduction." In *American Women: The Report of the President's Commission on the Status of Women and Other Publications of the Commission*. New York: Scribner's, 1963.

MEADOWS, D. H., MEADOWS, D. L., RANDERS, J., and BEHRENS, W. W. *The Limits to Growth: A Report for the Club of Rome's Project on the Predicament of Mankind*. New York: Universe Books, 1972.

MESAROVIC, J., and PESTEL, E. *Mankind at the Turning Point*. New York: Dutton, 1974.

MILLER, H. *Tropic of Capricorn*. New York: Grove Press, 1975.

MILLER, J. W. "Expanded Role of the Commission on Educational Credit of the American Council on Education." *Adult Leadership*, 1975, *23* (8), 251–255.

MILLER, S. M. "The American Lower Classes: A Typological Approach." *Sociology and Social Research*, 1964, *40* (3).

MINZEY, J. D., and LE TARTE, C. E. *Community Education: From Program to Process*. Midland, Mich.: Pendell, 1972.

MOODY, H. R. "Philosophical Presuppositions of Education for Old Age." *Educational Gerontology,* 1976, *1,* 1–16.

MOUSTAKAS, C. *Personal Growth: The Struggle for Identity and Human Values.* Cambridge, Mass.: H. A. Doyle, 1969.

MURPHY, G. *Human Potentialities.* New York: Basic Books, 1958.

MURPHY, J. T., and COHEN, D. K. "Accountability in Education: The Michigan Experience." *The Public Interest,* 1974, *36,* 53–81.

NADLER, L. A. *Developing Human Resources.* Houston: Gulf Publishing, 1970.

NADLER, L. A. *The NOW Employee.* Houston: Gulf Publishing, 1971.

NAGI, S. Z. "The Disabled and Rehabilitation Services: A National Overview." *American Rehabilitation,* 1977, *2,* 26–33.

NATIONAL ADVISORY COUNCIL ON VOCATIONAL EDUCATION. *Vocational Education: The Bridge Between Man and His Work.* Washington, D.C.: U.S. Government Printing Office, 1968.

NATIONAL ASSOCIATION OF EDUCATION, PROFESSIONS, DEVELOPMENT. "Mainstreaming: Helping Teachers Meet the Challenge, 1976." *Education Digest,* Nov. 1976, pp. 26–33.

NATIONAL CENTER FOR LAW AND THE HANDICAPPED. "The 504 Notice: Moving Towards a Civil Rights Act?" *Amicus,* 1976, *1,* 16.

NATIONAL CENTER FOR LAW AND THE HANDICAPPED. *"Disabled in Action of Pennsylvania, Inc., et al.* v. *Coleman et al."* *Amicus,* 1977, *2,* 29.

NATIONAL COUNCIL ON FAMILY RELATIONS. *CoFo* Memo, 1978, *1* (2), 1–2.

NATIONAL SELF-HELP RESOURCE CENTER. *UPLIFT: What People Themselves Can Do.* Washington, D.C.: National Self-Help Resource Center, 1976.

NELSON, H. "Critic Shakes Up Medical World." *Los Angeles Times,* Part I, June 25, 1976a, pp. 3, 35.

NELSON, H. "Many Executives in Trap." *Los Angeles Times,* Part II, October 27, 1976b, pp. 1–2.

NEUGARTEN, B. L. "Education and Life Cycle." *School Review,* 1972, *80* (2), 215.

NEUGARTEN, B. L. "The Future of the Young-Old." *The Gerontologist,* 1975, *15,* Part II, 4–9.

NEWMAN, P. M. "Inflation: A Particular Hardship for Handicapped Individuals." In *Programs for the Handicapped.* Washington, D.C.: Office of the Handicapped, U.S. Department of Health, Education and Welfare, 1974.

1971 WHITE HOUSE CONFERENCE ON AGING. "Part I—Section Recommendations: Education." In *Toward a National Policy on Aging: Final Report.* Vol 2. Washington, D.C.: U.S. Government Printing Office, 1973.

NORTHCUTT, N. *The Adult Performance Level Competency-Based High School Diploma Pilot Project.* Austin: University of Texas, 1976.

Occupational Safety and Health Act, Public Law 91-596, 1970.

O'DONNELL, M. P. *Advanced Information Reading Diagnostics Package.* Gorham: Right to Read Center, University of Maine Portland-Gorham, 1974.

OKES, I. E. *Participation in Adult Education: Final Report, 1969.* Washington, D.C.: National Center for Educational Statistics, 1974.

OKES, I. E. *Adult Education in the Public School Systems, 1968–69 and 1969–70: A Survey of the States and Outlying Areas.* Washington, D.C.: U.S. Government Printing Office, 1976.

OLSEN, D. H. *Treating Relationships.* Lake Mills, Iowa: Graphic Publishing, 1976.

OSBORN, R. H. "Characteristics, Motivation, and Problems of Mature Married Women College Students: A Status Study of Selected Students at The George Washington University." Unpublished doctoral dissertation, George Washington University, 1963.

OSIPOW, S. H. *Theories of Career Development.* New York: Appleton-Century-Crofts, 1968.

O'TOOLE, J. "Education, Work, and Quality of Life." In D. W. Vermilye (Ed.), *Lifelong Learners—A New Clientele For Higher Education.* San Francisco: Jossey-Bass, 1974.

O'TOOLE, J. "The Reserve Army of the Underemployed: II. The Role of Education." *Change,* 1975, *7* (5), 26–33.

OTTO, H. A. "New Light on Human Potential." *In Families of the Future*. Ames: Iowa State University Press, 1972.

OZAKI, Y. *National Congress on the Rehabilitation of Homebound and Institutionalized Persons, National Rehabilitation Association*. Chicago: Illinois Institute for DD, 1977.

PANEL OF CONSULTANTS ON VOCATIONAL EDUCATION. *Education for a Changing World of Work*. Washington, D.C.: U.S. Government Printing Office, 1963.

PARKER, W. *Parole Corrections Project*. Resource Document #1, ACA Parole-Correction Project. College Park, Md.: American Correctional Association, 1975.

PATTEN, T. H., JR. *Manpower Planning and the Development of Human Resources*. New York: Wiley, 1971.

PEARSON, D. B. "The Inconsistencies of Implementation." Paper presented at Conference on Continuing Education Requirements, National Association of State Boards of Accountancy, New York, 1975.

PENNINGTON, F. C., and MOORE, D. E., JR. "Issues Related to Mandatory Continuing Education for Professionals." *The NUEA Spectator*, March 1976, pp. 5–8.

PETERS, C. "Public, Not Doctors, Should Control Health Care." *Los Angeles Times*, Editorial Section, October 15, 1976, p. 5.

PETERSON, S. *A Catalog of the Ways People Grow*. New York: Ballantine Books, 1971.

PIDGEON, D. "A Self-Instructional Programme for Teaching Adults to Read English." *Literacy Work*, 1976, *5*, 47–48.

PIFER, A. "Is It Time for an External Degree?" *College Board Review*, 1970–71, *78*, 5–10.

PORTER, G. W., and COSTER, J. K. *Career Education in Six Selected States*. Raleigh: Center for Occupational Education, North Carolina State University, 1974.

POWNALL, G. A. *Employment Problems of Released Prisoners*. Prepared for the Manpower Administration, U.S. Department of Labor. Springfield, Va.: National Technical Information Service, 1969.

Public Works and Economic Development Act, 79 Stat. 552, 1965.

Rehabilitation Act of 1973, Section 504 (29 U.S.C. 794) as

Amended by Section 111(a) of the Rehabilitation Act Amendments of 1974, Public Law 93-516 (29 U.S.C. 706).

REHABILITATION RESEARCH FOUNDATION. *An Individually Prescribed Instructional System.* Elmore, Ala.: Draper Correctional Center, 1971.

REIFF, R., and RIESSMAN, F. *The Indigenous Nonprofessional: A Strategy of Change in Community Action and Community Mental Health Programs.* Monograph Series No. 1, *Community Mental Health Journal.* New York: Behavioral Publications, 1965.

REILLY, A. J. "Interview with Leland Bradford." *Group and Organizational Studies,* 1976, *1* (1), 12–25.

RIBICH, T. L. "The Effect of Educational Spending on Poverty Reduction." In R. J. Johns, and others (Eds.), *Economic Factors Affecting the Financing of Education.* Gainesville, Fla.: National Educational Finance Project, 1970.

RICHTER, M. L., and WHIPPLE, J. B. *A Revolution in the Education of Women: Ten Years of Continuing Education at Sarah Lawrence College.* Bronxville, N.Y.: Sarah Lawrence College, 1972.

RINGERS, J. J. *Community Schools and Interagency Programs: A Guide.* Midland, Mich.: Pendell, 1976.

ROBERTS, M. J. "On Reforming Economic Growth." *Daedalus,* 1973, *102,* 119–138.

ROBERTS, R. W. *Vocational and Practical Arts Education.* New York: Harper & Row, 1965.

ROGERS, C. R. *Freedom to Learn.* Columbus, Ohio: Merrill, 1969.

ROGIN, L. "Labor Education." In R. M. Smith, G. F. Aker, and J. R. Kidd (Eds.), *Handbook of Adult Education.* New York: Macmillan, 1970.

ROSE, M. *A Summary of Voluntary Education in the Armed Forces.* Washington, D.C.: Office of the Assistant Secretary of Defense for Manpower and Reserve Affairs, 1974.

ROTHMAN, S. "State Government, Social Problems and Systems Analyst: A Clash of Culture." *Educational Technology,* 1970, *10* (7), 18–19.

ROTTER, J. B. "Generalized Expectancies for Internal Versus External Control of Reinforcement." *Psychological Monographs: General and Applied,* 1966, *88,* 1–28.

RYAN, T. A. *Collection of Papers Prepared for 1970 National Seminars Adult Basic Education in Corrections.* Honolulu: Education Research and Development Center, University of Hawaii, 1970.

RYAN, T. A. *Model of Basic Adult Education in Corrections.* Honolulu: Education Research and Development Center, University of Hawaii, 1972.

SALISBURY, P. S. *An Evaluation of Lift, Inc., and Its Services to "Homebound" Individuals.* Springfield, Ill.: Division of Vocational Rehabilitation, 1977.

SATIR, V. C. *Peoplemaking.* Palo Alto, Calif.: Science and Behavior Books, 1972.

SCHEIN, E. H., and BENNIS, W. G. *Personal and Organizational Change Through Group Methods: The Laboratory Approach.* New York: Wiley, 1965.

SCHENSUL, S. L., PAREDES, J., and PEETO, J. "The Twilight Zone of Poverty." *Human Organization,* 1968, *27,* 47–53.

SCHRAMM, W. *Big Media, Little Media.* Beverly Hills, Calif.: Sage, 1977.

SCHUMACHER, E. F. *Small Is Beautiful: Economics As If People Mattered.* New York: Harper & Row, 1973.

SEIFER, N. *Absent from the Majority—Working Class Women in America.* New York: American Jewish Committee, 1972.

SELDON, W. K. "Implications for Society of Mandatory Continuing Education for the Professions." Paper presented at Conference on Mandatory Continuing Education for the Professions, Southern Methodist University, Dallas, 1976.

SHAW, M. B., and ROARK, M. *Everyday Everywhere Materials as Teaching Resources in Adult Basic Education.* Blacksburg: Virginia Polytechnic Institute and State University, 1977.

SHWORLES, T. R. "How Well Are We Doing Good?" *Occasional Papers,* 1977, *21,* 4.

SILVERN, L. *Principles of Computer-Assisted Instruction Systems.* Washington, D.C.: Education and Training Consultants, 1970.

SINGER, N. M., and WRIGHT, V. B. *Cost Analysis of Correctional Standards: Institutional Based Programs and Parole.* Standards and Goals Project. Washington, D.C.: Correctional Economics Center, American Bar Association, January, 1976.

SJOLUND, J. A. "Arts for the Handicapped." *American Rehabilitation,* 1976, *1,* 18.

SKELLEY, T. J. "Strategies in the Agencies." In E. J. Browne (Ed.), *Community Colleges, Community Services, and the Handicapped Citizens.* Chicago: City Colleges of Chicago, 1975.

SMITH, P. B. "Controlled Studies of the Outcome of Sensitivity Training." *Psychological Bulletin,* 1975, *82* (4), 597–622.

SMITH, R. F. W. "Uses of Sociology." In H. W. Burns (Ed.), *Sociological Backgrounds of Adult Education.* Chicago: Center for the Study of Liberal Education for Adults, 1964.

SMITH, R. M., AKER, G. F., and KIDD, J. R. (Eds.). *Handbook of Adult Education.* New York: Macmillan, 1970.

SMITTKAMP, J. E. "National Paraplegic Foundation." In *Feasibility Study for the Physically Handicapped: 1970–1971.* Chicago: Mayfair College, City Colleges of Chicago, 1972.

SMUTS, R. W. *Women and Work in America.* New York: Schocken Books, 1971.

SOMERS, G. G. (Ed.). *Retraining the Unemployed.* Madison: University of Wisconsin Press, 1968.

SPECIAL TASK FORCE TO THE SECRETARY OF HEALTH, EDUCATION AND WELFARE. *Work in America.* Cambridge: Massachusetts Institute of Technology Press, 1973.

SROLE, L. *Mental Health in the Metropolis.* New York: McGraw-Hill, 1962.

STEPHEN, V. *CA Vision.* Ithaca: New York State Colleges of Agriculture and Human Ecology, Cornell University, 1969.

STIX, H. "Occupational Hazard of Caring: Burnout." *Los Angeles Times,* Part IV, October 21, 1976, pp. 1–3.

SUBCOMMITTEE ON PUBLIC HEALTH SERVICE. *Health Manpower Credentialing.* Washington, D.C.: Health Manpower Coordinating Committee, U.S. Department of Health, Education and Welfare, 1976.

SUMMERS, A. A., and WOLFE, B. L. "Which School Resources Help

Learning? Efficiency and Equity in the Philadelphia Schools."
IRCD Bulletin, 1976, *11*.

SUPER, D. E., and OVERSTREET, P. L. *The Vocational Maturity of Ninth-Grade Boys*. No. 1960. Bureau of Publications. New York: Teachers College, Columbia University, 1960.

SURVEY RESEARCH CENTER. *A Study of Family Economics: Report Respondents*. Ann Arbor: University of Michigan, 1975.

TAYLOR, B., and LIPPITT, G. L. (Eds.). *Management Development and Training Handbook*. New York: McGraw-Hill, 1975.

THEOBOLD, R. *Beyond Despair*. Washington, D.C.: New Republic Book Company, 1976.

THORNDIKE, E. L., and others. *Adult Learning*. New York: Macmillan, 1928.

THORNDIKE, R. L. *Reading Comprehension Education in Fifteen Countries: An Empirical Study*. New York: Wiley, 1973.

TILGHER, A. *Homo Faber: Work Through the Ages*. Chicago: Regnery, 1930.

TOUGH, A. M. *The Adult's Learning Projects: A Fresh Approach in Adult Learning*. Toronto: Ontario Institute for Studies in Education, 1971.

TOUGH, A. M. "Self-Planned Learning and Major Personal Change." In R. M. Smith (Ed.), *Adult Learning: Issues and Innovations*. Inf. Series No. 8. DeKalb: Clearinghouse in Career Education, Northern Illinois University, 1976.

TRENT, C., KINLAW, R., *and* PINTOZZI, F. *The Effectiveness of Cartoon Booklets, Information Leaflets, and Circular Letters in Disseminating Basic Foods and Nutrition Information to Low-Income Families*. Raleigh: North Carolina Agricultural Extension Service, 1977.

TURNER, J. C. "Labor and Continuing Education." In *Proceedings of Invitational Conference on Continuing Education: Manpower Policy and Lifelong Learning*. Washington, D.C.: National Advisory Council on Extension and Continuing Education, 1977.

UNESCO. *UNESCO Adult Education Information Notes*. Paris: Division of Structures and Content of Lifelong Education, UNESCO, 1977.

U.S. DEPARTMENT OF LABOR. *Directory of National and Inter-*

national Unions. Washington, D.C.: U.S. Government Printing Office, 1975.

U.S. MARINE CORPS. *Voluntary Education Program.* Marine Corps Order 1560. Washington, D.C.: May 1977.

UNIVERSITY AND COLLEGE LABOR EDUCATION ASSOCIATION. *UCLEA Directory of Member Institutions and Professional Staff.* East Lansing: Michigan State University, 1977.

UNIVERSITY OF MINNESOTA. *Continuing Education for Women: A Five-Year Report of the Minnesota Plan.* Minneapolis: University of Minnesota, 1967.

VERNER, C., and DAVISON, C. V. *Physiological Factors in Adult Learning and Instruction.* Tallahassee, Fla.: Department of Adult Education, Florida State University, 1971.

VINCENT, C. *Sexual and Marital Health.* New York: McGraw-Hill, 1973.

VINES, C. A., and ANDERSON, M. A. (Eds.). *Heritage Horizons: Extension's Commitment to People.* Special bicentennial issue of the *Journal of Extension.* Madison, Wisc.: Journal of Extension, Inc., 1976.

Vocational Education Act (Smith-Hughes), 39 Stat. 929, 1917.

Vocational Education Act, 77 Stat. 403, 1963.

Vocational Education Amendments, 82 Stat. 1063, 1968.

WAKABAYASHI, R., and others. "Unique Problems of Handicapped Minorities." In *White House Conference on Handicapped Individuals. Vol. 1: Awareness Papers.* Washington, D.C.: U.S. Government Printing Office, 1977.

WALSTER, E., and WALSTER, G. W. "Equity and Social Justice." *Journal of Social Issues,* 1975, *31* (3), 21–44.

WANG, B. C. "An Inter-Ethnic Comparison of Educational Selection, Achievement, and Decision-Making Among Fifth-Form Students in West Malaysia." Unpublished doctoral dissertation, University of Chicago, 1975.

WARNER, D. C. "Fiscal Barriers to Full Employment." *Annals of the American Academy of Political and Social Science,* 1975, *418,* 156–164.

WARNER, W. L., MEEKER, M., and EELLS, K. *Social Class in America.* New York: Harper & Row, 1949.

WARREN, R. L. *The Community in America.* Chicago: Rand McNally, 1972.

WARREN, R. L. (Ed.). *Perspectives on the American Community.* Chicago: Rand McNally, 1973.

WATSON, E. R. "Interpersonal Changes Through Immediate Feedback Approaches." *Adult Education,* 1968, *16,* 251–269.

WEINTRAUB, F. "The Impact of Inflation on the Handicapped and Disabled." In *Programs for the Handicapped.* Washington, D.C.: Office of the Handicapped, U.S. Department of Health, Education and Welfare, 1974.

WEIR, J. "The Personal Growth Laboratory." In K. D. Benne, and others (Eds.), *The Laboratory Method of Changing and Learning.* Palo Alto, Calif.: Science and Behavior Books, 1975.

WELCH, F. "Human Capital Theory: Education, Discrimination, and Life Cycles." *American Economic Review,* 1975, *65* (2), 63–73.

WESTERVELT, E. M. *Report on Operation of New York State Guidance Center for Women.* Suffern, N.Y.: State Guidance Center for Women, 1968.

WETHEY, S. B. "Values and Social Change." *Organization for Cooperation and Development,* 1974, *1* (1), 21–32.

WIRTZ, W. *The Boundless Resource: A Prospectus for an Education-Work Policy.* Washington, D.C.: New Republic Book Company, 1975.

WOERDEHOFF, F. J., NELSON, N. J., and COSTER, J. K. *Vocational Education in Public Schools as Related to Social, Economic, and Technical Trends: I. The Analysis of Trends and Concepts.* Lafayette, Ind.: Purdue University, 1960.

WOLFENSBURGER, W. "The Principles of Normalization as a Human Management Model: Evolution of a Definition." In *The Principle of Normalization in Human Services.* Toronto: National Institute on Mental Retardation, 1974.

WOMEN'S BUREAU. *Continuing Education Programs and Services for Women.* Pamphlet 10, rev. Washington, D.C.: U.S. Department of Labor, 1971.

WORK, M. H. *The Negro Year Book.* Tuskegee, Ala.: Tuskegee Institute Press, 1936.

"wow: A Model for Encouraging Women's Potential." *Journal of the American Association of University Women,* 1970, *63* (2), 69–72.

YETMAN, N. R., and STEELE, C. H. (Eds.). *Majority and Minority.* Boston: Allyn & Bacon, 1971.

YOUNG, P., and MYERS, J. T. (Eds.). *Philosophic Problems in Education.* Philadelphia: Lippincott, 1967.

ZILLER, R. C. "Self-Other Orientations and Quality of Life." *Social Indicators Research,* 1974, *1* (3), 301–327.

Index